Visual Methodologies and Digital Tools for Researching with Young Children

International Perspectives on Early Childhood Education and Development

Volume 10

Early childhood education in many countries has been built upon a strong tradition of a materially rich and active play-based pedagogy and environment. Yet what has become visible within the profession, is essentially a Western view of childhood preschool education and school education.

It is timely that a series of books be published which present a broader view of early childhood education. This series, seeks to provide an international perspective on early childhood education. In particular, the books published in this series will:

- Examine how learning is organized across a range of cultures, particularly Indigenous communities
- Make visible a range of ways in which early childhood pedagogy is framed and enacted across countries, including the majority poor countries
- Critique how particular forms of knowledge are constructed in curriculum within and across countries
- Explore policy imperatives which shape and have shaped how early childhood education is enacted across countries
- Examine how early childhood education is researched locally and globally
- Examine the theoretical informants driving pedagogy and practice, and seek to find alternative perspectives from those that dominate many Western heritage countries
- Critique assessment practices and consider a broader set of ways of measuring children's learning
- Examine concept formation from within the context of country-specific pedagogy and learning outcomes

The series will cover theoretical works, evidence-based pedagogical research, and international research studies. The series will also cover a broad range of countries, including poor majority countries. Classical areas of interest, such as play, the images of childhood, and family studies will also be examined. However the focus will be critical and international (not Western-centric).

For further volumes:
http://www.springer.com/series/7601

Marilyn Fleer • Avis Ridgway

Editors

Visual Methodologies and Digital Tools for Researching with Young Children

Transforming Visuality

 Springer

Editors
Marilyn Fleer
Faculty of Education
Monash University
Frankston, VIC, Australia

Avis Ridgway
Faculty of Education
Monash University
Frankston, VIC, Australia

ISBN 978-3-319-01468-5   ISBN 978-3-319-01469-2 (eBook)
DOI 10.1007/978-3-319-01469-2
Springer Cham Heidelberg New York Dordrecht London

Library of Congress Control Number: 2013952934

Printed on acid-free paper

Springer is part of Springer Science+Business Media (www.springer.com)

Contents

Part I
Post-developmental Methodologies
for Researching with Young Children

Chapter 1
A Digital Turn: Post-developmental Methodologies for Researching with Young Children

Marilyn Fleer

Introduction

Niels Bohr (1885–1962) won the Nobel Prize for Physics in 1922. As a Danish physicist and pioneer in quantum physics, he was and still is viewed as a highly esteemed researcher. Interestingly, Bohr (1950) made the claim that there are huge limitations with the scientific method and its reliance on causal relations, arguing for a more holistic rather than reductionist view when undertaking research. He discussed the idea of complementarity, where he sought to remind the science community that 'it must never be forgotten that we ourselves are both actors and spectators in the drama of existence' (Bohr 1950: 51) and that complementarity 'aims at an appropriate dialectic expression for the actual conditions of analysis and synthesis in atomic physics' (Bohr 1950: 54). Fox Keller (1983) in looking at the life work of Barbara McClintock, noble laureate, stated that science is not as precise as one imagines. Instead 'new theories (or arguments) are rarely, if ever, constructed by way of clear-cut steps of induction, deduction, and verification (or falsification). But rather scientists work with intuition, aesthetics and a philosophical commitment' (p. 145). McClintock herself said she worked with the so-called scientific methods but only '*after* you know' (Fox Keller 1983: 203) the answer to your research question.

McClintock developed an approach to studying the genetics of corn that came to be known as developing a 'oneness of things' which pushed against the research traditions of her time: 'Basically, everything is one. There is no way in which you draw a line between things, what we [normally] do is to make these subdivisions, but they're not real' (Fox Keller 1983: 204). The methodological genius of her research was in creating 'a oneness' through bringing together all biological forms into a dynamic connectivity – the cell, the organism and the ecosystem. To do this,

M. Fleer, Ph.D., M.Ed., M.A., B.Ed. (✉)
Faculty of Education, Monash University, Melbourne, Australia
e-mail: Marilyn.fleer@monash.edu

M. Fleer and A. Ridgway (eds.), *Visual Methodologies and Digital Tools for Researching with Young Children*, International Perspectives on Early Childhood Education and Development 10, DOI 10.1007/978-3-319-01469-2_1,
© Springer International Publishing Switzerland 2014

she metaphorically stepped into her microscope to study what initially appeared as disorder stating that 'the more I worked with them the bigger and bigger [they] got, and when I was really working with them I wasn't outside, I was down there. I was part of the system. I was right down there with them and everything got big. I even was able to see the internal parts of the chromosomes-actually everything was there. It surprised me because I actually felt as if I were right down there and these were my friends' (Fox Keller 1983: 117).

In examining the methodological comments of these two well-known scholars of science research, we find that they (1) created a sense of the oneness with what is being studied; (2) gave a holistic or 'a oneness' view of research, rather than reducing and studying all the elements into separate categories; and (3) studied the connectivity of the system giving new insights, and only then did they test these through the scientific method.

In this book we draw upon these methodological insights but in the context of researching with children. We specifically seek to theorise how digital visual technologies support the idea of taking a holistic and connected view of research, where the subject under study remains part of a dynamic ecosystem of interactions. We draw upon a range of post-developmental (Blaise 2010) concepts, taken from cultural-historical theory (Hedegaard and Fleer 2008; Veresov, Chap. 8, this volume) and critical theory (e.g. Agbenyega, Chap. 9, this volume) to present a fresh new look at research in early childhood education and development.

Concepts that are introduced in this book have been generated through studies where digital visual tools for researching with children have been the focus. In this first chapter, a theoretical analysis of the key concepts that are later extrapolated in subsequent chapters in this book is given. This theoretical chapter concludes with a statement on the need for the concepts of *ethical validity, cultural validity* and *tool validity* when using digital visual tools for researching with children in the early childhood period.

Post-developmental Methodologies for Undertaking Research Using Digital Visual Tools

Evelyn Fox Keller wrote back in 1983 that 'Scientists make up many communities, and these communities vary by subject, by methodology, by place, and by degree of influence. Science is a polyphonic chorus. The voices in that chorus are never equal, but what one hears as a dominant motif depends very much on where one stands' (p. 174). This statement about science can be applied directly to research with young children. That is, in the field of early childhood education and development, we find a polyphonic chorus of methodological voices. Claims are made in support of how to gain 'the truth' in research as well as the opposite view about 'how the truth does not exist'. The opposition to truth has also been heard within science, as noted by Barbara McClintock, when she said the scientific method 'gives us relationships which are useful, valid, and technically marvelous; however, they are not a truth' (Fox Keller 1983: 201).

A post-developmental perspective as first mooted by Blaise (2010) for the field of early childhood education generally is a useful way of thinking about research. Inspired by this conceptualisation, the term is adopted and expanded directly in relation to research methodologies where digital visual tools are used. Usually the term postpositivist is applied to name the movement away from quantitative research and to qualitative research. However, the term postpositivist is too generic to capture the uniqueness of researching in the field of early childhood education because studying young children in the birth-to-five period is hard to do in educational research. The complexity of generating data with infants, toddlers and preschool participants is well recognised. That is, young children cannot read to fill in a survey, have limited language development and therefore it is difficult to respond to formal interviews, and have no sense of the need to stay for a 'testing process or procedure' and will therefore not necessarily stay seated for long periods to respond to set tasks organised by researchers (see Fleer, Chap. 2, this volume). What is required is a sense of a holistic research context for studying with children, where ethical and cultural validity is the norm.

Ethical Validity of the Data

Post-developmental research as theorised here specifically positions itself outside of the traditional child study paradigm where the researcher is viewed as being removed from the context (see all chapters on the role of the researcher). Rather, in post-developmental methodologies, the researcher takes an active role in the study context, not as someone who plays with children (anthropological or ethnographic view), or as someone who observes objectively (like a fly on the wall), but rather as holding the role of 'the researcher' with a specific position and task in the context. Sorensen (Chap. 11, this volume) makes the case that this means that the researchers take an ethically informed position, because they can help a child and still engage with a child, not ignoring the child, and therefore not being disrespectful to the child as a person, and through this ethical interaction gain more authentic data. She shows in her study that the *role of researcher* is a concept that is understood by children. She gives the example of a child who in physical activity seriously falls when playing outdoors and who asks the researcher if she caught this on her video camera. When the child discovered that the researcher had put down the camera in order to help her, the child offered to recreate the accident, so that the integrity of the study situation could be maintained (i.e. the research was about the studying physical sport in preschools).

We also see important elements of validity in the work of Quinones (Chap. 7, this volume), where she shows the different roles that a researcher can take when researching with children. She discusses the concept of the affective positioning of the researcher. She introduces nuanced positions that are emotionally charged to explain how researchers act when interacting with children during research. She has theorised a number of positions, including the researcher as a teacher, as a friend, one who is in the context of space, time and emotions and as a visual-emotional partner.

The role of the researcher has not been theorised in these ways before. In a developmental research tradition, the role of the researcher has been to be objective and invisible because the researcher might contaminate the data. In using a post-developmental research methodology, as is shown in this book, it becomes important to tease out a range of ways that the researcher is positioned, because the role they take gives different possibilities for building a respectful and genuine interaction between the child and the researcher, thus enhancing the validity of the data. This can be thought about as an *ethical interaction* because in a post-developmental research methodology the researcher is not distant and unnatural but rather has a specific role that is taken and linked explicitly to the data that is generated.

Data gathered about or with young children is framed in relation to what role the researcher was taking at the time when the data were gathered, thus increasing the validity of the data generated and determining a higher level of what I term as the *ethical validity of the data*. A search of this term suggests that it has been used (see Edwards et al. 2008) but in relation to what I would consider to be *cultural validity* (discussed further below). *Ethical validity of the data* as it is discussed in this chapter refers to the *relationship and interaction* between the researcher and the child. Here the actual position that the researcher takes when interacting in the research context is coded with the data and is discussed in relation to the findings. The digital visual data is deemed *ethically valid* because the researcher takes a respectful and engaging position with the child in the research context. The position the researcher takes is considered when the data is analysed. This gives a more authentic and holistic approach to researching with very young children.

Holistic View of Researching with Young Children

All the chapters of this book go beyond a reductionist view of studying children, as subjects to be carved up into developmental periods – as has been the norm in the child study movement that underpins the foundations of early childhood education. In this book Fleer (Chap. 2, this volume) shows how digital video observations can be examined iteratively and gives the example of studying a child who is learning to walk, where the physical activity is examined in the context of how the child feels about her achievements and what motives exist for her learning to walk. She shows how a much more holistic study of a child learning to walk can be obtained. Walking is not viewed as a physical activity but also as an emotional and cognitive exchange between the child, the family and the researcher. That is, a post-developmental approach to researching with children would conceptualise learning to walk as also an emotional and cognitive activity not just a physical action. This view of research is in direct opposition to the traditional approach to studying and reporting on research in relation to the domains of physical, social-emotional, cognitive and language development. Here only parts of the child are studied when this latter conceptualisation is taken.

Veresov (Chap. 8, this volume) in critiquing traditional quantitative research makes the case for conceptualising the development of the child as a qualitative and transformative change – not as a child to be carved up once development has already taken place (i.e. at the end of the process, as the fruits of development). Development can be researched through the experimental-genetic method originally outlined by Vygotsky, where the buds of development (not the fruit) are the focus, where the relations between the ideal and the real forms of development are included in the study and where the idea of a dramatic event is foregrounded as the central catalyst for development. According to Veresov, researching with children entails these principles and provides a foundation for studying development in motion and not retrospectively. This approach to researching with children is very different to the traditional child study movement that historically underpinned the nature of studying children's development in early childhood education.

Tool Validity in Researching with Young Children

A post-developmental view of research is also captured in the chapter by Agbenyega (Chap. 9, this volume) where Bourdieu's concepts of habitus, field and forms of capital are used to study children in Africa. Agbenyega demonstrates how the analytical tools used in critical theory for researching with children should also be applied directly to the researcher – their role, their tools and their fieldwork and the forms of engagement they have with the children, families and communities where they are researching. In studying children's perceptions of the disciplinary techniques used in families and the early years of school, Agbenyega argues that 'video is an option but it wouldn't work for me in this situation because the teacher and parents may alter their real punitive practices thereby defeating the purpose of the study; therefore I opted to use drawing' (Chap. 9, this volume). Casting the critical lens back onto the researcher and what tools they employ to gather data represents an important dimension of researching with young children. That is, for valid data to be generated when studying sensitive issues such as discipline, careful thought must be given to what kinds of visual tools will generate the most authentic data. Being mindful of what the tools will afford in relation to not just the research question but the specific context being researched represents a form of *tool validity in researching with young children.*

Tool validity was also the subject of analysis by Sumsion, Bradley, Stratigos and Elwick (Chap. 10, this volume). In their work critical reflexivity was central for determining how they could understand infants' perspectives in research. Their innovative approach of using *baby cam* for participatory research involved connecting a lightweight video camera to a headband and strapping it to an infant's head in order to capture the visual field of the infant, where the infant's intentions could be determined in relation to another video camera which captured the context that the infant and carer were jointly participating in. Conceptualising the infant's perspective through examining their gaze was possible through the use of digital visual tools. In this instance the tool afforded the best option for authentic data gathering. Once again, thought is directed to tool validity in researching with infants.

In considering the choices made by researchers in relation to tool use for gaining authentic data, it is possible to see how *tool validity* is important when researching with young children. We see a further example of this in the work of Monk (Chap. 5, this volume) where she chose to use visual tools but in relation to giving the tool to her participant families for capturing what mattered to them. In studying intergenerational learning and development in families, Monk used digital images to bring all members of the extended families together in order to create opportunities for dialogue around the images. Through this she positioned the family members as coresearchers, arguing that the families were the only ones that could accurately interpret the digital photographic images, where the dialogue acted as the source, and photographs as the site, of data generation. Through this conceptualisation of the tool, she was able to more authentically document beliefs, values and practices associated with child-rearing across generations. Here tool validity was conceptualised in relation to what it afforded as a tool for coresearching with the families of young children.

Ethical validity and tool validity in the context of a holistic framework for research is presented in this book as central principles of post-developmental methodologies for researching with young children in early childhood settings. We use this term post-developmental methodologies explicitly because the field of early childhood education in most European heritage communities has been *mind-locked* into a developmental view. This latter perspective of child development has guided and reinforced a view of the child as being reduced into pieces – social-emotional, cognitive, language and physical development. Like shadows from the past, developmental theory lives with us in the present. This period in our research history can be conceptualised as a *developmental methodology*. Post-developmental methodologies better capture the uniqueness of the research undertaken now in early childhood education. Post-developmental methodologies is a more accurate term for our field than the term postpositivist because it recognises the *developmental past that has enslaved our thinking about research*. It is a past that we work against each time we prepare and present our work in early childhood education publications. Each of the chapters in this book exemplifies and theorises the principles of post-developmental methodologies, making visible a new way forward with digital visual tools.

Dialectical Frameworks for Undertaking Research Using Digital Visual Tools

In post-developmental methodologies for studying with children, a dialectical model is adopted, where no one part of the system is studied independently of the whole system of interactions. Dialectical logic is used by the authors of the chapters in this book. Dialectics is understood in the Hegelian sense as both elucidating contradictions and concretely resolving them. Rather than dualisms, such as universal and particular, dialectical logic seeks to bring together binary opposites as a synthesis, where both the general and the particular are both-at-once the same thing – as resolving contradictions. For instance, dualisms are evident in research when researchers conceptualise their research as either to 'generalise across populations' or as a particular 'case study'. Cartesian logic (mind-body split – as dualism) would support this separation as a dualism that cannot be reconciled together. However, dialectical logic would seek to conceptualise the contradiction of the *general* and the *particular* together as a synthesis. For example, it is not possible to think about a *particular* case of a child, unless one also thinks about the child in relation to *general* childhood or humanity. A child is only conceptualised as a child if we know about a grown-up child – an adult. The *particular* child is part of a *general* population of people with all their complexity. We see an example of dialectical logic in the writings of Ridgway (Chap. 4, this volume) where the historical is conceptualised as part of the present context. She introduces the term past-present dialectic to name this movement. Through the use of digital visual tools for documenting and analysing how past practices manifest themselves in the present context, Ridgway was able to make visible how the fishing history of a preschool community she studied shaped the current practices of the children in an early childhood centre. It was through synthesising images of the past with the digital images of present that practices could be understood.

The concept of synthesis is also evident in Monk's chapter when family members bring past photographic images of everyday life across three generations together with recent digitally captured images by the researcher and the families of everyday life, where contradictions are made visible and taken-for-granted practices become understood as value positions for child-rearing. It is not just the past-present dialectic of preschool practices or intergenerational child-rearing practices that become better understood when dialectical logic is used for researching with children but broader understandings of culture and community are also realised.

Cultural Validity of Data When Researching with Children

Researching everyday life using digital video tools is exemplified across chapters and across cultures, for instance, poor families in Australia (Chaps. 2, 4, 5 and 10, this volume), Chinese-Australian families maintaining their heritage language (Chap. 3, this volume), rural families in Cambodia (Chap. 6, this volume), rural family in Mexico (Chap. 7, this volume), urban schools in Ghana (Chap. 9, this volume) and sports preschools in Denmark (Chap. 10, this volume). Pennay (Chap. 6, this volume) explicitly transcends the insider-outsider dualism in research by adopting an interactive-dialectical methodology (Hedegaard and Fleer 2008) where she examines motives and demands in relation to children's intentions in a rural Cambodian community. Pennay examines 'at once' the perspectives of the adults and the perspectives of the children during everyday activities in the morning, at school and in the evening. She draws out the dialectical relationship between the translator and the researcher, as an important form of conceptualising the research process in order to *ensure cultural validity of the data*. Here she notes rapport, respect, reliability and reflexivity for achieving this. It is through these principles that a holistic view of the research context is formed.

Li (Chap. 3, this volume) in specifically drawing upon and expanding Hedegaard and Fleer's (2008) model of a wholeness approach to data generation shows how to build cultural validity. Through spiralling the analysis of visual data from a common-sense interpretation, a situated-practice interpretation and a thematic interpretation, it becomes possible to visit the data iteratively and to better understand the perspectives of children, parents and the researcher within the research context of the family. She names this final iteration as the *spiral of synthesis analysis* of family practices. Here the researcher is someone who is both within the cultural community (insider) and outside of the family as a visitor (outsider). This is not a boundary, but a dialectic. Li states that her visual analysis seeks to dialectically frame simple and complicated, individual and collective, and researcher and researched, where all perspectives are examined at the one time, leading to greater understandings of cultural practices. Cultural validity of the data is increased through the process of a spiral analysis.

Conclusion

In this chapter it has been argued that a post-positivist view of research does not accurately reflect the history and development of research in early childhood education. Our research history can be termed as a *developmental research methodology*, and that which has followed can be conceptualised as part of what I have termed in this chapter as *post-developmental research methodologies*. This book fits within the latter.

The concepts of *ethical validity, cultural validity* and *tool validity* have been introduced in this chapter in relation to using digital visual tools when researching with young children. These concepts are exemplified in the chapters that follow in this book where dialectical logic was predominantly used to capture *a holistic view of researching with young children*. Taken together, these concepts represent some of the unique features of what it means to use digital visual tools in generating data related to early childhood education and development. Whilst many have written about how to use digital visual tools, few have conceptualised these tools in relation to increasing ethical, cultural and tool validity for early childhood education research. The chapters that follow theorise digital visual tools in new ways, giving insights into researching with young children across cultures, generations and time periods. As a result, this book forges new pathways for post-developmental research.

References

Blaise, M. (2010). New maps for old terrain: Creating a postdevelopmental logic of gender and sexuality in the early years. In L. Brooker & S. Edwards (Eds.), *Engaging play* (pp. 80–96). London: Open University Press.

Bohr, N. (1950). The notions of causality and complementarity. *Science, 111*(2873), 51–54.

Edwards, K., Lund, C., & Gibson, N. (2008). Ethical validity: Expecting the unexpected in community-based research. *A Journal of Aboriginal and Indigenous Community Health, 6*(3), 17–30.

Fox Keller, E. (1983). *A feeling for the organism: Life and work of Barbara McClintock.* New York: Freeman.

Hedegaard, M., & Fleer, M. (Eds.). (2008). *Studying children: A cultural–historical approach.* Berkshire: Open University Press.

Part II
Cultural–Historical Conceptualisations of Digital Visual Tools

Chapter 2
Beyond Developmental Geology: A Cultural-Historical Theorization of Digital Visual Technologies for Studying Young Children's Development

Marilyn Fleer

Introduction

Back in 1966, Barker and Wright asked "How can the student of psychological ecology keep the situation natural and observe naturally occurring behavior when it is not natural for an observer to be present?" (p. 6). I would like to suggest that the question we now need to ask is: How can a researcher using cultural-historical theory keep the situation natural and use a digital video camera to observe naturally occurring behavior when it is not natural for the researcher to walk around holding a video camera? Using digital video tools might look easy, but without a theoretical gaze or without methodological confidence, all that will be gained is hours and hours of video data, without knowing what to do with it. Building a methodology for the use of digital visual technologies has become an important research need for the study of young children's development.

Much of the work that has been written in early childhood education around the use of digital visual tools has either focused on the technical dimensions of the resources, such as what they offer researchers and teachers (e.g., Fukkink et al. 2010; Theobald 2012), or as a description of approaches used in particular research studies (e.g., Hsueh and Tobin 2003). Very little theoretical work has been directed toward knowledge generation through digital visual tools for the study of young children's development across a range of cultural communities (Rose 2007). However, important work outside (Derry 2007) and related (Angelillo et al. 2007; Hedegaard and Fleer 2008; Tobin and Hsueh 2007) to the field of early childhood education provides insights into video pedagogy (Tocho 2007), study of infants (see Johansson and White 2011), video and phenomenology (Erickson 2007), peer learning (Hmelo-Silver et al. 2007), and informal learning environment, such as

M. Fleer, Ph.D., M.Ed., M.A., B.Ed. (✉)
Faculty of Education, Monash University, Melbourne, Australia
e-mail: Marilyn.fleer@monash.edu

M. Fleer and A. Ridgway (eds.), *Visual Methodologies and Digital Tools for Researching with Young Children*, International Perspectives on Early Childhood Education and Development 10, DOI 10.1007/978-3-319-01469-2_2,
© Springer International Publishing Switzerland 2014

museums (Palmquist and Crowley 2007; vom Lehn and Heath 2007). Consequently, the field of early childhood education has had to mostly draw upon work outside of its area when conceptualizing digital visual research (Johansson 2011a) from a cultural-historical perspective. Significantly, a theoretical space has emerged where digital video tools need to be studied in relation to cultural-historical theory, the research problem, and the study methods. We urgently need to build a cultural-historical methodology for digital tools when researching children's development (e.g., Quinones and Fleer 2011; Vygotsky 1998).

In this chapter it will be argued that digital visual tools when conceptualized from a cultural-historical perspective and applied to the study of child development will allow researchers to document and analyze a child's intentions and engagement across a variety of activity settings. As children move between home, community, preschool, and school, different practice traditions create conflicts and demands that create different conditions for children's development which can be captured in motion using digital video observations (Fleer 2008a, b, c). How these shape children, and how children contribute to these demands, conflicts, and transitions, can be studied in new ways and theorized differently when using digital video tools conceptualized by cultural-historical theory.

In the first part of this chapter, it will be argued that standard approaches to making observations of children have been dominated by traditional views of development where progression is captured as a linear movement following maturational developmental norms constituted in Western middle class communities. It is well understood within the field of early childhood education that these child development theories are limiting and have been called into question. Digital video observations and simple computer video editing tools give the possibility for conceptualizing development differently. I theorize how this might be possible.

In the second part of the chapter, a theoretical discussion will ensue, framed as a methodological rationale focused specifically on the use of digital visual technologies for researching children's development. The social situation of development for Louise, an 18-month-old toddler (Fleer 2010), will be used to illustrate the different features of a cultural-historical methodology for the use of digital visual technologies for studying young children's development.

Transcending Linearity and Capturing Change

When research focuses on studying change of some kind, then it is important to make explicit how change is captured and analyzed. This is usually theorized as some form of "development over time." But one of the fundamental problems facing the field of early childhood education is the need for a new theory of child development to replace the exiting and heavily critiqued maturational theory of how children develop (e.g., Dahlberg et al. 1999). The latter theory affords the documentation of biologically determined developmental milestones that are used as the benchmark for analysis. So how can cultural-historical theory inform research into child's development in ways which offer something new and help with gaining new understandings of children's development? For example, what would a cultural-historical study of a child learning to walk look like? Would a cultural-historical theory better inform our research practices than traditional maturational theory?

Temporality, rather than dynamic motion, is foregrounded in traditional thinking about development. Bringing together both development as change and development as an overarching theory of child development adds richness and context to a theoretical investigation of digital video technology as a methodological construct. This is particularly so for digital observations and analyses (see Lemke 2007), because as will be argued, *change does not need to be measured by time.*

Standard tools used for making observations of children within the field of early childhood education, such as paper and pencil, have been dominated by traditional views of development where progression is captured as a linear progression. Assumptions about children's development have mostly followed maturational developmental norms constituted in Western middle class communities (for a critique see Rogoff 2003). For instance, developmental milestones are often used as markers of "expected development over time," such as when a baby crawls at 6 months, walks at 12–14 months, and runs thereafter. Vygotsky (1997) argued that much of the research and theorization in traditional psychology sought to understand human development as a fused mix of biological and cultural development, where the biological developmental pathway is privileged because it is more visible. For example, when a child does not walk at an expected age, then this is viewed as a lack of developmental progression. Originally development was seen and researched in relation to growth and maturation. However, Vygotsky's thinking ran much deeper.

Unlike maturational theories of development, a cultural-historical conception of development is not linear. Vygotsky argued against a maturational or biologically driven view of development, stating that this theory only ever represented one side of development. He argued that although this theory acknowledges "the external influences on the biological plan (natural)," he stated that the biological plan does not go far enough because it does not show how "culture itself profoundly refines the natural state of behavior of the person and alters completely anew the whole course of his [sic] development" (Vygotsky 1997, p. 223). For instance, community beliefs about how babies are held ready to support communication or walking (e.g., see Nsamenang and Lamb 1998) determine the conditions for not only an infant's opportunities for social engagement and willingness to walk, but how they can physically respond or interact, completely changing the nature of what might be learned or developed. For example, in Cameroon babies are held outward facing the community, ready for social engagement, while in many European heritage communities, babies are held facing their caregiver, ready for one-to-one intimate communication.

Vygotsky (1997) articulated a theory that focused on a holistic model of development that included the dialectical relations between psychological, biological, and cultural dimensions as noted through motives, cognition, and the social situation of development (Bozhovich 2004, 2009; Kravtsova 2005). In a dialectical and revolutionary view of child development as discussed by Vygotsky (1997), the child's relations to their environment are the central source of development. For example, when an infant is constantly held to keep it safe because it lives within a family where older siblings and pets move rapidly about (Fleer 2010), the opportunities to learn to walk are different to an infant who is placed on the floor with an expectation of moving about by themselves. In a cultural-historical reading of child development, walking is culturally defined and enacted and not just biologically determined. Video observations can capture the complexity of the dynamics that surround the material conditions and social expectations that make up the cultural nature of a child's development.

Vygotsky (1997) stated that "the process of cultural development itself must be understood as a change in the basic original structure and the development of new structures" where cultural development "represent a genetically more complex and higher form of behavior" (Vygotsky 1997, p. 83). When using video tools, "video re-presentations may never be raw data in the sense that we once understood that phrase…" raw data deines all that which is captured "from the moment the video camera is turned on" (Goldman 2007, p. 17), and re-presentations of how this raw data is worked in layers. For example, digital video observations of an infant learning to walk are better understood when data are layered to determine the relations between individual motives, family interactions and demands, societal expectations of when children are "expected to walk," and the material conditions available to the infant. The video data are saturated with interpretation across each of these layers, but these interpretations can only be understood in relation to each other. One level of analysis (i.e., at the individual child level) is given meaning by an analysis at another level (i.e., the community expectation of when children should walk).

Vygotsky (1997) argued that maturational theories of development when used by educators position the person "to take slow, smooth steps" (p. 223) along a particular development trajectory, as an *evolutionary pathway* of child development. However, in Vygotsky's alternative theorization, he suggested that development could be captured through the metaphor of *skipping*, where development is nonlinear and revolutionary. For example, a dynamic form of analysis is needed when we see an infant who is positioned centrally within a family, always being held, placed into a high chair, or pram, for extended periods, and where siblings are constantly moving about the house circling the mother and infant, the high chair, or the pram, engaging with the baby and each other and the material environment. In this example, there is no need for the infant to walk and no motive for learning to walk. The infant does not develop walking in relation to an expected age, but rather in relation to the material conditions and social need for walking. Digital video tools capture this engagement and interaction and give a new approach for dynamic analysis of development. Goldman (2007) argued that "Video representations seem to be a different kind of re-presentation than textual representations. They display and illustrate a person's expression and experience in the context of a community as an event is taking place" (p. 16). Knowledge production about human development

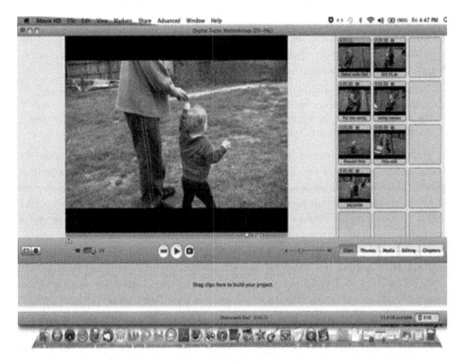

Fig. 2.1 Screen dump capturing a child learning to walk

is viewed "as a series of dynamic and interactive events," and this perspective "trumps the linear, causal, and internal explanation" (p. 22) and problematizes linearity (see Tobin 2007). The metaphor of *skipping* transcends linearity as measured by time, and video tools help realize this new dynamic way of thinking about capturing change.

Capturing change as *skipping* is central to Vygotsky's (1997) dynamic methodology where child development is viewed as a dialectical process between the child and their social and material world as a form of cultural development. Vygotsky (1997) argued that "Culture is both a product of social life and of the social activity of man [sic] and for this reason, the very formulation of the problem of cultural development of behavior already leads us directly to the social plane of development" (Vygotsky 1997, p. 106). Important here for understanding skipping as a metaphor for cultural development is the concept of *social mediation*. Social mediation is the relations between the child and their material world, and mediation with all its complexity can be easily captured in digital visual form as a copy of social reality. An example of what this might look like when using simple technologies, such as Imovie on a Macintosh, is shown in the screen dump depicted in Fig. 2.1. Here the example of a child learning to walk is shown. An electronic copy of these social relations that become higher mental functions allows for the possibility of an iterative analysis as conceptualized through the metaphor of *skipping*. In this theorization, it is important to acknowledge that Vygotsky had a specific scientific meaning for the term social because to do otherwise would be to risk reducing the interpretations of Vygotsky's theory to a superficial or everyday reading of this term:

> The word "social," as applied to our subject, has a broad meaning. First of all, in the broadest sense, it means that everything cultural is social. ...Further, we could indicate the fact that the sign found outside the organism, like a tool, is separated from the individual and serves essentially as social organ or social means. (Vygotsky 1997, p. 106)

Hence, all "higher mental functions are the essence of internalized relations of a social order, a basis for the social structure of the individual. Their composition, genetic structure, method of action – in a word, their entire nature – is social; even in being transformed into mental processes, they remain quasisocial" (Vygotsky 1997, p. 106). Digital visual technologies capture the social order and structure of the individual in the process of its formation.

Digital video observations provide detailed accounts of how, in everyday life, cultural development is shaped by and shapes the social situations that the child finds themselves in. Digital video analysis allows these cultural interactions to be examined and reexamined, in ways which include the researcher and the researched, the material world, and the past events that are active in the moment. Categories are held visually together within a system of concepts and are not separated out. For instance, to examine the "demands" upon a child, one can also examine the "demands" and "expectations" that the child makes upon an adult. For example, when an infant who cannot yet walk wishes to be on a swing, the infant will make demands upon the adult to carry her to the swing and give support. The adult creates the conditions by providing the swing. But when the adult does not have time to support the infant to go on to the swing, this places demand upon the infant to try to stand in order to go onto the swing. This in turn may lead to the development of a motive to learn to walk (Fleer 2010). The complexity of this kind of analysis, common in cultural-historical research, can be understood when the techniques of digital analysis are considered.

In situ video observations gained through digital video recording, and the mirroring of this process later through digital video analysis, allow many possibilities for analysis which seek to keep data connected and not disembedded from context, activity, and the lived nature of everyday life where development occurs. In digital video work, the layers of analysis are iterative and present themselves within the mirror image of the real situation being researched (as shown in Fig. 2.1).

To document the cultural nature of development as *revolutionary rather than evolutionary* process requires tools, such as digital visual technologies, that will make visible the nature of the dynamic interaction conceptualized in the *skipping* metaphor. Vygotsky (1997) states that "It is obvious that the uniqueness of this process of changing behavior that we call cultural development requires very unique methods and ways of research" (Vygotsky 1997, p. 27). A cultural-historical conception of digital visual technologies for the study of child development gives this possibility.

A Cultural-Historical Method for Using Digital Technologies in the Study of Child Development

In 1997 Joseph Glick in his prologue of the 4th volume of the Collected Works of L. S. Vygotsky spoke of Vygotsky's account of the history of the development of higher mental functions as a form of *developmental geology*. In this book, Vygotsky (1997) uses the metaphor of the "fossil" to make visible to the reader how the study of development in his time had focused primarily on the study of what had already formed and was complete, rather than what was in the process of development. Vygotsky (1997) argued that the research tools and their accompanying methodologies were designed to study *psychological fossils* "in a petrified and arrested form in their internal development" (p. 44). He suggested that "The beginning and end of development is united in them. They actually are outside of the process of development. Their own development is finished. In this combination of plasticity and fossilization, initial and final points of development, simplicity and completeness lies their great advantage for research, making them incomparable material for study" (Vygotsky 1997, p. 44). As a result of Vygotsky's work, a whole new approach to researching children's development has emerged, and new theoretical insights have been generated, particularly for early childhood research. It is timely that new digital visual technologies, unavailable in Vygotsky's time, be theorized so that early childhood researchers can more rigorously employ these new tools for data gathering and analysis in the theoretical field of cultural-historical theory.

Technological advances have generated a range of digital visual tools that have been posited as being useful to researchers. Digital video observations are fluid, dynamic, and rich with analytical possibilities that are always in flux. Digital video technologies through both their familiarity with research participants and their possibility for uniting rather than dividing data represent a contemporary technology not previously available. Consequently, it is important that these new digital tools be theorized and their potential for studying children be excavated. In Fig. 2.2 the central elements of digital video technologies for studying child development from a cultural-historical perspective are brought together as a model.

In this model the dialectical relations between methodology and method are central. Here the study design transcends linearity and seeks to capture change in motion. The left side of the model suggests a strong relationship between the research problem, the use of digital technologies (i.e., digital video observations and analysis), and the study of change in a recursive, iterative, and concurrent manner (as shown at the bottom of the model). The right-hand side of the model conceptualizes the researcher as not only part of the study design but as a central force in orchestrating the capturing of dynamic motion in action, the unity of affect and intellect, where emotionality can signal noteworthy data for recording and later analysis. The central features of this model collectively interact to capture change

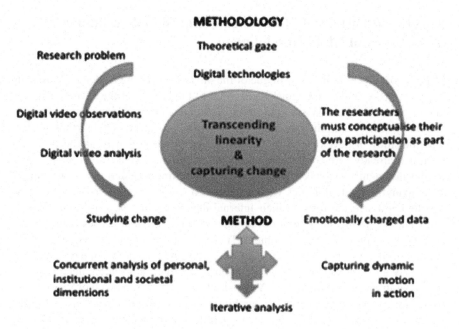

Fig. 2.2 A cultural-historical model for the use of digital technologies

in nonlinear motion as exemplified through the *skipping* metaphor. The uniquely cultural-historical features of digital video technologies which are exemplified in the model include, how:

1. The researcher is conceptualized as intertwined within the activity setting, but always as the researcher who is obviously using a digital video camera to gather data.
2. Digital video technologies by their very nature copy social reality and capture emotionality in association with actions, activity, and social mediation as a form of emotionally charged data.
3. Digital video analysis lends itself to iterative analysis where the researcher can concurrently examine personal, institutional, and societal dimensions associated with the specific research question under investigation, and trawl backward and forward through visual data as new elements emerge that were not originally conceptualized within the design, but which can be examined because the digital video technologies capture detail not possible through traditional approaches employed in research.

These elements are discussed in an interrelated way within the following three themes that make up the model shown in Fig. 2.2: conceptualizing the role of the researcher in digital observations, emotionally charged data, and digital video analysis.

Conceptualizing the Role of the Researcher in Digital Observations

In video observations the researcher becomes intertwined with the activity setting because she/he moves about within the setting following with the camera the movement and activity of the participants (Fleer 2008c). This is particularly significant for research in early childhood, where young children are likely to be physically active, not stopping for the researcher, but rather actioning what they wish to do (e.g., video recording of infant's nonverbal actions; White 2011a). Hedegaard (2008a) argues that the researcher "enters into a social situation with other persons where she has to *understand* what is going on as a participant in everyday practice" (p. 202). The researcher has to follow the intent of the child and understand the context in which she has entered in order to know how to make digital video observations. The researcher cannot simply be seated absent from the activity, because the situation demands that for quality video observations and sound, the researcher must stay in close proximity to the child. In research by Degotardi (2011) she was known as the "camera lady" and in Hedegaard's (2008a) work she was positioned as the "children's researcher." The positioning of the researcher by the participants through the identification of their role means that everyone is clear about what role the researcher is taking. Significantly, this also names the relationship that has formed between the participants and the researcher.

Hedegaard (2008a) argues "the social scientist both participates in activities in everyday settings paying attention to her needs and motives and, at the same time, includes these activities as her object of study – with the focus on the participants' motives, projects and intentions" (p. 202). In relation to digital technologies, a researcher must conceptualize his or her own participation as part of the researched activities and note this in the edited digital video clips created as part of the analysis. Here the researcher's motives, project, and intentions are documented as text, and these form the relational links between the raw video material and edited video clips. An example is shown in Fig. 2.3 where the analysis framework is given. In this example, the digital video observations were made of everyday family life over 12 months, organized around three periods of data gathering. This particular video observation has been made over a 1 h period of family interactions in the after-school period. The example shown has been taken from the second observation period, and this observation is the first one being undertaken after not visiting the family home for 3 months. The father is showing the researcher the youngest child's achievements (Louise) in learning to walk. A series of video clips have been made, and the following dialogue represents one clip:

Transcript: Achievements in learning to walk

Dad: She won't walk by herself.
Researcher: But she is crawling fast.
Dad: She will walk around everywhere doing this (walks with father, holding his hand).
Researcher: Wow

Family: _Pen_ Period: _2_ Time: _4.30 pm_ **Researcher filming:** _Marilyn_ Code for digital video record: (_P2 V1 MF_) **Transcript:** _Dad: She won't walk by herself._ _Researcher: But she is crawling_ _fast...._. **Relations to observer:** _Ex-_ _change. Researchers help chil-_ _dren who are all wanting the_ _snacks provided by the research-_ _er_ **Relations to observer:** _Louise_ _looks to observer for response to_ _her walking. Father wants to_ _show Louise's walking achieve-_ _ments_	**Description overview:** _The research-_ _ers meet the family at their home. Th e_ _children have been home for an hour_ _and are playing outside....the father_ _leads the researchers to the new slid e_ _and swing set where Louise is swing-_ _ing....._ **Digital video log:** **00–0.5:** _Arrival and greetings_ **0.5–0.25:** _____ etc **Activities (summary):** - _Arrival and greetings_ - _Louise walking with father_
Focus child(ren): _____ **Relations to siblings:** _____	**Commonsense interpretations** **Individual** _____ **Institutional** _____ **Societal:** _____

Categories
 	
Cultural-historical concepts
 	
   Engagement/motives:
 	
   Emotions:
	Links to Video Project (raw data)
	
	(clip1): Louise walking 1 

Points of interest:	**Situated interpretations:** Links within records (clips in other records)
	Thematic interpretation: Links across records (clips in other records)

Fig. 2.3 A cultural-historical _analysis framework_ for digital technologies

Louise: Smiles broadly
Dad: But when you let go of her hand...
Researcher and Dad: She drops down (Louise sits down).
Louise: Drops down and signals for help by raising her arm towards her father
(extract Period 2, Visit 1)

The role of the researcher is captured in the analysis framework and that is shown in the first column. This framework is a type of pro forma that is used for organizing and then analyzing all digital video data. For each hour of video data, the researcher records details of who is being researched (i.e., which family) and when the observation was made (period; time). Each video observation is summarized and logged, and the activities are recorded as a list (this is shown in the second column). The focus of the observation is given (i.e., child, parent), and the relations between the researcher and the participants are noted in connection with the specific activities that have been video recorded. Coding, and the interpretations that are shown below, is discussed later in the chapter.

Writing the researcher into the material gathered is rarely undertaken in the research process. Exceptions include Cosaro and Molinaro (2000), Hedegard and Fleer (2008c), and Christensen (2004). These researchers write themselves into data (Hedegaard and Fleer 2008) or into the narrative that forms as a result of the analysis (Cosaro and Molinari 2000) or as the initiator of an ongoing intervention (Christensen 2004). In most research the role of the researcher is made invisible or wiped from the scene. This was also noted by Vygotsky (1987) in traditional psychological research where he determined that researchers frequently set up an experimental condition, but they never included in their data or the analysis details of how the researcher introduced the intervention. Vygotsky's (1987) advice is pertinent:

> Usually the decisive moment of the experiment – the instruction – is left outside the research. The researcher, forgetting the origin of the artificially elicited process, naively trusted that the process went forward in exactly the same way as if it had appeared of itself without instruction. (Vygotsky 1987, p. 36)

In video observations of naturalistic settings, the researcher continues to record even when he/she is asked by the child about the technology (i.e., can they see themselves in the video camera) or when they ask for help, or in the case where the researcher intervenes in the activity because of a health or safety issue, such as when children pick up and use a dangerous piece of equipment where they could hurt themselves. When or if to turn off the camera is an important and central question in research which primarily uses digital video observations (Johansson 2011b). Despite interruptions to what would be deemed as the normal course of events, the researcher using video tools continues to record the events because they form the connected whole that makes up the video observation. The camera is not turned off because as a child meets new demands, capturing these as data could be of significance for answering the research question.

Cultural-historical observations offer what Hedegaard (2008a) termed the *doubleness of the researcher*, where the researcher acts as a researcher but also has a relationship to the children and the other adults in the research context. In digital video research this *doubleness* is captured explicitly by not turning off the video camera when the researcher interacts with the participants, but also when the researcher seeks meaning during analysis where the researcher's role is considered when viewing the digital video data. Here the researcher's contributions to the activity setting must be noted and examined as a relation between the raw data and the video clips through the textual analyses that are created (see Fig. 2.3). How the relations between the researcher and the researched develop throughout the research project is important to capture in cultural-historical research. In video observations it is possible to check for this by listening to the dialogue between the researcher and the participants at different points within the data set (or as nonverbal interactions when viewing video clips). As with other forms of qualitative research, in video observations the researcher must also code for the development of the relations between the participants and the researcher.

Cultural-historically framed studies which use digital video tools must show how the relationship between participants was formed and developed so that all subsequent video observations can be analyzed with this backdrop in mind. Confidence that the research has generated valid results emerges when the perspectives of the participants are considered when analyzing the material in relation to the perspective of each participant. It is through an analysis of their relations and perspectives, alongside of the role that the researcher took at different points within the video observations, that validity is established. With this conception, digital video tools offer a significant method for undertaking research into child development. Yet, there is more to digital video observations than simply capturing "motion." The emotionality of the context being filmed and how these affect the researcher during and later within the analysis period also need to be included within the *dynamic analysis framework*. We now turn to a discussion of the emotional nature of video technologies.

Emotionally Charged Data

> Video is often pushed as a research tool in term of its virtues of being an efficient way of telling a story ("a picture is worth a thousand words") and its utility as a data-recording tool (providing opportunities for multiple coding slowing down action, etc.). These claims are true, but they leave something out: video can be very pleasurable, both to make and to watch. These need not be guilty pleasures. Why not name and acknowledge them? (Tobin and Hsueh 2007, p. 90)

Emotions in research is not a topic that is generally valued or discussed. However, Hsueh and Tobin (2003) deal with this explicitly. Twenty years ago Jo Tobin pioneered the use of analogue video for research in early childhood education. His video ethnography has been conceptualized as a reflective tool for stimulated interviews across cultures, where early childhood teachers are shown cross-cultural examples of early childhood practices and are asked to comment on what they see.

Fig. 2.4 Emotional exchange
captured and analyzed
through digital video
technologies

As part of his own reflections with colleagues, he has highlighted an important
aesthetic and emotional dimension of video work, usually not discussed in research
reports, primarily because it appears to be too subjective. He has argued that video
recording is an "artistic process and that editing videos can be a tedious process, but
that on the whole it is a pleasurable way of working." He has suggested that the
"written word both as something we create and consume is not as visceral or immediate as something we listen to or watch" (Tobin and Hsueh 2007, p. 90).

Digital video analysis is a tactile process that captures the tone of interactions
between people and material conditions that are often missed when paper and
pencil approaches are adopted. For example, videotaping an infant walking for the
first time is loaded with emotions, not just for the child but also for those who
mediate this practice. There is a kind of emotional energy that is captured with the
video data and which is retained as an important factor in undertaking the analysis.
The emotionality of the data can give clues and direction for how the data is to be
worked and what might be noteworthy for analyses across data sets – moving
beyond pre-established categories. An example of this is shown in Fig. 2.4 where
this image represents a still frame taken from the raw data represented in Fig. 2.1
and transcribed (see earlier transcript) and tagged in Fig. 2.3. Collectively, these
figures illustrate that the father is showing the researcher with great pride that his
daughter Louise is now able to walk with just some assistance. The researcher is
clearly being invited to observe, comment, and share this moment of achievement.
This is evident because Louise looks back to the researcher as she is walking to
"check" the researcher's response to her achievement. Video observations capture
not just the walking but the emotional exchange between all three people documented in this observation. In Fig. 2.4 we see the emotional exchange between the
infant, the father, and the researcher.

Emotionality captured as a system of exchanges is made possible through video
observation and analysis. Consequently, it becomes possible to examine how "Every
idea contains some remnant of the individual's affective relationship to that aspect
of reality which it represents" (Vygotsky 1987, pp. 50–51). Video analysis allows

the researcher to hold constant many different dimensions of an event, activity, or social exchange. It allows the researcher to go back and forth between data sets to find possibilities that contributed to an emotional exchange from previous contexts and exchanges captured on digital video. The researcher codes these exchanges and tries to make meaning of the everyday interactions that have "somehow" become emotionally charged activities in ways that are not always visible to the observer on first viewing of the data, or which may be missed if traditional paper and pencil observations are used.

Cultural-historical scholars who have revisited Vygotsky's writings on the unity of emotions and intellect are now including this unity in their work (see Roth 2011). Quinones and Fleer (2011) found that when a child is participating in learning experiences that they find boring, emotionality matters when interpreting the data. Similarly when children are engaged in play where they show joy, they can also express fear when they are role-playing being the patient who is about to get a needle from a nurse. Two kinds of emotions are concurrently experienced – fear and pleasure. Cultural-historical researchers have noted a gap in their work, finding that *emotions* are an important and rich dimension of any research project, and that its absence reduces the quality of the analysis and interpretation (see Gonzalez Rey 2012). Vygotsky (1987) drew attention to this problem a long time ago when he noted that by "isolating thinking from affect at the outset, we effectively cut ourselves off from any potential for a causal explanation of thinking" (p. 50), but rather, there "exists a dynamic meaningful system that constitutes *a unity of affective and intellectual processes*" (pp. 50–51). Digital video tools allow for the capture and the close study of this dynamic. How this is realized in the practice of analysis is shown in the next section.

Digital Video Analysis

In the previous sections it was shown that digital video observations bring together the dynamics of the whole in motion, as exemplified through the skipping metaphor, in ways that demand analysis in layers and as action movements which are nonlinear and not static. Analysis seeks to find the relational dimensions, as is symbolized in Fig. 2.5, where the raw data, the edited video clips, and the interpretations are simultaneously shown on screen. Participants' verbal language and bodily movements need to be viewed in relation to their social relations and intentions (particularly with the researcher) and the material interactions as presented. Digital video observations keep these data "together" during the analysis, as depicted in Fig. 2.5, where analysis is kept as a *relational whole.*

Digital analysis is dislocated from the actual research site, and the analysis becomes progressively more abstract, despite the fact that raw data captures a copy of reality, as shown in Fig. 2.5. With written observations Hedegaard (2008b) has

Fig. 2.5 Screen dump depicting the unity in analysis

defined these layers into three processes. However, in digital visual analysis these three layers are together in the *one* system:

1. A common sense interpretation
2. A situated practice interpretation
3. A thematic interpretation

Digital video analysis at the first level is coded by examining the digital video data and writing an overall interpretation of what is evident in relation to the 1 h of video data (discussed in relation to Fig. 2.3). Situated practice interpretations in digital analysis involve linking raw data, video clips, and written interpretations together on the one screen (see Fig. 2.5). Finally, a thematic interpretation goes beyond individual digital video files and seeks to bring together multiple examples to build evidence across data sets (see over the page Fig. 2.6). While it is possible to undertake the three layers of analysis for any data set, when using digital video observations and analyses, all three levels of interpretation occur concurrently, moving back and forth across the data, adding more and more visual layer to the analysis as the material is worked. How this is realized in practice is shown across the figures in this chapter.

Figure 2.5 shows both the digital video program Imovie introduced in Fig. 2.1 together with the analysis framework shown in Fig. 2.3. Digital technologies allow the researcher to simultaneously consider the individual child's experience in the

Fig. 2.6 Thematic interpretations formed through simultaneous viewing of digital video data

moment, family expectations, demands upon the child, and the material conditions, while also including across institutional contexts where different expectations and material conditions exist, the latter being determined by societal expectations of child-rearing (in addition to expectations of preschool education), how children should behave, and the resources that are directed to the activity. For example, documenting the significance of the infant's achievement in learning to walk must also be understood in relation to how the family was being positioned by staff from the Department of Human Services, where expectations of when a child should be walking were being expressed directly to the parents. This was understood because multiple files were brought together to show thematic interpretations. This is visually represented in Fig. 2.6 (see folder of files marked as Visit 4). This digital analysis includes interview data, video data, video clips, stills, and sets of files across data sets, though this layering can depict parents' perceptions of societal expectations of child development (in this example, as expressed through the Department of Human Services who visited the family and had specific expectations of children's development, see Fleer and Hedegaard 2010).

All of these dimensions (individual, institutional, and societal) can be made visible at all points in an analysis and when contemplating findings. It is very easy to move the digital video images forward and backward by simple mouse movements. Still images of important interaction sequences can be captured and loaded directly into word documents. Digital video logs make transparent patterns across raw data, and multiple digital video records provide a layered patterning across data files. All of these can be held together at one moment when using digital video tools. This cultural-historical approach to the study of young children builds upon earlier work (see Hedegaard and Fleer 2008) because relational dimensions of the individual, the institutions, and the society (Hedegaard 2008a) are theorized in relation to how digital video technologies provide a tool for data contemplation that foregrounds their *unity in analysis*.

In digital video analysis, these relational demands can be viewed in terms of the conditions that the context creates, such as the rules and expectations of child-rearing and how children and adults shape or are shaped by these societal or community expectations. These dialectical relations can be viewed in each moment of raw data, and the differing perspectives make visible and can be considered concurrently, interpreted, stills created, and other raw data files opened and interrogated in the same manner in order to see thematic patterns across data sets. This type of analytical connectedness dispenses with linearity and creates the possibility for fusing and holding together elements that are often disconnected. This is made possible through the aid of digital video technologies. Digital tools make dialectical research more easily executed because data can be visually displayed and visually revisited for detail not originally thought important to code or to document during observations, but which are present because the raw data captures more detail than other traditional tools.

Conclusion

> In studying any new area, it is necessary to begin by seeking and developing a method. In the form of a general position, we might say that every basically new approach to scientific problems leads inevitably to new methods and ways of research. The material and method of research are closely related. For this reason, research acquires a completely different form and course when it is linked to finding a new method suitable to the new problem; in that case, it differs radically from those forms in which the study simply applies developed and established scientific methods to new areas. (Vygotsky 1997, p. 27)

Although this statement was made more than 80 years ago, it is as pertinent now as it was then. Digital tools theorized as a particular methodological construct from a cultural-historical perspective bring to light the need for capturing the *full dynamics* and *revolution* of the social and material world within which the child is located. This contrasts with an approach which sees attention directed toward studying the process of development when it has already concluded, solidified, or as Vygotsky (1997) noted has become *fossilized* (p. 71). Traditional approaches to research represent a *postmortem* approach.

In this chapter we have sought to better understand how a cultural-historical perspective on the use of digital video tools can inform the study of child development. I have specifically drawn upon cultural-historical theory for analyzing these digital tools for use in contemporary contexts and with young children, and through this to theorize how digital visual technologies can act as a research methodology that transcends linearity and captures change. As noted by White (2011b) "the visual means employed never stand alone – they are determined by the theories that underpin them" (p. 197). A cultural-historical theorization of digital video technologies provides a contemporary and powerful tool for studying young children's development. Through these tools of observation and analysis, new knowledge and understandings are possible and new insights into child development can be determined.

Acknowledgment Monash University Research Committee provided funds for inviting a professional writing consultant, Dr. Barbara Kamler, to contribute to building writing expertise within the Faculty of Education. A methodology chapter is very different to writing an empirical paper and hence very difficult to write. I am very appreciative of the amazing expertise of Dr. Kamler and wish to acknowledge her insightfulness for the redevelopment of my chapter.

References

Angelillo, C., Rogotff, B., & Chavajay, O. (2007). Examining shared endeavors by abstracting video coding schemes: With fidelity to cases. In R. Goldman, R. Pea, B. Barron, & S. J. Derry (Eds.), *Video research in the learning sciences* (pp. 189–206). Mahwah: Lawrence Erlbaum Associates.

Barker, R. G., & Wright, H. F. (1966). *One boys' day – A specimen record of behavior*. New York: Harper and Brothers Publishers.

Bozhovich, L. I. (2004). L. S. Vygotsky's historical and cultural theory and its significance for contemporary studies of the psychology of personality. *Journal of Russian and East European Psychology, 42*(4), 20–34.

Bozhovich, L. I. (2009). The social situation of child development. *Journal of Russian and East European Psychology, 47*(4), 59–86.

Christensen, P. H. (2004). Children's participation in ethnographic research: Issues of power and representation. *Children and Society, 18*, 165–176.

Cosaro, W. A., & Molinari, L. (2000). Entering and observing in children's worlds: A reflection on a longitudinal ethnography of early education in Italy. In A. James (Ed.), *Researching with children: Perspectives and practices* (pp. 179–200). London: Falmer Press.

Dahlberg, G., Moss, P., & Pence, A. (1999). *Beyond quality in early childhood education and care: Postmodern perspectives*. London: Falmer Press.

Degotardi, S. (2011). Two steps back: Using Bourdieu's theory of practice to explore observer identity and presence. In E. J. White & E. Johansson (Eds.), *Educational research with our youngest: Voices of infants and toddlers* (pp. 15–38). New York: Springer.

Derry, S. J. (2007). Video research in classroom and teacher learning (standardize that!). In R. Goldman, R. Pea, B. Barron, & S. J. Derry (Eds.), *Video research in the learning sciences* (pp. 305–320). Mahwah: Lawrence Erlbaum Associates.

Erickson, F. (2007). Ways of seeing video: Toward a phenomenology of viewing minimally edited footage. In R. Goldman, R. Pea, B. Barron, & S. J. Derry (Eds.), *Video research in the learning sciences* (pp. 145–158). Mahwah: Lawrence Erlbaum Associates.

Fleer, M. (2008a). Interpreting research protocols – the institutional perspective. In M. Hedgeaard & M. Fleer (Eds.), *Studying children: A cultural-historical approach* (pp. 65–87). Berkshire: Open University Press.

Fleer, M. (2008b). Interpreting research protocols – the child's perspective. In M. Hedegaard & M. Fleer (Eds.), *Studying children: A cultural-historical approach* (pp. 88–103). Berkshire: Open University Press.

Fleer, M. (2008c). Using digital video observations and computer technologies in a cultural-historical approach. In M. Hedegaard & M. Fleer (Eds.), *Studying children: A cultural-historical approach* (pp. 104–117). Berkshire: Open University Press.

Fleer, M. (2010). *Concepts in play*. New York: Cambridge University Press.

Fleer, M., & Hedegaard, M. (2010, April–June). Children's development as participation in everyday practices across different institutions: A child's changing relations to reality. *Mind, Culture and Activity, 17*(2), 149–168.

Fukkink, R. G., Louis, W. C., & Tavecchio, L. W. C. (2010). Effects of video interaction guidance on early childhood teachers. *Teaching and Teacher Education, 26*, 1652–1659.

Glick, J (1997). Prologue (M. J. Hall, Trans.). In R. W. Rieber (Ed.), *The collected works of L.S. Vygotsky: The history of the development of higher mental functions* (Vol. 4, pp. v–xvi). New York: Plenum Press.

Goldman, R. (2007). Video representations and the perspectivity framework: Epistemology, ethnography, evaluation, and ethics. In R. Goldman, R. Pea, B. Barron, & S. J. Derry (Eds.), *Video research in the learning sciences* (pp. 3–38). Mahwah: Lawrence Erlbaum Associates.

Gonzalez Rey, F. (2012). Advancing on the concept of sense: Subjective sense and subjective configurations in human development. In M. Hedegaard, A. Edwards, & M. Fleer (Eds.), *Motives in children's development. Cultural-historical approaches* (pp. 45–62). Cambridge/New York: Cambridge University Press.

Hedegaard, H. (2008a). The role of the researcher. In M. Hedegaard & M. Fleer (Eds.), *Studying children: A cultural-historical approach* (pp. 202–207). Berkshire: Open University Press.

Hedegaard, H. (2008b). Principles for interpreting research protocols. In M. Hedegaard & M. Fleer (Eds.), *Studying children: A cultural-historical approach* (pp. 46–64). Berkshire: Open University Press.

Hedegaard, M., & Fleer, M. (Eds.). (2008). *Studying children: A cultural-historical approach.* Berkshire: Open University Press.

Hmelo-Silver, C. E., Kati, E., Nagarajan, A., & Chernobilsky, E. (2007). Soft leaders, hard artifacts, and the groups we rarely see: Using video to understand peer learning processes. In R. Goldman, R. Pea, B. Barron, & S. J. Derry (Eds.), *Video research in the learning sciences* (pp. 255–270). Mahwah: Lawrence Erlbaum Associates.

Hsueh, Y., & Tobin, J. (2003). Chinese early childhood educators' perspectives on dealing with a crying child. *Journal of Early Childhood Research, 1*(1), 73–94.

Johansson, E. J. (2011a). Introduction: Giving words to children's voices in research. In E. Johansson & E. J. White (Eds.), *Educational research with our youngest: Voices of infants and toddlers* (pp. 1–14). Dordrecht: Springer.

Johansson, E. J. (2011b). Investigating morality in toddler's life-worlds. In E. Johansson & E. J. White (Eds.), *Educational research with our youngest: Voices of infants and toddlers* (pp. 39–62). Dordrecht: Springer.

Johansson, E., & White, E. J. (Eds.). (2011). *Educational research with our youngest: Voices of infants and toddlers.* Dordrecht: Springer.

Kravtsova, Y. Y. (2005). The concept of age novel formation in modern developmental psychology. *Journal of Cultural-Historical Psychology, 1*(2), 23–24.

Lemke, J. (2007). Video epistemology in-and-outside the box: Traversing attentional spaces. In R. Goldman, R. Pea, B. Barron, & S. J. Derry (Eds.), *Video research in the learning sciences* (pp. 39–52). Mahwah: Lawrence Erlbaum Associates.

Nsamenang, A. B., & Lamb, M. E. (1998). Socialization of Nso children in the Bamenda Grassfields of Northwest Cameroon. In M. Woodhead, D. Faulkner, & K. Littleton (Eds.), *Cultural worlds of early childhood* (pp. 250–260). London: Routledge.

Palmquist, S. D., & Crowley, K. (2007). Studying dinosaur learning on an island of expertise. In R. Goldman, R. Pea, B. Barron, & S. J. Derry (Eds.), *Video research in the learning sciences* (pp. 271–286). Mahwah: Lawrence Erlbaum Associates.

Quinones, G., & Fleer, M. (2011). "Visual Vivencias": A cultural-historical tool for understanding the lived experiences of young children's everyday lives. In E. Johansson & E. J. White (Eds.), *Educational research with our youngest: Voices of infants and toddlers* (pp. 107–134). Dordrecht: Springer.

Rogoff, B. (2003). *The cultural nature of human development.* Oxford: Oxford University Press.

Rose, G. (2007). *Visual methodologies: An introduction to the interpretation of visual materials* (2nd ed.). London: Sage.

Roth, W.-M. (2011). Emotion, motives, motivation. In W.-M. Roth (Ed.), *Possibility: At the limits of the constructivist metaphor* (pp. 185–203). Dordrecht: Springer.

Theobald, M. A. (2012). Video-stimulated accounts: Young children accounting for interactional matters in front of peers. *Journal of Early Childhood Research, 10*(1), 32–50.

Tobin, J. (2007). An anthropologist's reflections on defining quality in education research. *International Journal of Research and Method in Education, 30*(3), 325–338.

Tobin, J., & Hsueh, Y. (2007). The poetics and pleasures of video ethnography of education. In R. Goldman, R. Pea, B. Barron, & S. J. Derry (Eds.), *Video research in the learning sciences* (pp. 77–92). Mahwah: Lawrence Erlbaum Associates.

Tocho, F. V. (2007). From video cases to video pedagogy: A framework for video feedback and reflection in pedagogical research praxis. In R. Goldman, R. Pea, B. Barron, & S. J. Derry (Eds.), *Video research in the learning sciences* (pp. 53–66). Mahwah: Lawrence Erlbaum Associates.

vom Lehn, D., & Heath, C. (2007). Social interaction in museums and galleries: A note on video-based field studies. In R. Goldman, R. Pea, B. Barron, & S. J. Derry (Eds.), *Video research in the learning sciences* (pp. 287–301). Mahwah: Lawrence Erlbaum Associates.

Vygotsky, L. S. (1987). Thinking and speech (N. Minick, Trans.). In R. W. Rieber & A. S. Carton (Eds.), *The collected works of L. S. Vygotsky: Problems of general psychology* (vol. 1, pp. 39–285). New York: Plenum Press.

Vygotsky, L. S. (1997). The history of the development of higher mental functions. In R. W. Rieber (Ed.), *The collected works of L. S. Vygotsky* (Vol. 4). New York: Plenum Press.

Vygotsky, L. S. (1998). Child Psychology (M. J. Hall, Trans.). In R. W. Rieber (Ed. English Trans.), *The collected works of L. S. Vygotsky* (Vol. 5). New York: Kluwer Academic/Plenum Publishers.

White, E. J. (2011a). 'Seeing' the toddler: Voices or voiceless? In E. Johansson & E. J. White (Eds.), *Educational research with our youngest: Voices of infants and toddlers* (pp. 63–86). Dordrecht: Springer.

White, E. J. (2011b). Summary: Lessons learnt and future provocations. In E. Johansson & E. J. White (Eds.), *Educational research with our youngest: Voices of infants and toddlers* (pp. 185–202). Dordrecht: Springer.

Chapter 3
A Visual Dialectical Methodology: Using a Cultural-Historical Analysis to Unearth the Family Strategies in Children's Bilingual Heritage Language Development

Liang Li

Introduction

> Out of such a methodological crisis, from the conscious need for guidance in different disciplines, from the necessity – on a certain level of knowledge – to critically coordinate heterogeneous data, to order uncoordinated laws into a system, to interpret and verify the results, to cleanse the methods and basic concepts, to create the fundamental principles, in a word, to pull the beginnings and ends of our knowledge together, out of all this, a general science is born. (Vygotsky 1997a, p. 233)

Every research process aims to generate knowledge and find the laws, the principles and the rules that hide in everyday reality. However, in order to uncover these hidden principles, an effective methodological tool needs to be developed within the research process. This chapter puts forward the claim that a visual methodology is an effective tool for conducting and contributing to cultural-historical studies on families' involvement in children's bilingual heritage language development.

In recent years the empirical studies on bilingualism have paid close attention to the issue of crosslinguistic interaction and transfer in preschool-aged bilingual children (Cheung et al. 2010; Cummins 2005; Nicoladis et al. 2010). Such studies confirm that heritage language proficiency can become a resource for learning a second language. While empirical studies have investigated the effects of weekend heritage language schools on children's heritage language learning (Li 2005; Liao and Larke 2008), not many researches focus on the ways in which adult interactions and communication contribute to children's heritage language development. Those studies ignored 'the real conditions that determine the development of speech, specially, speech interaction' (Vygotsky 1998, p. 270). In studying children's bilingual heritage language development, we must not ignore the situation of development and the

L. Li, Ph.D. ME (EC), ME (TESOL International), Grad. Dip ECE, B. Law (✉)
Faculty of Education, Monash University, Melbourne, Australia
e-mail: liang.li@monash.edu

M. Fleer and A. Ridgway (eds.), *Visual Methodologies and Digital Tools for Researching with Young Children*, International Perspectives on Early Childhood Education and Development 10, DOI 10.1007/978-3-319-01469-2_3,
© Springer International Publishing Switzerland 2014

situation of speech interaction in the home context. In this chapter we specifically look at research in this area in terms of family pedagogy. Research findings show that weekend school-based programmes alone are not enough to maintain and develop children's heritage language across generations (Fishman 1991). Therefore, it is up to immigrant parents to take responsibility for improving children's heritage language development and language practice within a home context, as this becomes a determining factor for children's heritage language development (Hakuta and Pease-Alvarez 1994; Lao 2004). In order to show preschoolers' heritage language development under the support of their parents through their everyday practices, a new way of thinking of researching bilingual heritage language development is needed. Vygotsky's cultural-historical concepts of mediation and the zone of proximal development (ZPD) offer important methodological directions for illustrating how parents interact with their children through storytelling practices at home.

Visual methodology in early childhood education research, which is framed by cultural-historical theory, makes an important contribution to understanding child development. Visual technology increases the cultural-historical researcher's awareness of research context while investigating children's development (Fleer 2008b). This chapter begins with a discussion of why the cultural-historical study of visual data is important for investigating communication and interactions between parents and children in the home context; then, it focuses on how visual data supports the cultural-historical analysis of everyday family practice; and, finally, the chapter concludes with the implications of using visual data for theory building and family pedagogy.

Visual Methodology Is Driven Theoretically

The most important thing to acknowledge is that a research methodology must be driven theoretically. Vygotsky (1994) emphasises that

> The child's higher psychological functions, his [sic] higher attributes which are specific to humans, originally manifest themselves as forms of the child's collective behaviour, as a form of co-operation with other people, and it is only afterwards that they become the internal individual functions of the child himself. (p. 349)

Regarding studies on children's heritage language development, the child's collective behaviour and performance are produced in everyday family activities. Jones (2008) argues that language communication can only take place through the social interaction of natural situations with linguistic meaning. A child's language acquisition results from the 'process of creating with others this meaningful substance in daily interactions' (p. 86). In other words, children are able to name, remember and categorise objects, not as a result of innate capabilities, whereby meanings exist in some kind of prior 'language of thought', but because of the process of their interactions with others using communicative language, which verbalises these psychological processes. From this point of view, the methodological approach to studying children's bilingual development must be oriented by children's interactions and dynamic movements within their surroundings. Visual methodology offers a platform to support the researcher in capturing children's communication and interactions with their families at home, so as to discover how they develop their bilingual heritage language in relation to family pedagogy.

Furthermore, Vygotsky (1997b) argues that 'all higher processes arise by way of associative combination of a series of elementary processes' (p. 67). Therefore, it is necessary to develop a wholeness approach to understanding child development as a holistic and dynamic process as the basis for a methodological approach to child development research. That is, children's everyday activities need to be taken into account as a whole process, including subconscious family beliefs. Video research using the wholeness approach enables multiple viewpoints by recording 'the dynamic and evolving nature of the social situations' and interactive events in which children are located, where they construct their knowledge across institutions (family, community groups and preschool) (Fleer 2008a, p. 106). Thus, visual methodology is driven by cultural-historical theory.

Research Sample

The researcher conducted the research with three Chinese-Australian immigrant families who were with children 4–5 years of age who were involved in the overall study. The children were born in Melbourne and attended a weekend Chinese school programme. Their parents had immigrated to Australia more than 5 years earlier. The data referred to this chapter is about a girl, Lin, aged 4 years old, who has a younger sister aged 18 months old. Lin attended an English-based childcare from Monday to Friday, excepting Thursdays when she stayed home with her mother. Lin's parents spoke to their daughters in Chinese most of time at home, and English was used on occasion. Chinese is Lin's heritage language in the English-speaking Australian context. The overall study seeks to determine how parents support their children's heritage language development at home and will show how visual methodology supports the researcher in reaching family strategies.

The Position of the Researcher

Vygotsky's (1986) cultural-historical approach suggests that human developmental processes emerge when participating in cultural, linguistic and historical contexts such as family life, school settings and various other environments. To examine how young children interact with adults and other peers within the family, community and educational institutions they participate in, cultural-historical research requires the researcher to be an active partner with the researched person within the activity (Hedegaard 2008a). In Chap. 7 of this book, Quinones proposes that the active role of the researcher is shown by the researcher's 'affective positioning', which is given by the participants from the visual data collection. The argument has further examined how researching child development does not only involve the child but all those involved, including the researcher, child and families. In this chapter, it is argued that the researcher also takes herself an active role, building good relationships with the researched families in order to have a strong understanding of their everyday practices.

Furthermore, visual methodology creates the conditions for the researcher to be an insider of the research setting in order to investigate young children's activities and engage in the social practices of everyday life, as well as examine people's different perspectives, including the researcher's own point of view. To put it another way, visual methodology provides a new dimension for understanding the dynamic interactive process between parents and children in order to find out how parents engage in children's bilingual heritage language development.

The digital video observation and photographs as methods of data collection can help to:

- Capture the dynamics of parents' and children's participation at home within their everyday family practices.
- Identify the conflicts and interactions within family activities.
- Share and discuss the visual data with participants in order to comprehend the multiple perspectives of the participants.
- Allow for collaborative interpretation and advances in understanding children's interactions with others and their development.

Because of physical constraint, video cannot show every moment that has occurred, only the range permitted by the camera lens. It is a fact that 'the camera's field of vision is so much more limited than the human eyes' (Tudge 2008, p. 92). Furthermore, Goldman (2007) observes the notion of *being there/being with* in video research. *Being there* means that the viewer is able to make sense of what is happening in the video by conducting research *on* the children and family. *Being with* means that the viewer can find the whole given situation by researching *with* children and family. Goldman (2007) argues that 'it is more important for the readers to 'be with' rather than 'be there'' (p. 30). Thus, when considering the limitations of range and the idea of *being with*, how to video the social setting and where the researcher points the video camera becomes very important. In the study, two cameras were organised. One focused on the researched child's interactions with others filming by the researcher, and the other filmed the whole setting by the research assistant, capturing the family/school activities and the interactions between parents, teachers, children and siblings as much as possible. This approach is designed to capture children's interactions with others within a whole situational context.

A Wholeness Approach to Data Generation

As already stated, the visual methodology discussed in this chapter is driven by a cultural-historical approach and a wholeness approach to research. Why and how visual data is generated through these approaches needs to be further discussed.

As mentioned early, an interview was conducted with the researched family using photographs or video clips that the researched family took during the first

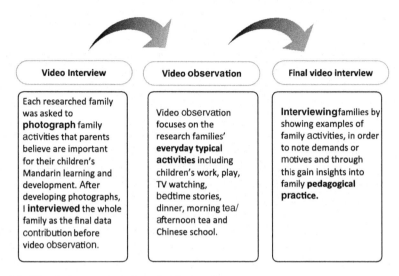

Fig. 3.1 The wholeness approach to visual research

2 weeks in the research field. On the one hand, the photos acted as a visual tool to direct the interview topics in order to try to find out what the family's beliefs on children's bilingual education were. The visual data on the other hand provided a basic idea of what activities the family thought were important to their children's language learning at home before the interview, and supported the development of interview questions to expand the interview dialogue.

This interview dialogue allowed the researcher to understand the parents' beliefs regarding their children's Mandarin learning at home. However, how the child learns Chinese through everyday family activities is still a question that needs to be explored. Specifically, how parents and children interact, and how parents mediate their child's learning Chinese, needs to be further discussed in order to uncover the family pedagogy. In order to see closely the interaction between children and parents, multiple visual tools are needed. According to Burke (2008), 'Visual methods offer accessible, flexible and inclusive tools fit for purpose' (p. 25). The research project being discussed considers the functions of multiple tools in the visual methodological approach. There are three components to the wholeness approach which are interrelated: (a) the photo-based video interview, (b) video observation and (c) snapshot-based video interview method as shown in Fig. 3.1.

As previously mentioned, the first interviews helped the researcher ascertain a basic understanding of the researched families, especially the family's values and beliefs concerning children's bilingual heritage language development. This created a foundation which shaped the next stage. The video observation, as the second stage of data generation, helped the researcher to capture typical everyday family activities within the home context and children's performance in the Chinese classroom. As Hedegaard (2008a) has elaborated, 'Research that is culturally and historically framed takes into account all of these multi-dimensional elements of children's participation in everyday life' (p. 30). In order to study children's language development within the home context, it is necessary to video everyday activities that children engage. In doing so, it is possible for the researcher to understand families' child-rearing practices in terms of children's home language development and to notice the crises caused by societal change and the change in social relations in new institutions children participate in (Hedegaard 2008a, p. 32). Meanwhile, the researcher also communicated with parents and children within the video context and even discussed the videoed activities they participated in, which also supported the researcher in building a positive relationship with the researched family. Video data can capture casual communication with the researched family during observations, which allows the researcher to further their understanding of family activities as they occur while still recording every moment.

In order to attain a good understanding of the historically located family practices in an everyday home context, it was necessary to arrange additional interviews as the third stage of data generation. After the initial data analysis, the researcher chose some important video clips covering typical everyday activities within the home context to show during a second interview with the researched families. The images, photographs, video clips and family's dialogue in the interview provide insights into the complex ways dynamic family interactions occur. This enabled the researcher to gain further knowledge of why the family organised such an event in the everyday context. Meanwhile, the researcher could confirm the initial understanding of the data with the researched family and receive the families' feedback and comments.

The Four Spirals of Visual Data Analysis

This study draws upon Hedegaard's (2008a) dialectical-interactive approach to interpret and analyse the visual data. By using the wholeness approach, the researcher interpreted the data dialectically. Adapting Hedegaard's (2008b) ideas of different forms of interpretation, the researcher developed a dialectical visual analysis approach. The researcher analysed the visual data from a *common-sense interpretation, situated-practice interpretation and thematic interpretation.* In Chap. 2 of this book, Fleer has considered these three spirals of interpretation as one system in the digital analysis. In agreement with this, this study also needed a fourth spiral of *synthetic analysis* in this analytical system to draw comparisons between cross-family pedagogy (see Fig. 3.2), which Hedegaard does not include. The progression of visual data interpretation is a kind of 'ladder of abstraction' (Carney 1990, cited in Miles and Huberman 1994), whereby the ladders of progress show our progress of understanding the visual data conceptually to reach our research destination by answering the research questions. This kind of process of interpretation and analysis supports the researcher in investigating the communication and interplay between child and parents within their family's everyday life on a deeper and deeper level.

Four spirals of visual analysis

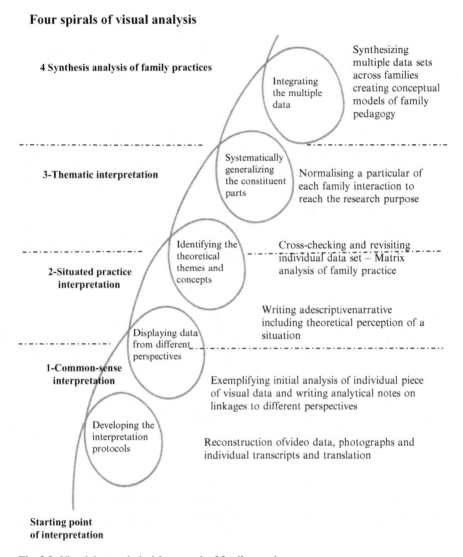

Fig. 3.2 Visual data analytical framework of family practice

Figure 3.2 shows a progress of the analytical model of family practice. It is interpreted from multiple perspectives, including the child's, parent's and researcher's perspectives, based on the interpretation protocols. Then, the researcher moves to the next spiral of situated-practice interpretation with regard to theoretical concepts. The more complex theoretical themes and trends are identified, including situation explanation, motives, conflicts and interaction patterns. The whole analysis process moves in a spiralling line.

Additionally, the process of understanding is not linear, but is dialectical in essence, conceptualised as a continuing upward spiral of progress. As the philosopher Bacon (1985) notably stated, all rising to great places is by a winding stair. Each step of visual data analysis links together, showing a dialectically interpreted progress of understanding. The spiral has been used in representing the interpretation to work against linear explanation, showing the analytical thinking dialectically (see Fig. 3.2).

Figure 3.2 shows the upward spiral progress of visual analysis as a dialectical process. It represents the way to dialectically interpret the visual data upward to the final synthesis. Hedegaard's (2008b) principle of interpretation (from *common-sense interpretation, situated-practice interpretation to the thematic interpretation*) indicates the process of interpretation. In this chapter the spiralling line shows the power of the tool for understanding families' involvement in children's bilingual heritage language development. The following section will clarify how the visual data support the spiral cultural-historical analysis and interpretation by using an empirical study example of storytelling as a family practice.

Spiral 1: Common-Sense Interpretation

The common-sense interpretation comments on my understandings of the interactions in the activity setting. According to Hedegaard (2008b), this kind of interpretation does not focus on theoretical concepts, but rather, obvious relations are drawn out, where simple patterns in the interaction can be identified. The data is objectively interpreted and the researcher is outside of the shared activity settings, which can be shown in the following example. This reading vignette happened during the first visit to videotape Lin's family. This is only part of video transcript.

On the first spiral the researcher initially interpreted and displayed the visual data from the child's, parents' and researcher's perspectives in each particular moment in order to have a basic understanding of the small visual data and to be ready for the further analysis-situated practice interpretation, which is shown by the explanation in the square brackets [] (Table 3.1).

Through this video clip, it can be seen that the visual data enables the researcher to closely see the dynamic physical moment when Lin pointed to the picture and how Lin's father responded and asked questions.

Spiral 2: Situated-Practice Interpretation

After making common-sense interpretations of case example 1, the data analysis moves to the second spiral of interpretation, which is the situated practice using theoretical concepts (Hedegaard 2008b). During this process, the researcher first watched the video clips *without* sound; this enabled the researcher to focus on their

Table 3.1 Common-sense interpretation of shared book reading

Verbal communication	Visual images
... *Father:* 嗯。她在看什么呢? *<Yes. What is she looking at?>* *Lin:* 她在看那个....那个**goose**. *<She is looking at the 'goose' (in English).>* *Father:* **Goose** 就是鹅。*<Goose (in English) is 'e' in Chinese.>* *Lin:* 鹅,鹅,鹅。*<E, e, e.>* *Father:* 她走路时有什么动物在跟着她?*<What animal is following her when she is walking?>* [She imitated 'goose' in Chinese three times. The shared book reading with her father enhanced her vocabulary.]	 **Fig. 3.3** Lin looking at the goose
Lin: 那个...鹅。*<It is a...'e'.>* *Father:* 有几只鹅?*<How many 'e' are following her?>* [*Lin moved and sat on the edge of the book and started counting the geese by looking at the picture.*]	 **Fig. 3.4** How many 'e'?
Lin pointed to the geese in the book. *Lin:* 1, 2, 3, 4, 5. *<One, two, three, four, five.>* *Father:* 五只鹅啊。那还有个动物在偷看? *<Five e. What animal is spying on them?>* *Lin:* 猪。*<Pigs.>* [Lin did not use her finger to count the geese. It seemed that it was difficult for her to count the geese just by looking. So, her father suggested that she look at the geese closely and count them. Then, she figured out how many geese there were in the picture.]	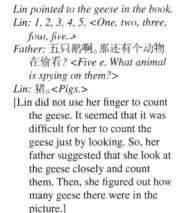 **Fig. 3.5** Lin pointing to the picture

physical movements, which were shown in the highlighted part of the transcript. *The pictures* on the storybook become a psychological tool to mediate Lin's exploration and thinking. Lin could apply the pictures in the book as tools to make the Chinese word 'e' conscious. When Lin appropriated the image and the action, she actually remembered the words and her thinking became verbalised, demonstrating how 'Action, word, and image constantly grow into each other, and interweave and enrich each other, creating the fringes of forms' (Zinchenko 2007, p. 238). Next, the researcher watched the video clip again *with* sound, and the visual data helped the researcher further understand the relationship between Lin and her father. The way of communicative interactions between Lin and her father became much clearer, as shown below using the relevant images in relation to cultural-historical concepts including social situation, motives, conflicts and mediation (Table 3.2).

The second spiral of visual analysis is based on theoretical concepts. Important cultural-historical concepts such as motive, interaction, transition and the situation of child's development are understood by revisiting the visual data.

Through revisiting the video clips, the researcher was able to write the above descriptive narrative to capture the whole view of interaction patterns between Lin and her father. Hence, it can be seen that visual data plays a key role in allowing the researcher to revisit the research activity many times in relation to the theoretical concepts. Vygotsky (1997a) argues that 'sooner or later for each science the moment comes when it must accept itself as a whole, reflect upon its methods and shift the attention from the facts and phenomena to the concepts it utilizes…from this moment…it is organised in a qualitatively different way' (p. 247). Within this process, visual data can be seen as a mediating tool for the researcher to understand family interactions and see how Lin's Chinese vocabulary developed, by providing contextual information to develop a complete view of family shared book reading activity and children's learning progress.

Spiral 3: Thematic Interpretation

Thematic interpretation is related to the research purpose and allows the visual data to be understood on a deeper conceptual and theoretical level. In Lin's shared book reading, it shows that 'two-way' engagement, as a manifestation of family pedagogy, is applied to this activity. Lin's father not only asked Lin questions but also responded to her actions and words. Lin also initiated their book reading. The 'two-way' engagement helped them achieve intersubjectivity conceptually and contextually. The visual data allows for the assessment of the previous spiral of interpretation for quality and for the analysis of why the parent and child interacted in such a way. Up to this spiral of interpretation, the visual data also can be shared with other experts in the field and the researched families. The visual analysis thus comes under the close scrutiny of the researcher, other experts and research participants. In doing so, it increases the reliability and validity of the research.

Table 3.2 Situated-practice interpretation of Lin's shared book reading

Situation explanation (social situation)	Lin and her father shared their reading by observing the *pictures* on the book rather than her father reading the written words	

Fig. 3.6 Shared book reading

Motives/ competence	Lin actively engaged in their book reading, which showed her interest in the storybook. Lin was able to answer her father's *questions* in Chinese most of the time	

Fig. 3.7 Lin pointed the geese to answer the question: '1, 2, 3, 4, 5'

Conflicts/ transition (values and interests)	Her father was provided with the opportunity to support and motivate Lin's Chinese reading	

Fig. 3.8 Lin's father supported Lin to read by looking at the picture

(continued)

Table 3.2 (continued)

| *Interaction patterns (mediation)* | Lin's father used *exploratory talk* to engage Lin in Chinese book reading. Her father mediated Lin's enhancement of Chinese vocabulary, such as *goose* in Chinese |  |

Fig. 3.9 The picture of geese is considered a psychological tool

Furthermore, approaching the dialectical visual methodology, all the video data of the family can be cross-checked and revisited in order to conduct a matrix analysis of family practice. Lin's own storytelling in another video clip can be linked to the shared book reading activity. It is not hard to find the reason why Lin had the competence to use her own words to read a Chinese storybook, although she did not know a lot of written Chinese words (see Figs. 3.10 and 3.11).

The pictures in the book mediate her imagination and thinking, enabling her to make up her own story, which is consistent with the shared book reading practice with her father. Additionally, the process of Lin's interaction with her father and the pictures in the book showed how she had learned about reading and how she read the story on her own. The most important change is that she developed the skill of reading, which can be shown from her own storytelling. In other words, the 'two-way' engagement supported her reading skills development. This point is clearly demonstrated by Arievitch (2008), who states that 'Individual development is based on acquiring social ways of dealing with reality and on learning how to carry out activities in a shared social world and in constant dialogue with this world' (p. 54).

How can we draw conclusions from the shared book reading activity? We must first recognise the powerful tool of how visual technology catches every typical moment and the way children communicate with their surrounding world, so that the researcher can cross-check the data from Lin's family and make connections with other family activities, in order to establish the family pedagogy regarding children's language development. As Vygotsky (1997c) argues, 'the crisis of methods…begins precisely when they [methods] turn from the foundation, from the elementary and simple, to the superstructure, to the complex and subtle' (p. 45). Revisiting and cross-checking the visual data allows the researcher to identify the more complex interactions in the seemingly simple and elementary small data set. Hence, the research findings are developed dialectically through upward spiral of interpretation.

Fig. 3.10 Lin's storytelling 1

Fig. 3.11 Lin's storytelling 2

Spiral 4: Synthesis Analysis of Family Practices

One of the greatest challenges when dealing with qualitative multiple disparate visual data is how to integrate them together into a whole in order to reach the research aims. Vygotsky (1997c) also argues that the research analysis can be called *Reflexes*, which 'do not exist separately, do not act helter-skelter, but band together in complexes, in systems, in complex groups and formations that determine human behavior' (p. 39). Thus, the interpretation at this spiral is the integration of multiple visual data sets in each shared family activity and, through this synthesis, the creation of a conceptual model of family pedagogy. In each family practice, findings from the multiple visual data sets of the three researched families are displayed and integrated into family strategies relating to children's heritage language development. The visual data are powerful in allowing the researcher to compare the different interactions between parents and children across three families when they take part in similar family activities such as storytelling (see Figs. 3.12, 3.13, 3.14 and 3.15).

These visual images have caught the intimate storytelling movements of the three families, showing the different family strategies in relation to the children's Chinese-language capacities.

Yi's mother was a primary school teacher in China before she immigrated to Melbourne 6 years prior to the study. Her way of telling the story to her daughter was like a teacher and was very formal (see Figs. 3.12 and 3.13). She initiated the reading progress and Yi did not like to ask the questions during the reading. But Yi was very interested in correcting inaccuracies in stories. It can be shown from the following interview dialogue (Table 3.3).

Fig. 3.12 Yi's storytelling

Fig. 3.13 Yi's mother
reading story to her

Fig. 3.14 Lin's shared book
reading

Fig. 3.15 Lin's father shared
book reading with Lin

Yi's father attempted to elicit the story by stating an inaccurate fact and asking false questions, demonstrating their conscious methods to help Yi within her zone of proximal development. This is based on their understanding that Yi's motivation is to correct others, so they were able to offer the appropriate scaffolding to encourage

Table 3.3 Yi's interview dialogue

*Researcher: Yi,*你能告诉我,在故事
里三只小猪做什么了?
*<Yi, can you tell the researcher what the three little pigs
do in the story?>*
Yi: 我不知道。*<I don't know.>*
Father: 我知道的。三只小猪都在睡
觉。*<I know. The three little pigs are sleeping.>*
Yi: 不对。三只小猪自己在做一个小房
子。*<No. Each of them built a smal house.>*

Fig. 3.18 Yi's storytelling with
her parents

Fig. 3.16 Wen's book
reading

her story-retelling and support her to engage in expansive social conversation. Their parents made conscious choices of which communicative style best supported the extension of Yi's language.

In contrast, the images of Lin and her father participating in the reading activity demonstrate their intersubjectivity and the family's bilingual practice of reading an English book in Chinese (see Figs. 3.14 and 3.15). Based on the first three spirals of analysis as above, drawing upon cultural-historical concepts, Lin's family reading practices show how her father and Lin engaged in shared book reading and how her father consciously supported her storytelling and language practice from Lin's perspective. Her father considered the pictures in the storybook as a pedagogical tool to support their shared book reading. The exploratory talk sustained their shared book reading.

Wen's family showed a different style of storytelling, where the family preferred to read the story together around their round table. It is obvious from the positions they sat in around the table that the mother was leading the storytelling as she was closest to the book (see Figs. 3.16 and 3.17). Wen was sitting at the opposite end of the table and tried to read the story. He held toys while doing so. Meanwhile, his younger sister sat on the table. According to their parents, they did not ask questions because of their Chinese developmental level. His Chinese was not good enough to ask his mother questions. She read the Chinese story and

Fig. 3.17 Wen's mother
reading story to him and his
siblings

supported Wen's understanding through further explanation. It can be shown from the following conversation. The conversation occurred after Wen's mother read the story 'The monkey and the peach'.

Mother: 哦!它又看到了西瓜。它又捡了西瓜,又忘了摘桃子。 *<Oh. It was a watermelon. He picked the watermelon and totally forgot to pick the peach.>*
Wen: 兔子。 *<A rabbit.>*
Mother: 哦,后来又看到兔子。结果它就去追兔子。对吧?追到最后,有没有追上啊? <Oh, after that, he saw a rabbit. So, he ran after the rabbit. Right? Finally, did the monkey catch the rabbit?>*
Wen shook his head to express 'No'.
Mother: 没有。它什么都没有得到。是不是啊?那我们文儿能不能像聪聪一样呢?*
     <No. The monkey did not get anything, did it? Can we behave like this monkey?>
Wen: No.

It can be seen that Wen's mother kept the leading position to ask the follow-up questions to further explain the story to Wen and his siblings. When the child needs a high level of help and information to be given, the adults need to take the leading/above position to support the child's engagement within their zone of proximal development (Kravtsova 2009). In Wen's case, when compared to Yi and Lin's Chinese level, Wen and his siblings had a lower level of Chinese, as their home language is not Chinese; hence, they needed more of their mother's support. This is the reason why their mother takes the leader position and Wen and his sister listened to the story without asking questions.

The synthesis of visual analyses shows that researchers are able to see the whole interplay between child and parents across families in relation to similar everyday family activities. The visual data helps us to see the different family strategies employed in Chinese-language storytelling practices (see Table 3.4).

The four spirals of visual analysis show how visual methodology supports the researcher in accessing the data dialectically from the simple to the complicated, from each individual factor to their synthesis. An effective analysis requires the researcher to interpret the data from different perspectives and to develop their analytical thinking in a progressive spiral of progress.

Table 3.4   Three families' strategies in storytelling and reading practices

Family	Child's engagement	Family strategies
Yi's family	Correcting others' inaccuracies in stories	Expansive social conversation Asking false questions Encouragement
Lin's family	Initiative Asking the questions Shared understanding of the story	Collaborative strategies Engagement Shared book reading Exploratory talk
Wen's family	Low level of Chinese Listening to mother's storytelling Answering the questions by using simple Chinese words	Mother taking leading position to read the story and ask the questions Further explanation after reading the story

Conclusion

The purpose of this chapter is to explore why and how visual methodology is an effective tool to understand child development and family pedagogy. Drawing upon Vygotsky's cultural-historical concepts, by investigating the visual data of storytelling practices in three Chinese-Australian immigrant families, this chapter reveals that a cultural-historical theory of visual methodology is a substantial means to investigate children's bilingual development in regard to family pedagogy.

First of all, unlike previous linguistic approaches to bilingual studies, this chapter shows how visual methodological tools are theoretically driven by cultural-historical concepts and how it helps to seek the family pedagogy scientifically.

By discussing the empirical study of Lin's family's shared book reading practice, it can be concluded that the visual tools supported the researcher in catching the dynamic physical moments and even their affective movement.

Furthermore, visual data analysis of the shared book reading or storytelling practices of the three families highlights that the way parents guide children to read stories is as an important pedagogical issue. The visual methodology provides an effective way to investigate family pedagogy to support children's Chinese development. Therefore, this methodology is a way to investigate as well as illustrate family pedagogy.

Acknowledgements   I would like to show my gratitude to Professor Barbara Kamler, who has offered expert support in developing writing workshops. Professor Marilyn Fleer provided invaluable support as supervisor of my doctoral research from which this paper was developed. I would like to thank all the authors for their comments and contribution to this chapter. I also acknowledge my three researched families' participation and thank them for welcoming me to video-observe their everyday activities.

References

Arievitch, I. M. (2008). Exploring the links between external and internal activity from a cultural-historical perspective. In B. V. Oers, W. Wardekker, E. Elbers, & R. V. D. Veer (Eds.), *The transformation of learning: Advances in cultural-historical activity theory* (pp. 38–57). Cambridge/New York: Cambridge University Press.

Bacon, F. (1985). Of great place. In M. Kiernan (Ed.), *The essayes or counsels, civill and morall* (Vol. 15). Oxford: Clarendon.

Burke, C. (2008). 'Play in focus' children's visual voice in participative research. In P. Thomson (Ed.), *Doing visual research with children and young people* (pp. 23–36). London/New York: Routledge.

Cheung, H., Chung, K. K. H., Wong, S. W. L., McBride-Chang, C., Penney, T. B., & Ho, C. S.-H. (2010). Speech perception, metalinguistic awareness, reading, and vocabulary in Chinese-English bilingual children. *Journal of Educational Psychology, 102*(2), 367–380.

Cummins, J. (2005). A proposal for action: Strategies for recognizing heritage language competence as a learning resource within the mainstream classroom. *The Modern Language Journal, 89*(4), 585–592.

Fishman, J. (1991). *Revising language shift: Theoretical and empirical foundations of assistance to threatened languages.* Clevedon: Multilingual Matters.

Fleer, M. (2008a). Interpreting research protocols-the institutional perspective. In M. Hedegaard, M. Fleer, J. Bang, & P. Hviid (Eds.), *Studying children: A cultural-historical approach* (pp. 65–87). Maidenhead/New York: Open University Press.

Fleer, M. (2008b). Using digital video observations and computer technologies in a cultural-historical approach. In M. Hedegaard, M. Fleer, J. Bang, & P. Hviid (Eds.), *Studying children: A cultural-historical approach* (pp. 104–117). Maidenhead/New York: Open University Press.

Goldman, R. (2007). Video representations and the perspectivity framework: Epistemology, ethnography, evaluation, and ethics. In R. Goldman, R. Pea, B. Barron, & S. J. Derry (Eds.), *Video research in the learning science* (pp. 3–37). London: Lawrence Erlbaum Associates.

Hakuta, K., & Pease-Alvarez, L. (1994). Proficiency, choice, and attitudes in bilingual Mexican-American children. In G. Extra & L. Verhoeven (Eds.), *The cross-linguistic study of bilingual development* (pp. 145–164). Amsterdam: Royal Netherlands Academy of Arts and Sciences.

Hedegaard, M. (2008a). Developing a dialectic approach to researching children's development. In M. Hedegaard, M. Fleer, J. Bang, & P. Hviid (Eds.), *Studying children: A cultural-historical approach* (pp. 30–45). Maidenhead/New York: Open University Press.

Hedegaard, M. (2008b). Principles for interpreting research protocols. In M. Hedegaard, M. Fleer, J. Bang, & P. Hviid (Eds.), *Studying children: A cultural-historical approach* (pp. 46–64). Maidenhead/New York: Open University Press.

Jones, P. E. (2008). Language in cultural-historical perspective. In B. V. Oers, W. Wardekker, E. Elbers, & R. V. D. Veer (Eds.), *The transformation of learning: Advance in cultural-historical activity theory* (pp. 76–99). Cambridge/New York: Cambridge University Press.

Kravtsova, E. (2009). The cultural-historical foundations of the zone of proximal development. *Journal of Russian and East Europeon Psychology, 47*(6), 9–24.

Lao, C. (2004). Parents' attitudes toward Chinese-English bilingual education and Chinese-language Use. *Bilingual Research Journal, 28*(1), 99–121.

Li, M. (2005). The role of parents in Chinese heritage-language schools. *Bilingual Research Journal, 29*(1), 197–209.

Liao, L.-y. J., & Larke, P. J. (2008). The voices of thirteen Chinese and Taiwanese parents sharing views about their children attending Chinese heritage schools. *US-China Education Review, 5*(12), 1–8.

Miles, M. B., & Huberman, A. M. (1994). *Qualitative data analysis: An expanded source book* (2nd ed.). Thousand Oaks: Sage.

Nicoladis, E., Rose, A., & Foursha-Stevenson, C. (2010). Thinking for speaking and cross-linguistic transfer in preschool bilingual children. *International Journal of Bilingual Education and Bilingualism, 13*(3), 345–370.

Tudge, J. (2008). *The everyday lives of young children: Culture, class and child rearing in diverse societies*. Cambridge/New York: Cambridge University Press.

Vygotsky, L. S. (1986). *Thought and language* (A. Kozulin, Trans.). Cambridge, MA: The MIT Press. (Original work published 1934).

Vygotsky, L. S. (1994). The problem of the environment. In R. V. Veer & J. Valsiner (Eds.), *The Vygotsky reader* (pp. 338–354). Cambridge: Blackwell.

Vygotsky, L. S. (1997a). The historical meaning of the crisis in psychology: A methodological investigation. In R. W. Rieber & J. Wollock (Eds.), *The collected works of L. S. Vygotsky* (Vol. 3, pp. 233–344). New York/London: Plenum Press.

Vygotsky, L. S. (1997b). The history of the development of higher mental functions (M. J. Hall, Trans.). In R. W. Rieber (Ed.), *The collected works of L. S. Vygotsky* (Vol. 4). New York/London: Plenum Press.

Vygotsky, L. S. (1997c). The methods of reflexological and psychological investigation. In R. W. Rieber & J. Wollock (Eds.), *The collected works of L. S. Vygotsky: Problems of the theory and history of psychology* (Vol. 3). New York/London: Plenum Press.

Vygotsky, L. S. (1998). Early childhood (M. J. Hall, Trans.). In R. W. Rieber (Ed.), *The collected works of L. S. Vygotsky: Child psychology* (Vol. 5, pp. 261–282). New York/London: Plenum Press.

Zinchenko, V. P. (2007). Thought and word. In H. Daniels, M. Cole, & J. V. Wertsch (Eds.), *The Cambridge companion to Vygotsky* (pp. 212–245). Cambridge: Cambridge University Press.

Chapter 4
The Past-Present Dialectic: A New Methodological Tool for Seeing the Historical Dynamic in Cultural-Historical Research

Avis Ridgway

Introduction

For the researcher to more fully understand child development, it is important to account for the significance of culture and pay attention to its historical context (Vygotsky 1987). In cultural-historical research, studying the historical dynamic in its cultural context implies a need to understand changing institutional practices in a way that shows them in motion, in their iterations, reiterations and transformations. Historical influences in child development are embedded over time, in dynamic but usually invisible forms of institutional practices. In this chapter, a new methodological tool is used to unearth the historical dimensions of child development. It aims to expand the researcher's capacity for seeing how institutional practices are formed, both temporally and dynamically, and thereby influence child development.

The chapter opens with an example of juxtaposed travel images, to illustrate how dialectical methodology may be applied to read meaning into historical development of local practices. This is followed by foregrounding the research context to show why the need arose for a new methodological tool. The tool is then discussed, applied and illustrated through visual narrative methodology and proposed as a productive and generative method for researching influences in historical child development.

Image Juxtaposition: Culture and History

Time cannot be seen, days pass quickly and historical development becomes embedded in local practices. Time is 'invisible' and cannot measure change, but when the

A. Ridgway, Ph.D., M.Ed., GDEA, B.Ed. (✉)
Faculty of Education, Monash University, Peninsula Campus,
PO Box 527, Frankston, VIC 3199, Melbourne, Australia
e-mail: avis.ridgway@monash.edu

M. Fleer and A. Ridgway (eds.), *Visual Methodologies and Digital Tools*
for Researching with Young Children, International Perspectives on Early
Childhood Education and Development 10, DOI 10.1007/978-3-319-01469-2_4,
© Springer International Publishing Switzerland 2014

Fig. 4.1 Harvested field

Fig. 4.2 Scythes and rakes
harvest folk dance

researcher uses cultural-historical theory to frame visual documentation from the
perspective of temporal practices, it is argued that capturing moments in time
becomes possible and new meanings can be construed. This chapter seeks to do this.
Applying a visual research method of image juxtaposition with the notion of practices
over time in mind raises important questions about embedded relationships
and meaning. An example is given in Figs. 4.1 and 4.2. Taken on the same day in
Strasbourg, France, in 2009, it was only when these images were juxtaposed that
local practices made sense and were given new meaning. Visual method using
image juxtaposition realised a cultural-historical interpretation of phenomena.

In the field outside the French town, the patterns of mechanical harvesting
techniques were captured. In the image of the harvested field shown in Fig. 4.1 lay
an explanation for the historical origins of Fig. 4.2, the *scythes and rakes* harvest
folk dance being performed for tourists in Strasbourg's town square.

This simple example is given to illuminate the power of image juxtaposition as a method for making sense of historically embedded local practices. Here, my researcher's eye looks to the social source of a local practice in the dialectically arranged images, and it becomes possible to speculate on the relationship of past to present practices. In the research study site referred to in this chapter, the method of image juxtaposition was initially experimental. It later underwent conceptual development and became an important tool for uncovering relationships of past to present practices.

Seeing Beyond What Is Simply There

From experimental beginnings of image juxtaposition, a tool was sought for 'seeing' the historical dimensions of a present social situation of development (Vygotsky 1997).

> ...the present stands in the light of history and we find ourselves in two planes: that which is and that which was. It is the end of the thread that ties the present to the past, the higher degrees of development to the elementary. [41]

In using visual methods we need to give attention to the notion of what and how we are 'seeing': 'To alter our particular personal construct requires a substantial leap of imagination as we need to see things from a new angle' (Fletcher 2001, p. 197). All researchers see things differently, and in the 'seeing', accounting for local community context results in generation of rich background data. *Seeing beyond what was simply there* involves awareness of context. In the study site discussed below, this awareness involved personal knowledge as 'locally produced' (Nowotny 2002, p. 26), and produced in a place well known to me, as a researcher returning to a former site of work. Awareness of the origins of site practices formed (as suggested by Nowotny) 'a kind of dynamic map onto which the reality one seeks to grasp, understand, manipulate or control is projected' (2002, p. 27). My 'dynamic map' of this study site was understood as both 'over time' and involved experiences and 'memories of specific local practices'. This map produced local knowledge, embedded in the epistemological origins of the location.

Study Background

The broader study referred to in this chapter used a cultural-historical approach to studying child development where the historical dimensions that are embedded in current practices became visible in the research. The study took place in an Australian community pre-school site, an institution where I taught over 30 years ago (1976–1979). In returning to the site as a researcher in 2005–2008, past experiences (e.g. use of the fishing boat) were filtered by present perspectives on local practices in the pre-school and its community. A feature of this situation was the support given by community members known to me and the ready availability of personal archival material. These historic data included minutes of committee meetings, handwritten reports and photographs from the 1960s (pre-school opened) and the 1970s in my teaching time there. The juxtaposition of images and meeting notes for interviews with current and former staff members prompted historical commentary and generated narrative data.

Seeing Historical Development

My former employment in the site linked past institutional practices to the present time and prompted the idea of a *keeper of local knowledge*. One present staff member who had worked continuously in the site for over 30 years was viewed as a *keeper of local knowledge*. She had visually recorded community and demographic change and, without conscious awareness, carried earlier ways of working with children, materials and equipment into current institutional practices (Ridgway 2009). Her visual records and matching narratives played a pivotal role in understanding family, institutional and community perspectives over time.

Focus on Practices over Time

Historic practices in the site prompted questions associated with the use and reuse of particular artefacts, that is, how the past appeared to be still present. The possibility of better understanding historical elements in child development therefore lay in conceptualising how recorded changes to practices had occurred in the site.

The use of juxtaposition of archival materials as part of *visual narrative methodology* enabled me to see current practices in new ways. Creating visual documentation of my reconnaissance experience in the community and reorientation to the research site supported this process.

Visual Narrative Methodology

In this study, historic images and narrative memory of past experiences were filtered simultaneously through generating recent images and stories, using a process of visual reorientation to the site and its community.

Reorientation to Practices over Time

By comparing earlier images with images collected through a visual reconnaissance of the site, it showed the social fabric of the fishing village had shifted significantly. These new images (Fig. 4.3a) were important as they were used in interviews that led to the gathering of up-to-date narratives.

Fig. 4.3 Research community context – former fishing now a tourist village. (**a**) Old boat sheds. (**b**) New charter boat. (**c**) New facilities. (**d**) Tourist village

Prior to entering the pre-school site, this visual reconnaissance of the coastal village and tidal inlet gave me a dialectical frame of reference. The village now and the village of 30 years ago were different, but the village had held close to its historical past because of its location and the essential qualities of the place.

Fishing boats on the inlet were now pleasure cruisers moored near jetties (Fig. 4.3b), and there were no fishing boats pulled up in muddy mangroves, smelling of mud crabs and whiting. The community foreshore had been redeveloped for educational tours, and signs identified birds, fish and the special local mangrove environment. Picnic tables and shelters provided public amenity, and former fishing shacks transformed into weekenders. The research site community had changed from being a fishing village to a place serving the needs of tourists.

By contrast, re-entering the pre-school site was like stepping back in time. This moment was experienced as if time had stood still. There were familiar qualities of place, like a fishing boat present in the yard and a set of six little red chairs, still in use. Remarkably, a door handle to the adult toilet remained broken, despite an application 30 years ago for its repair. In the storeroom, dust settled on shelves with familiar puzzles, and old books were arranged as they had been placed by me 30 years ago. The playroom spaces were still constrained by the building's original inconvenient design with seven doors leading off the main room. Having previous experiences as a teacher in the site provided a unique opportunity to see beyond the present reality, apply dialectical thinking and contextualise, for example, how artefacts and rituals were being reiterated in new ways. Also evident, but less visible to current site participants, was the continuity of long-standing values of frugality and embedded habits (including family expectations) reflected in present site practices. My researcher's curiosity was sparked as to how this happens. How is it that the *past is present*? There ensued a struggle to make sense of how continuity and change occur in institutional practices and what this means for children's learning and development.

A Cultural-Historical Lens

When using cultural-historical theory to frame visual methodology, particular notice is taken of the relational elements that are reflected in site and community practices. In this case, it was possible for me to use the dialectic formed by having prior knowledge of past site elements and seeing these in present time.

Fig. 4.4 The past is present. (**a**) Boat full of children, 1977. (**b**) Boat-shaped stage, 2008

In particular, one past but still present element in the community and pre-school stood out in my mind. This was the fishing boat. Historic images from the past showed fishing boats moored in the inlet and bait and tackle supply shops prominent, but new digital images showed pleasure boats, a retail area with café facilities and advertising of bay cruises and availability of fresh fish (Fig. 4.3c). The social setting of the site had changed from a fishing village to a drive-through community with special stay-a-while tourist amenities (Fig. 4.3d). With the change, there existed new relations to transform learning and development opportunities for children and family life in this community. One photograph on its own, as Pink (2001) suggests, 'has no single meaning' [51], but when used in the context of a methodological approach that uses juxtaposed images and dialectical thinking, there is capacity to generate new temporal meanings. Meanings of artefacts/ objects change over time, according to their contexts. For example, a fishing boat in the pre-school yard in past times was still present, but in a new stage form. The historic archival photograph on the left (Fig. 4.4a) shows a fishing boat full of children with me (as a youthful staff member), taking part in an annual site ritual: a pre-school group photograph in the fishing boat. The recent digital image on the right (Fig. 4.4b) shows a fishing boat in abstraction as a flat stage but clearly representative of the shape of a fishing boat. The juxtapositioning of these images prompts the question of how a phenomenon such as a fishing boat undergoes dynamic changes of form and becomes embedded in the historical development of this research site.

For me, the notion of time standing still and the past being present were persistent thoughts that raised curiosity about how to conceptualise the dynamic social and cultural practices that influence historical child development. My research, framed by a cultural-historical approach, used visual methodology to illustrate the consistently identified presence of fishing boats in different forms over time, in order to investigate what influenced historical child development in the site.

Seeing Historical Development

Artefacts like the fishing boat are not just in the environment. They facilitate learning and development as they hold a capacity to transform thinking. In cultural-historical theory, the historicity of situational context and of participant's institutional practice activity is understood to influence learning and development. Interactive forces, historically located, are a *dynamic-form* of becoming something (with new meanings), and this idea offered me as the researcher two opportunities:

(a) To understand why historical dimensions of environment and practices are invisible and difficult to unearth
(b) To create a method for seeing beyond what is taken for granted and simply there

If, as Vygotsky (1997) had suggested, '…the past and present' are 'inseparably merged' [41], then a methodological tool was needed to vividly capture the nature of the relationship of past to present and what this may mean for child development. As will be shown, past *dynamic-forms* of socially mediated interactions are embedded in present institutional practices.

Focusing on Practices: Fishing Boat as Phenomena

In the study site, I saw children's learning and development in historical light and as being situated across institutional contexts of family, community and society. Different institutional practices were being played out in new ways by staff and children. Choosing to focus on the iconic fishing boat, I was able to examine practice activity around the real fishing boat in the 1970s and found that it centred on fishing trips play and using the boat for annual photographs. The new stage version of the boat however brought very different affordances for play activity. The dynamic movement to different forms and uses of the fishing boat provided me with evidence that different uses of the fishing boat over time had affected change to institutional practices in this site.

The institutional practices around an artefact, person, cultural tradition or ritual relate to both a historic past and the present. Ratner (1997) clarifies this notion of mediated social relations when he reports on how Vygotsky moved his thinking about artefacts from a descriptive and empirical framework to one more concerned with their internal essence. This is a really helpful idea for understanding child development because in being able to unearth the formative underlying relations, it is possible to capture an essential part of the social construction of mind. Hedegaard (2009) confirms this in her conceptualisation that the wider perspectives of societal conditions play an important part in understanding the influences of changing institutional practices on children's development. My participation in institutional practices across different historical times involved changes in daily life contexts and

the various affordances for learning within the different practice activity settings. Vianna and Stetsenko (2006) comment on the role of the researcher as someone who (as in this case) looks to the historical in the light of the present. As one, for instance, who

> ...lays foundations for a dialectical view of history as an ongoing fluid and dynamic process that is always here in the present, existing in the unending and ever-expanding dynamic layering of social practices in which the past and the present interpenetrate one another. [82]

Theorising institutional practices around the fishing boat in the study site over a 30-year time span represents an example of a common symbolic thread tying the past to the present. It effectively captures historical institutional practices in research data for the study, drawing on the use of *visual narrative methodology* which will now be explained further.

Creating Visual Narratives

In this study, I gathered both historical and current data in relation to contemporary practices. Using a dialectical methodology allowed visual narratives to remain continuously open to me for 'seeing' in new ways. Narratives were generated through *photo elicitation interviews* (using images as prompts) with two past and three present staff members and one family. Drawing on Hedegaard's (2009) model of a wholeness approach, particular attention in the interviews was given to generating understandings of societal, personal and community practices over time. Looking at visual images and interview narratives gave the capacity to reveal tensions between intersecting motives and ideas. These relations and tensions could be expressed, reiterated and regenerated within the day-to-day institutional practices. The question that emerged for me was how to read meaning for historical child development in visual narrative dialectics.

Narrative data from interview transcripts, photographs, archival records and field notes were also juxtaposed in order to create a visual narrative where images could be labelled. These told an illustrated story of practices over time. The visual narrative created in Fig. 4.5 by juxtaposing images one to six shows how the fishing boat, an iconic artefact, had become an 'abstract symbol system' (Nelson 2007, p. 164) shown in new logo and art forms that were identified by research participants as being associated over time with child development in the study site and its community.

Knowing that fishing boats had always been a feature of this community research site, these images offered localised, interpretative opportunities. The visual narrative formed in Figs. 4.5a–f showed practices over time around the fishing boat that were dynamic in form and subject to constant change. These images triggered narrative memories, from present and past staff interviewed in the study.

Fig. 4.5 (**a–f**) Visual narrative of fishing boat (1978–2008). (**a**) Fishing community. (**b**) Class in boat. (**c**) Boat logo. (**d**) Logo uniform. (**e**) Boat mosaic. (**f**) Boat stage

Table 4.1 Conceptualising practices over time

	Dynamic-forms	Historical development	Becoming
Interactive forces	*Action*	*Interaction*	*Re-enactments*
Keepers of local knowledge			
Places and qualities of place			
Memory and identity			

Conceptualising Practices over Time

How the researcher sees things, Nelson (2000, 2007) suggests, is to consider the local perspective of 'finding oneself in time' (2007, p. 179). By creating a visual narrative of temporal practices around the fishing boat, I was able to conceptualise these practices (Table 4.1) as having dynamic-forms identified as *keepers of local knowledge, place and qualities of place,* and *memory and identity*.

These general concepts are:

1. *Keepers of local knowledge*: including traditions, governance, discourses, values and narratives
2. *Places and qualities of place*: including artefacts/objects, signs and symbols in local community
3. *Memory and identity*: including photographs, historical archival documents, personal expressions, recall and reflection

Table 4.2 Analysing narrative data using three concepts of interactive forces

	Dynamic-forms	Historical development	Becoming
Interactive forces	*Action*	*Interaction*	*Re-enactment*
Keepers of local knowledge	Original teacher, the wife of local fisherman, role-plays taking a fishing trip in pre-school boat with playgroup children	1980–1990s long-serving assistant teacher JR designs a logo for pre-school uniform that symbolised a boatful of children	JR's boat logo design applied to newsletter head and used by subsequent parent committees and staff reiterating site identity in symbolic forms
Places and qualities of place	1960s playgroup established. Original teacher's husband provides an old fishing boat for the yard	1970–2008 Annual pre-school photographs taken near/in boat in yard	Wall mosaic of boat logo assembled and installed by JR with 2007 teacher, children and families
Memory and identity	Original teacher Ro replays her everyday life as fisherman's wife with children, reflecting community life of the time	Photos taken in boat are visual keepsakes and memory for children and their families	Boat represented symbolically in stage form holds memory and identity of site and community

As a conceptual guide, Table 4.1 was formed to frame the analysis of a visual narrative.

In mediating practices over time, interactive forces conceptualised as *keepers of local knowledge, place and qualities of place,* and *memory and identity* become clearly evident when narrative data is inserted. For example, when the visual narrative shown in Figs. 4.5a–f is expanded in Table 4.2, a unified understanding of what influences historical development is generated. Temporal practices have dynamic-forms that become something new with new meaning.

This conceptualisation offers a new methodological tool with three conceptual hooks to unearth influences on practices over time that can affect child development in its historical sense.

New Methodological Tool: A Past-Present Dialectic

The new methodological tool is fully applied to the *visual narrative dialectic process* in Table 4.3. Data were formed into a *past-present dialectic* for analysis, in order to trace the transformed fishing boat historically, in terms of its positioning in the reality of local community, family and pre-school practices. The dialectic is about the theorisation of these institutional practices and how they are interiorised over time by children, families and staff, thereby influencing historical child development.

A *past-present dialectic* using the fishing boat identifies in conceptually fresh ways the essential elements of change in practices over time.

Through theorising visual narrative data, *temporal practices* are seen to be mediated by three interactive forces, identified through visual narratives and conceptualised as *keepers of local knowledge, places and qualities of place* and *memory and identity*. Each of the three interactive forces has *dynamic-forms* that historically vary over time and place, in the process of 'becoming', and show how the fishing boat (or any artefact for that matter) continues its historic process of constantly 'becoming'.

Looking to the Past to Understand the Present: Past-Present Dialectic

In Table 4.3 visual narrative data analysis is focused around the fishing boat, an icon recognised by the former fishing village community and those in the research site as symbolic of the place. These data show how institutional practices in the research site move through iterative dynamic-forms over time, which can influence child development. This addresses the question of how researchers can use new visual methodology to understand child development not just in a maturational way but in its fuller historical sense by looking to the past to understand the present. The *past-present dialectic* is a tool that enables the reviewing of dialectical relations in institutional practices, which influence historical child development.

Temporal practices when analysed through the three general concepts, (keepers of local knowledge, place and qualities of place and memory and identity) can be understood to have many *dynamic-forms*. For example, institutional practices are dynamic as they are acted and re-enacted, told and retold, iterated and reiterated. In the discussion below, the methodological tool's use is illustrated by reviewing concrete, abstract and symbolic *temporal practices,* around the fishing boat.

Transformed Phenomena

There was a continuous reiteration of the iconic fishing boat in new forms. The community discourse around fishing boat phenomena changed as the community changed.

> Communities of learners within which communities of discourse evolve are contexts for the constant negotiation of meaning. (Daniels 2007, p. 327)

Table 4.3 data showed that in relation to the pre-school site, the fishing boat became an example of 'transformed phenomena'. Used and reused symbolically in

Table 4.3 Analysis of temporal practices: theorising the relations in a *past-present dialectic*

Temporal practices		Keepers of local knowledge	Places and qualities of place	Memory and identity
	Interactive forces		Orient	Tell
	Dynamic-forms	Act Re-enact	Reorient	Retell
Community practices		Fishing village boat, 1960s	Selling local fish, 1990s	Tourist village, 2000s
Family practices		Father and son/boat captains, 1970s	Windcheater uniform logo, 1990–2000s	Family newsletter logo, 2000s

Pre-school practices

Class photos taken in boat, 1960s–1990s

Boatful of children mosaic installed in pre-school entrance, 2007

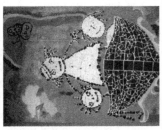

Boat as platform stage in yard, 2008

the pre-school site, the fishing boat was an object/artefact imbued with different senses and meanings. Over time, its presence had become one of the special qualities of the place. The various forms of fishing boat phenomena were subject to *interactive forces* that mediated its use in institutional practices, over time. In particular, actual fishing boats were used in official pre-school photos, and these images were valued mementos kept by children, staff and families, from the community. For example, long-serving staff member (JR) had a photograph album of all official annual pre-school group photos. These were kept as a reminder of the many groups of children she had worked with, over a 32-year time span. The practice of having annual photos taken in this way was very consistent. JR's documentation was a vivid example of why the *keeper of local knowledge* is such an important conceptual source for anyone seeking to understand historical child development. In the collection of photos, children and staff were posed in various fishing boats in the pre-school yard, with the iconic fishing boat images becoming the phenomena that cemented a historical link between community and institutional practices. This illustrates the equally useful concept of *place and qualities of place* as another key to understanding child development in its cultural and historical sense.

The fishing boat image remained a thread of consistency and an embedded and essential quality of this place, and it characterised teaching and institutional practices over time and continues to do so in new ways. The fishing boat and its iconic status can also be understood as an *interactive force,* when seen in the light of the concept of *memory and identity.* Institutional practices, dynamically formed over time and mediated by *interactive forces,* became more abstracted (as in the design logos) and symbolic (as in the mosaic and boat stage). Local *temporal practices* of the pre-school and community were shown as representative re-enactments that had moved from very concrete beginnings. The usefulness of the three concepts for identifying historical elements in child development is illustrated in Table 4.3 that shows how these concepts operate simultaneously and can offer a researcher, using visual methodology, some conceptual hooks for making sense of cultural-historical practices over time.

Reiterations in Abstract and Symbolic Forms

The interview narrative of institutional practices by the foundational teacher Ro (self-identified as a local fisherman's wife) exemplifies how the concept of *keeper of local knowledge* supports trying to make sense of historical child development. Recognised as a *keeper of local knowledge,* she told stories of how a generation ago she would take imaginary fishing trips in the little wooden fishing boat in the yard. Ro had built a local curriculum for children, through role-playing imaginary fishing trips, trips she had in reality experienced with her husband, a local fisherman. Her first-hand knowledge, actively shared with the original small class of pre-school children and their families, became a clear starting point of the reiterated fishing boat phenomena. The fishing boat remains strongly identified with the site today, as phenomena expressed in new abstract and symbolic forms (logo, mosaic, stage). The original fishing boat became changed, transformed and modified over time as shown in Table 4.3, and the practice activities of staff, children and families are closely linked to those changes. As a researcher revisiting a familiar site, a new awareness had unfolded for me about understanding child development in its historical and cultural, as well as biological, dimensions. Knowing the starting point of the fishing boat narrative, where knowledge was kept, re-presented, re-enacted and reiterated symbolically over time, allowed me to see and understand the *dynamic-forms* of phenomena that influence child development.

Unifying Visual Narratives

It can be said that the *dynamic-forms* of change influencing child development were invisible in the research site, until the *past-present dialectic* was applied to data. Its application unified the visual narratives and thus supported my analysis of them. Through the *past-present dialectic*, I was able to make sense of site data and be better informed about historically and culturally embedded forms of child development.

An example of the reiterative nature of the visual narrative around fishing boat phenomena featured the boat mosaic. On a study site visit in 2007, a new wall mosaic (shown in Fig. 4.5f) was first noted. It was a welcoming sight identifying the place and had been installed beside the entry to the pre-school building. It came into my visual field when entering the front door and reminded anyone entering of the essence of this place. The wall mosaic fishing boat image used the logo design created by a long-serving staff member (JR). This design represented a boat full of happy children. The mosaic visually narrated the essence of children's past historical play, still present in this site. The long-serving staff member (JR) in the role of a *keeper of local knowledge* had worked with the 2007 parent committee, staff and children to design, construct and install the wall mosaic as a community endeavour. In doing so, JR provided another reiteration and re-enactment of the past in the present, expressed in the wall mosaic's form, function and shape.

Seeing Cultural and Historical Elements in Child Development

The application of the *past-present dialectic* to data permitted a reading of meaning across visual narratives (Table 4.3). These narratives illustrated the centrality of children playing in the fishing boat as abstractions of this practice over time. *Temporal practices* had been mediated by *keepers of local knowledge* through close attention to *place and qualities of the place* and *memory and identity* of play and community in the site. In this process, the visual narratives of fishing boat play that influenced historical changes to child development in the site could be seen. Visual narrative analysis showed how reiterations and re-presentations of institutional practices occur over time, not as a fossilised repetition, but in *dynamic-forms* as noted in Table 4.3. We see another example of this in Monk's Chap. 5 (this volume).

With local knowledge and using cultural-historical theoretical perspectives over generational time, children's development in this site was seen from a cultural-historical view, one that significantly enriches the maturational and biological views commonly held about child development. This finding shows that using the *past-present dialectic* as a methodological tool supported my research as I looked for answers to the problem of accounting for the significance of changes in cultural and historical context in child development. The tool shows how cultural-historical theory can be used in a methodological dialectic to solve problems of understanding the historical dimensions of child development.

Conclusion

Using a visual narrative methodology in a *past-present dialectic* as research tool allows me as a researcher to factor in temporal, cultural and local historical perspectives of child development. The *past-present dialectic* shows the invisible relations of the 'past-present' in an early childhood site and its community.

Through anchoring research in a more general historical framework, new local perspectives may be built. In examining the epistemological origins of practices around the fishing boat, as phenomena over time through the *past-present dialectic*, a coherent visual narrative analysis tool is provided. This tool, for example, also speaks to the notion of collective memory (Wertsch 2008), which in this site was carried in concrete and symbolic re-enactments by *keepers of local knowledge* around fishing boat play. Visual image juxtapositioning identified concrete and symbolic re-enactments, prompted memory, launched narratives and acted as a stabilising process for reflecting about the past and present dialectically. Using the methodological tool with the artefact/fishing boat demonstrated the complexity of the process of 'becoming' over time.

The *dynamic-forms* around fishing boat phenomena were seen to be in iconic and identifying signs and manifested in designs that captured the pre-school's original boat play. Figure 4.6 illustrates the dynamically formed fishing boat visual narrative in the research study site. All manifestations were abstractions of the original fishing boat and represent re-enactments unearthed through application of the methodological tool, the *past-present dialectic*.

Framing visual narrative data using cultural-historical theory created a methodology for showing dialectical relations that revealed influences of historical child development. Using the *past-present dialectic* as a visual narrative methodological tool enabled the showing of relations visually, in support of understanding the process of 'becoming', and this is the new methodological tool for *seeing* the historical dynamic in cultural-historical research. This tool has been applied successfully to other local site phenomena, such as traditional institutional practices (Ridgway 2009) and intergenerational family practices (Ridgway 2010).

Fig. 4.6 Seeing fishing boat as phenomena – process of becoming (1977–2008)

To summarise, the visual narrative tool is conceptualised as a *past-present dialectic*, formed through the notion that *temporal practices* are influenced by *interactive forces* conceptualised as *keepers of local knowledge, places and qualities of place, memory and identity* and their *dynamic-forms*. The *past-present dialectic* supports analysis of written and visual data, using a cultural-historical framework. This visual narrative methodology captures phenomena as historical development and allowed me to unearth invisible influences in child development. This is a new conceptual system using *visual narrative methodology* for analysing cultural-historical data and provides researchers with support for *seeing beyond what is simply there*.

Acknowledgements   The Australian Research Council discovery grant project won by Professor M. Fleer with Professor R. Gunstone in 2005 enabled the field research experiences from which this study grew. Professor Marilyn Fleer supervised the unpublished doctoral thesis from which this paper was developed. Professor Barbara Kamler offered expert support in developing the writing process as did fellow workshop participants. Research site staff, past and present, willingly provided interview times, archival photos and materials and offered generous hospitality.

References

Daniels, H. (2007). Pedagogy. In H. Daniels, M. Cole, & J. Wertsch (Eds.), *The Cambridge companion to Vygotsky* (pp. 193–211). New York: Cambridge University Press.

Fletcher, A. (2001). *The art of looking sideways*. London: Phaidon Press Ltd.

Hedegaard, M. (2009). Children's development from a cultural-historical approach: Children's activity in everyday local settings as foundation for their development. *Mind, Culture and Activity, 16*(1), 64–82. London: Routledge. Accessed 3 Mar 2009.

Nelson, K. (2000). Narrative, time and the emergence of the encultured self. *Culture and Psychology, 6*,183–196. http://cap.agepub.com. doi:10.1177/1354067X0062007. Accessed 2 Mar 2009.

Nelson, K. (2007). *Young minds in social worlds. Experience, meaning and memory*. Cambridge/London: Harvard University Press.

Nowotny, H. (2002). Shifting contexts, science, art and their audiences. In A. Goehler & B. Loreck (Eds.), *Remote sensing laboratories of art and science* Baumann. Berlin/Hannover: International Women's University GmbH.

Pink, S. (2001). *Doing visual ethnography, images, media and representation in research*. London/California/New Delhi: Sage.

Ratner, C. (1997). Prologue to the collected works of Vygotsky, Volume 5. Child Psychology. http://webpages.charter.net/schmolzel/vygotsky/childpsych.html. Accessed 2 June 2006.

Ridgway, A. (2009). Santa's buckle. Using a cultural-historical framework to show societal, institutional and personal influences on learning in an Australian early childhood community. *Journal of Australian Research in Early Childhood Education, 16*(1), 73–86.

Ridgway, A. (2010). How can cultural-historical theory be used as a methodological dialectic? *European Early Childhood Education Research Journal, 18*(3), 309–326.

Vianna E., & Stetsenko, A. (2006). Embracing history through transforming it: Contrasting Piagetian versus Vygotskian (activity) theories of learning and development to expand constructivism within a dialectical view of history. *Theory and Psychology 16*, 82–89. Sage. http://tap.sagepub.com

Vygotsky, L. (1987). *The collected works of L.S. Vygotsky. (Prologue by Carl Ratner): Vol. 5. Child Psychology*. Boston/Dordrecht/London/Moscow: 1998 Publishers, Kluwer Academic/Plenum.

Vygotsky, L. S. (1997). *Research method in the collected works of L.S. Vygotsky: Vol. 4. The history of the development of higher mental functions* (R. W. Rieber, Ed., pp. 27–63). New York/London: Plenum Press.

Wertsch, J. V. (2008). The narrative organization of collective memory. *Ethos, 36*(1), 120–135. American Anthropological Association.

Chapter 5
Intergenerational Family Dialogues: A Cultural Historical Tool Involving Family Members as Co-researchers Working with Visual Data

Hilary Monk

Introduction

Over the last 50 years, the field of family research has accumulated a wealth of data related to families and family relationships. Considerable knowledge has been generated concerning increasingly diverse family structures, the multifaceted relationships of individuals within families and the variations of family relations that occur within and across different cultural groups and societies (Bengston et al. 2005). Government-initiated and government-funded longitudinal studies have been established in a number of countries to investigate the learning and development of children, family functioning, health and education (e.g. the Longitudinal Study of Australian Children which began in 2004 and has 10,000 children involved across two cohorts and the Norwegian Institute of Public Health study which began in 1993 with 1,081 families). Here the child is the focus with data being generated by the children themselves, family members (parents and possibly grandparents) and their teachers all of whom discuss different aspects of the child's life, learning and development. Other family studies focus on the relations occurring between family members within or across generations.

Intergenerational family studies mostly involve participants spanning two generations with data generated from both generations simultaneously, for example, parents and their children (Yi et al. 2004) or children and their grandparents (Chun and Lee 2006; Wise 2010). Less common are studies spanning three or four generations with researchers citing the difficulties in recruiting participant families as the main reason for not attempting multigenerational research. In many societies and especially in western European families, it is common for family members of different generations to reside in different locations, and often residences are a long distance

H. Monk, Ph.D., M.Ed. (Adult Ed), B.Ed. (✉)
Faculty of Education, Monash University, Melbourne, Australia
e-mail: hilary.monk@monash.edu

M. Fleer and A. Ridgway (eds.), *Visual Methodologies and Digital Tools for Researching with Young Children*, International Perspectives on Early Childhood Education and Development 10, DOI 10.1007/978-3-319-01469-2_5, © Springer International Publishing Switzerland 2014

apart possibly in a different state or country. Under these circumstances researchers often experience difficulties when attempting to meet participants face-to-face unless the family members and researchers are willing to travel to a central location. The need for more multigenerational family studies with participants spanning three or four generations has been expressed for some time (Fine and Norris 1989; Hill 1970; Sabatier and Lannegrand-Willems 2005), yet this gap in the literature continues to exist (Monk 2010).

Intergenerational family research is complex. Commonly quantitative methods are used to generate data with family researchers preferring questionnaires and surveys involving large numbers of participants (e.g. Bailey et al. 2009; Bengtson and Roberts 1991; Dingus 2008; Harrel-Smith 2006; Maré and Stillman 2010; Schönplug 2001). Katz, Lowenstein, Phillips and Daatland (2005) argue that 'one of the most enduring puzzles in family research is how to conceptualise and theorize intergenerational relationships' (p. 393). These authors argue that no single theoretical or methodological approach can facilitate such understanding. To capture and investigate the complexity of intergenerational family relationships holistically in their richness and diversity, a variety of theoretical approaches and methodological tools are needed. One method that is not commonly used in intergenerational research is the generation and analysis of visual data. As digital technologies become more affordable and easy to use, families, particularly in western societies, often document their everyday lives and development over time as informal photographs and video clips sharing these images amongst themselves and with their friends. Yet, although researchers are beginning to explore the use of digital technologies in their research with children and families, the use of these tools is still in its infancy and requires further conceptualisation and theorisation (Pauwels 2011). In addition, few studies have attempted to involve family members of three generations as co-researchers generating and analysing visual data as a means of exploring their everyday family practices.

This chapter draws on examples from an intergenerational study of three Australian families (Monk 2010) and offers a new methodological tool for use in intergenerational research. Framed within cultural-historical theory, this qualitative tool (the intergenerational family dialogue) combines the use of visual and verbal methods while involving family members (adults and children) as co-researchers generating and analysing data. Intergenerational family dialogues engage family members and researchers in unique ways as both groups relate dialectically influencing and being influenced by one another. The tool offers a new approach to researching everyday family practices holistically highlighting, and at the same time uncovering, the complexity and uniqueness of individual intergenerational families while providing a means to study intergenerational development and learning in motion. The chapter begins by exploring the concept of the intergenerational family dialogue and situating it as a methodological tool within cultural-historical theory. The second part of the chapter explicates the use of digital photography and video footage as data generation methods within the framework of the intergenerational family dialogue. This section highlights how the use of visual methods can foreground the dialectic development of everyday family practices. The chapter concludes with examples from the study that illustrate the involvement of family members as co-researchers, their use of digital technology and their participation in intergenerational family dialogues.

Intergenerational Family Dialogues

The term *intergenerational family dialogue* brings together the nature of the participants and the broad concept of dialogue or conversation where two or more people share understandings and points of view. The family dialogue incorporates aspects of the research interview which is a well-recognised qualitative data generation method (Bryman 2004; Creswell 2003; Denzin and Lincoln 2005; Yin 2009) yet moves away from a researcher and question-led format to an emphasis on interactive exchange of ideas between the family members themselves as well as the family members and the researcher. The dialectic nature of the dialogue is central. Although the researcher prepares a focus for the dialogue, for example, a discussion around a series of photographs or video clips, the preselected focus topics are used to open the dialogue, not to control it. One aspect of the role of the researcher is that of a facilitator who carefully listens and prompts providing opportunities for the family members to share knowledge construction and deconstruction amongst themselves while conversing with the researcher. The dialogue is formed and informed by all those participating, not only the researcher. In addition, when a study design includes successive intergenerational family dialogues, each dialogue has the potential to inform subsequent dialogues allowing for the development and revisiting of ideas over time.

Framing the Intergenerational Family Dialogue in Cultural-Historical Theory

Studying development in motion over time is a central aspect of cultural-historical theory (Vygotsky 1987, 1997, 1998) (see Fleer Chap. 2 and Veresov Chap. 8 this volume). Vygotsky (1997) argued that 'what must interest us is not the finished result, not the sum or product of development, but the very *process of genesis or establishment … caught in living aspect*' (p. 71). Vygotsky's desire to study the process of development required methods of investigation that moved away from studying separate and developed functions to methods that were suitable when studying multifaceted, dynamic, socially formed whole processes. For Vygotsky 'the past and present were inseparably merged … the present stands in the light of history and we find ourselves simultaneously in two planes: that which is and that which was' (Vygotsky 1997, p. 41). His life work led him to the study of relations, transitions, processes, motion and history, dialectically. (Ridgway has explored the past/present dialectic in detail in Chap. 4 this volume.)

The dialectic nature of the intergenerational family dialogue situates it as a methodological tool within a cultural-historical framework on a number of different levels. Firstly, the participants span three generations; they bring funds of family knowledge that cross generational boundaries providing opportunities to investigate the development and change of everyday family practices over time. These socially formed practices can be discussed and reflected upon, drawing from 'that which is and that which was' (Vygotsky 1997, p. 41) – experiences past and present. Secondly the intergenerational family dialogue allows for participants to relate to each other in an open discussion thereby influencing and being influenced by one another, rather than individually answering a set of preselected questions controlled by the researcher. The family members and the researcher actively participate in the discussions, thereby forming and reforming the relations and transitions within the group. Thirdly, when the study design includes a series of intergenerational family dialogues, there is the potential for iterative relations to occur within, across and between the dialogues. These relations may be intentional and planned by the researcher, or they may be initiated by the family members themselves as they refer to comments made on previous occasions. Finally, the researcher and the family members are involved in separate but dialectically related roles. The researcher engages in two roles that of research partner with the family members and researcher undertaking an investigative study (Hedegaard 2008). While engaged in the inter-generational family dialogue, the researcher must conceptualise his or her participa-tion within the research setting moving in and out of these two roles (see Quinones Chap. 7 this volume for further discussion on the role of the researcher). The family members also participate in two roles: they are active participants in their everyday lives while at the same time they have been asked to act as researchers generating and analysing visual data concerned with their everyday family practices.

The Intergenerational Family Dialogue and Digital Photography

A vital element in the development of the intergenerational family dialogue as a cultural-historical methodological tool is the use of visual digital technology. Photographs and video clips are used to capture the multifaceted, relational and dynamic everyday family practices holistically 'in living aspect' (Vygotsky 1997, p. 71), by family members in their homes and communities before each family dialogue meeting. Everyday family life is alive with activities and practices that are in constant motion, development and change. For example, the activities associated with eating a meal such as the preferred food, cooking methods, use of utensils and seating arrangements may all change over time. 'With photography we can make a more complete, reliable and comprehensive record of the change process than we could without it' (Rieger 2011, p. 144). Digital photography can be used to capture in detail the present family mealtime practices multiple times, in a range of locations such as the family or grandparent's home, the local park, beach or other community setting. The resulting photographs or video footage can then act as a mediator during the intergenerational family dialogue, stimulating discussion related to past and present practices foregrounding the process and trajectory of change within and across generations. In addition, with the intergenerational family dialogue taking place in the family home, it is possible for family members to refer to and include photographs and artefacts to support the data under discussion. For example, while viewing a short video clip of the family eating a meal, it is possible for a family member to go to the family photograph album and show a photograph of a birthday dinner leading to a discussion of favourite foods and celebrations across generations.

The use of visual methods in intergenerational research affords opportunities for children, parents and grandparents to participate in the generation of data in different locations. This is particularly important when family members reside in different suburbs or cities making observational visits by the researcher difficult. The portability of the digital camera allows family members engaged in everyday activities in different locations to be captured as research data by the family members themselves. If the family chooses the data can be viewed immediately on site. The family members make the decision to save or delete the data before it is passed to the researcher for viewing during an intergenerational family dialogue meeting. Involving all family members in the generation of visual data brings a sense of family ownership to the data that is shared with the researcher. It also provides a point of interest for the children involved in the research. Later the children can contribute to the discussion and analysis of the data during the family dialogue session. Spencer (2011) argues that 'there is something indefinable about the visual, grounding it in material reality. It is an immediate and authentic form which verbal accounts are unable to fully encompass' (p. 32); 'images and video open up complex, reflexive and multifaceted ways of exploring social realities' (p. 35). The verbal account and visual data combine during the intergenerational family dialogue meeting to provide a rich platform for the investigation of the relations, transitions and processes of learning and development occurring in intergenerational families.

The Study

The larger study from which this chapter draws investigated how family values, knowledge and practice traditions relate, transition and transform within and between generations during child-rearing (Monk 2010). Of particular interest were how family members participated in the shaping of their own and their family's development and culture, the motives of family members and what social and/or cultural signs and tools mediated the family's everyday practices. Three intergenerational families from southeast Melbourne, Australia, participated in the study over a period of 9 months. Family members spanned three generations: young children, their parents and grandparents (Fig. 5.1). The participant families were recruited through a local university full day childcare centre and a

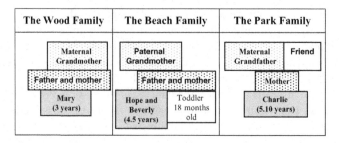

Fig. 5.1 Participant families

community sessional crèche. The grandparents of each of the families resided in separate homes approximately 1–3 h' car travel from the parents and children. Family members regularly visited one another. A pseudonym given by the researcher identifies each family group, and family members choose the pseudonyms used to identify the children.

In addition to the family members participating in the study, the toddler in the Beach family was normally present at the family dialogues with his family and on one occasion a family friend joined a family dialogue with the Park family. As much as possible the family dialogue sessions were arranged at times that were suitable for all members of a family. However, there were times, because of distance or other commitments that individual family members were unable to attend. All three generations of the Beach Family attended each family dialogue meeting; the father of the Wood family missed one meeting as did the grandfather of the Park family. The grandmother of the Wood family had a 3-h commute to attend the family dialogue sessions so was only present at one meeting however she participated by telephone when that could be arranged.

The Iterative Nature of the Research Design

The study design centred around three intergenerational family dialogues; it was sequential as shown by the bold arrows and iterative as shown by the fine arrows in Fig. 5.2. The first level of iteration (indicated by the fine arrows at the top of Fig. 5.2) related to the three family dialogues. Each family dialogue built on the previous one. Topics discussed at the first dialogue meeting were revisited and received further elaboration at the second and third dialogue meetings. This revisiting was sometimes initiated by me (the researcher) and at other times by the family members.

The second level of iteration (indicated by the fine arrows at the bottom of Fig. 5.2) was data generated by the family. Before the first dialogue I asked the family to choose one or two artefacts, treasures or items of family interest to discuss when we met. (The first family dialogue and the data generated for it are not

Fig. 5.2 Iterative study design

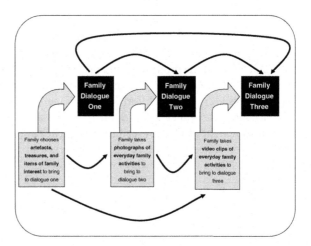

discussed in this chapter.) Between the first and second dialogues, I provided the families with a digital camera to take photographs of their everyday family practices, and between the second and third family dialogues, I requested that the families film short video clips of their everyday practices. These data generation activities were designed to build one upon the other potentially providing richer and deeper data as the study progressed. Initially the families were asked to photograph important or favourite activities that the children do with their parents or grandparents. The request was open-ended with no specific activities alluded to by the researcher. I explained to the families that any member of the family could take as many photographs as they chose, at any time at home or in their wider community. These photographs were viewed, sorted and discussed during the second family dialogue. In preparation for the third family dialogue, I requested family members to consider the initial activities they had photographed and choose a small number of these activities to video for between 5 and 10 min. The examples explicated in this chapter relate to family dialogues two and three.

The family dialogue meetings took place at the child's home or in the early childhood setting as convenient for the families. Families often preferred to meet in the weekend. Dialogue meetings mostly lasted 1–1½h, were audio taped and were followed by afternoon tea that I provided. The time between meetings varied from 2 weeks to 1 month depending on family commitments.

Involvement of Family Members as Co-researchers Working with Visual Data

Using intergenerational family dialogues as a methodological tool provides unique opportunities for family members (children, parents and grandparents) to work alongside researchers as co-researchers generating and analysing data. Family members of all ages are 'experts in their own lives' (Clark 2010, p. 117) and as such are capable and competent decision makers able to generate and analyse research data of their own choosing. Increasingly researchers are recognising the value of involving both children and adults in the production and discussion of visual research data. In the past, the obstacles to involving young children (their chronological age and levels of ability) have been cited in an effort to discourage their involvement; however, more recently researchers such as Clark (2010) claim these difficulties or challenges rest with the researcher and the research design. The children and adults involved in my study demonstrated confidence and competence in generating and analysing rich data derived from their everyday family practices.

Data Generation

Before each family dialogue family members were requested to generate photographic or video data. Children, parents and grandparents generated photographic data; however, mostly video data was generated by the mother of each family. Occasionally the camera was set up to film and then placed on a table or shelf so that no one was left out of the family activity because they were operating the camera. At times family members choose to ask other people to photograph them involved in specific activities; this approach also provided opportunities for family members to be photographed while involved in the family activities. I was not involved in the generation of this visual data, family members choose when, where, how and what to capture of their everyday activities in photographs and video clips. The family members influenced and were influenced by taking part in the study as participants and co-researchers. The children and adults moved in and out of these roles making decisions about the data they were generating.

Table 5.1 illustrates some of the choices made by the Beach family regarding the photographic data they choose to generate for the second family dialogue. On these occasions, the family members chose what was to be photographed and requested the assistance of others to achieve their objectives. Bev (the 4-year-old) requested the assistance of her twin sister; the mother of the family asked a local shopkeeper to photograph her and the twins while they were out shopping; and the grandmother of the family who had taken the camera to her home when the twins were visiting asked her neighbour to photograph them as a group putting the laundry on the clothes line to dry.

Simultaneously the family members were aware of their own participation in the activity and their role as a researcher generating data to investigate their participation in the activity. They were also aware that they needed the assistance of others within their social environments to achieve their objectives. Not only did the family members relate to the situation as participants *in* the activity and researchers *of* the activity, they also *influenced* and *were influenced* by the social situations in which they participated. They each arranged for someone else to assist them in generating data that they were unable to generate themselves; they rearranged the social

Table 5.1 Generation of photographic data by the Beach family

Family member	Photographer and location	Photograph
Child – Bev	Twin sister Child's home	Snail
Mother	Shopkeeper Local shopping centre	Shopping trip with the twins and toddler
Grandmother	Neighbour Grandparent's home	Pegging out the laundry with the twins

environment they were in to achieve their objectives. They were confident and competent participants in their social situations. They generated rich data that formed a platform for the discussions that occurred in the second family dialogue. In addition, the family members built on this initial data when they generated video footage for the third family dialogue.

Between the second and third family dialogues, the families were requested to generate some short video footage of their everyday family practices. Where possible they were asked to build on the data they had generated as still photographs. Some of the video footage generated by the Beach family related to the photographs discussed in this section. Table 5.2 shows the extension of the original photographic data by including relevant video data generated by the family.

Table 5.2 Generation of related video data by the Beach family

Family member	Photographer and location	Photograph	Camera person and location	Video clip
Child – Bev	Twin sister Family home	Snail	Mother Family home	Gardening
Mother	Shopkeeper Local shopping centre	Shopping trip	Mother Family home	Baking biscuits
Grandmother	Neighbour Grandparent's home	Pegging out the laundry	Mother Family home	Sock races – pairing and putting laundered socks away in drawers

The iterative study design created opportunities for the rich complexity of everyday family practices to emerge while at the same time providing opportunities for this complexity to be uncovered, analysed and revisited. The three examples provided in Tables 5.1 and 5.2 all relate to domestic activities around the home. However, as the data were discussed during the family dialogues, these socially formed practices could be understood as multifaceted expressions of change across the generations. One example is the photograph of the snail. The photograph itself was extremely difficult to interpret; when I first viewed the photograph, I had no idea of its object or subject or its relevance to the everyday practices of the family. During the second family dialogue, Bev (the 4-year-old twin from the Beach family) told a story of how she was afraid of snails and had only recently overcome this fear. This led to a discussion of various fears and anxieties different members of the family had and how they had overcome them with the help of parents and grandparents. In particular, the

Fig. 5.3 Children, parents and a grandparent from the Beach family can be seen sorting photographs on the *left* and viewing video clips on the *right*

father of the family expressed his desire for the children to understand the difference between creatures and animals that might harm them and those that would not. In response to Bev's fear of garden creatures, her parents and grandmother were encouraging her to participate in gardening activities (the subject of a short video clip) to aid her in overcoming this fear. The photograph and video footage recorded her development. 'In the cultural-historical perspective, children's development is seen as a consequence of participation in practices, and conceptualised in terms of personality development' (Chaiklin and Hedegaard 2008, p. 198). Bev's photograph of the snail recorded a special moment in her development that was cause for celebration. The video clip showed her ongoing participation in the family practice of gardening. The complexity and richness of the data became apparent during the family dialogues where family members from three generations discussed, analysed and reflected on that 'which is and that which was' (Vygotsky 1997, p. 41) as development and learning were captured holistically through everyday family practices.

Data Analysis

Traditionally data analysis work involved in research has been carried out by the researcher or research team away from the research site, as a separate activity that does not involve the participants of the study. However, during intergenerational family dialogues, family members and researchers have opportunities to work with and analyse data together. Children, parents and grandparents become involved in sorting, analysing and categorising the photographs as well as viewing and interpreting the video footage they had generated (Fig. 5.3).

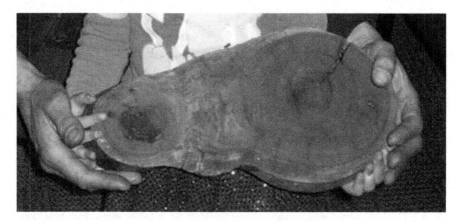

Fig. 5.4 A piece of wood

The technique of photograph sorting used in the second family dialogue (Fig. 5.1) provided opportunity for family members to dialogue together while interacting with the photographs. I asked the family members to select a series of photographs (three or four) that they would like to share with the group. Before the family dialogue meeting, prints of all the photographs had been numbered by me, for easy reference. My intention was for the family members to have the opportunity to discuss, analyse and categorise the data with minimal involvement from me. Once sorting had begun, conversation flowed easily between family members. Family members tended to ask each other 'where is the photograph of...' which led to 'why do you want that one?', 'I want that one because...' or 'here is another one that shows... do you want that one too?' The dialogue that took place indicated that 'much of the analytical framing is done in the initial choice or construction of the image ... but as more in-depth analysis proceeds, the relationships within and between images [photographs and video clips] ... begin to become clearer' (Spencer 2011, p. 133). This was evident in the Beach family's discussion of Bev's snail photograph and the gardening video clip. The clarity of the relations between photographs as well as photographs and video footage unfolded as family members discussed, questioned and critiqued the images during the second and third family dialogues.

The richness of involving three generations (children, parents and grandparents) in the family dialogues was also apparent as images are open to interpretation and can therefore be understood from different viewpoints. For example, the Wood family had a photograph of a piece of wood (Fig. 5.4); as a researcher I could not understand the significance of the photograph, it was just a piece of wood being held by a child and adult. Mary (3-year-old) explained that it was 'daddy's piece of wood'; mother added 'he likes the colour ... we put cheese and biscuits on it when friends come over'; Gran went on to explain 'he has just got a thing with wood'.

The narrative continued to develop as Gran told about the origins of the wood, that it came from the farm wood pile where she lived; the woodpile was stacked carefully and separated into 'dry' wood and 'wet' wood. She explained how her husband (Mary's grandfather) had a particular way of stacking wood that had been collected around the farm and that Mary's father was known in the family for 'messing with the wood pile'. From an outsider's viewpoint, it was a piece of wood; from Mary's viewpoint, it was an artefact associated with her daddy; from mother's viewpoint, it had a use domestically in the home; from father's viewpoint, wood was something he enjoyed as a hobby; and from Gran's viewpoint, it was associated with family dramas when Mary and her family came to visit. Analysis is an iterative process; it does not start and stop in a particular linear sequence. Analysis weaves together the sequences involved in image production, sorting and coding of images, as well as historical, contextual and cultural knowledges of artefacts and social situations.

When family members are co-researchers (active participants and research partners) new opportunities for analytical interpretation of the data arise. Family members can draw on different sets of knowledge, for example, participation knowledge (the image is of a familiar activity in which they participated), researcher knowledge related to image production (choice of subject, location and time), historical knowledge (family history of circumstances locations and practices) and reflective interpretative knowledge (viewing the image from a researcher perspective). These rich and meaningful perspectives are dynamic and complex; they create new avenues of interpretation and analysis that would not normally be available to a single 'outsider' researcher. New understandings of the *living aspect* (Vygotsky 1997, p. 71) [emphasis added] of intergenerational family life caught in action, movement and process are possible.

Challenges and Limitations

Working with participants of very different ages spanning three generations is very demanding and can be challenging for researchers. Designing research procedures that are suitable for a diverse group of participants including young children (3–6 years) and older people (grandparents of 60 years and older) as well as parents in the middle age range involves levels of flexibility and adaptability. Initially I found that the parents and grandparents would give total focus to the children. On one occasion early in the study, the mother of the Wood family took the role of 'child interviewer' during a family dialogue meeting asking a series of 'quick fire' questions that required 'one-word' answers from her child who was 3 years old. For a short time, the child obliged but then lost interest. On that occasion the child's father intervened and I was able to suggest the child have some afternoon tea at the table with the family so she could remain in the room and rejoin the conversation as she choose. Providing snacks for the family seemed to create a more relaxed atmosphere allowing family members particularly the young children, to move in and out of the dialogue as they preferred. Quiet activities (such as threading beads and drawing) that could be undertaken at the table or close by offered a similar situation for the children. The meeting venue of the child's home or early childhood centre provided flexibility for the children as they could move from room to room in a familiar environment. Overall the children in my study found the visual data engaging and their involvement in the family dialogues was very focused for considerable periods of time as they listened to other family members and contributed to the conversations. On one occasion, Charlie (the 6-year-old from the Park family) was so focused on the video clips we were watching that he worked out the sequence of viewing or reviewing ensuring none were missed. His involvement in this way lasted for over an hour. At the same time he commented on what was being seen giving his perspective which opened up a number of insightful conversations.

Alongside the challenges of researching with young children, their parents and their grandparents is the limited number of families whose members span three generations, live in reasonably close proximity and are willing and able to participate in a project for several months. Although many older people are living longer, they are often residing some distance away from their children and grandchildren, making it difficult for all three generations of the one family to meet together regularly over a period of a few months to generate or to view visual data. It is possible for technology to bring people together even though they are not present in the same room however often older people find using modern technological tools a challenge. In this study the grandmother of the Wood family participated by phone on one occasion; however, this became more of an interview than a dialogue as she had a hearing difficulty and there were no visual clues that would normally be available for her during a face-to-face meeting. Nevertheless, she was actively involved in the data generation for the study because her granddaughter and family regularly drove the 3 h to her home to stay during the weekends. On one occasion she was present at a family dialogue meeting.

Conclusion

Embarking on visual research with intergenerational families as co-researchers is an exciting and rewarding pursuit. What is unique about the study examples discussed in this chapter is the way in which intergenerational family dialogues afford family members and researchers the opportunity to generate and explore holistic, rich and complex data related to everyday family practices. The intergenerational family dialogue offers a new methodological tool situated within cultural-historical theory, as a means of studying intergenerational development and learning in motion. This methodological tool allows for theory and research about intergenerational family practices to be generated. Hedegaard, Fleer, Bang and Hviid (2008) argue that to do this a 'methodology must be anchored in a concrete historical setting and at the same time contribute towards an understanding of the *general conditions* that support child development' (p. 4) [original emphasis]. The intergenerational family dialogue does this; the methodology is situated in the specific everyday practices of individual families that have been formed and transformed across generations.

At the same time, these specific practices are indicative of the everyday practices occurring in the wider society of which the family is a part.

As our research approaches continue to develop, there is so much to explore about the everyday lives of intergenerational families. Some time ago Lefebvre (1991) urged his readers to open their eyes to the everyday, recognising that what is so familiar is not necessarily known, that 'it is in the most familiar things that the unknown not the mysterious – is at its richest' (p. 132). Family members are experts in the own everyday lives, inviting them to participate in intergenerational family dialogues as co-researchers using visual methodologies within cultural-historical frameworks opens up new research possibilities for the family researcher.

Acknowledgements I acknowledge the expertise offered by Dr. Barbara Kamler who led a series of writing workshops and provided guidance on the redevelopment of this chapter. Professor Marilyn Fleer provided invaluable support as supervisor of my doctoral research. The Beach, Park and Bush families kindly gave of their time as participants of the study. Financial support was afforded as recipient of the Monash Silver Jubilee Postgraduate Scholarship (2007–2010).

References

Bailey, J. A., Hill, K. G., Oesterle, S., & Hawkins, J. D. (2009). Parenting practices and problem behaviour across three generations: Monitoring, harsh discipline, and drug use in the intergenerational transmission of externalizing behaviour. *Developmental Psychology, 45*(5), 1214–1226.

Bengston, V. L., & Roberts, R. E. L. (1991). Intergenerational solidarity in aging families: An example of formal theory construction. *Journal of Marriage and the Family, 53*(4), 856–870.

Bengston, V. L., Acock, A. C., Allen, K. R., Dilworth-Anderson, P., & Klein, D. M. (2005). Theory and theorizing in family research. In V. L. Bengston, A. C. Acock, K. R. Allen, P. Dilworth-Anderson, & D. M. Klein (Eds.), *Sourcebook of family theory and research* (pp. 3–33). Thousand Oaks: Sage.

Bryman, A. (2004). *Social research methods* (2nd ed.). Oxford: Oxford University Press.

Chaiklin, S., & Hedegaard, M. (2008). Radical-local teaching and learning: A cultural-historical perspective on education and children's development. In M. Fleer, M. Hedegaard, & J. Tudge (Eds.), *World yearbook of education 2009: Childhood studies and the impact of globalization: Policies and practices at global and local levels* (pp. 184–201). New York: Routledge.

Chun, J., & Lee, J. (2006). Intergenerational solidarity in Korean immigrant families. *Journal of Intergenerational Relationships, 4*(2), 7–21.

Clark, A. (2010). Young children as protagonists and the role of participatory, visual methods in engaging multiple perspectives. *American Journal of Community Psychology, 46*, 115–123.

Creswell, J. W. (2003). *Research design: Qualitative, quantitative, and mixed methods approaches* (2nd ed.). Thousand Oaks: Sage.

Denzin, N. K., & Lincoln, Y. S. (Eds.). (2005). *The SAGE handbook of qualitative research* (3rd ed.). Thousand Oaks: Sage.

Dingus, J. E. (2008). 'Our Family business was education': Professional socialization among intergenerational African-American teaching families. *International Journal of Qualitative Studies in Education, 21*(6), 605–626.

Fine, M., & Norris, J. E. (1989). Intergenerational relations and family therapy research: What can we learn from other disciplines. *Family Process, 28*(3), 301–315.

Harrel-Smith, J. A. (2006). *An exploration of intergenerational connections.* Unpublished Doctor of Philosophy thesis, The Claremont Graduate University, Claremont.

Hedegaard, M. (2008). The role of the researcher. In M. Hedegaard, M. Fleer, J. Bang, & P. Hviid (Eds.), *Studying children: A cultural-historical approach* (pp. 202–207). Berkshire: Open University Press.

Hedegaard, M., Fleer, M., Bang, J., & Hviid, P. (2008). Researching child development – An introduction. In M. Hedegaard, M. Fleer, J. Bang, & P. Hviid (Eds.), *Studying children: A cultural-historical approach* (pp. 1–9). Maidenhead: Open University Press.

Hill, R. (1970). *Family development in three generations: A longitudinal study of changing family patterns of planning and achievement*. Cambridge, MA: Schenkman.

Katz, R., Lowenstein, A., Phillips, J., & Daatland, S. O. (2005). Theorizing intergenerational family relations: Solidarity, conflict, and ambivalence in cross-national contexts. In V. L. Bengston, A. C. Acock, K. R. Allen, P. Dilworth-Anderson, & D. M. Klein (Eds.), *Sourcebook of family theory and research* (pp. 393–420). Thousand Oaks: Sage.

Lefebvre, H. (1991). *Critique of everyday life: Introduction* (Vol. I). London: Verso.

Maré, D. C., & Stillman, S. (2010). *Passing it on: The intergenerational transmission of human capital in New Zealand families*. Wellington: New Zealand Families Commission, Kōmihana ā whānau.

Monk, H. (2010). *Learning and development across the generations: A cultural-historical study of everyday family practices*. Unpublished Doctor of Philosophy thesis, Monash University, Melbourne.

Pauwels, L. (2011). An integrated conceptual framework for visual social research. In E. Margolis & L. Pauwels (Eds.), *The SAGE handbook of visual research methods*. Los Angeles: Sage.

Rieger, J. H. (2011). Rephotography for documenting social change. In E. Margolis & L. Pauwels (Eds.), *The SAGE handbook of visual research methods* (pp. 132–149). Los Angeles: Sage.

Sabatier, C., & Lannegrand-Willems, L. (2005). Transmission of family values and attachment: A French three-generational study. *Applied Psychology: An International Review, 54*(3), 378–395.

Schönpflug, U. (2001). Introduction: Cultural transmission – A multidisciplinary research field. *Journal of Cross-Cultural Psychology, 32*(2), 131–134.

Spencer, S. (2011). *Visual research methods in the social sciences: Awakening visions*. London: Routledge.

Vygotsky, L. S. (1987). *The collected works of L.S. Vygotsky: Vol. 1, Problems of general psychology* (R. W. Rieber, A. S. Carton, (Eds. English Trans.) & N. Minick, Trans.). New York: Plenum Press.

Vygotsky, L. S. (1997). *The collected works of L.S. Vygotsky: Vol. 4, The history of the development of higher mental functions* (R. W. Rieber (Ed. English Trans.) & M. J. Hall, Trans.). New York: Plenum Press.

Vygotsky, L. S. (1998). *The collected works of L.S. Vygotsky: Vol. 5, Child psychology* (R. W. Rieber (Ed. English Trans.) & M. J. Hall, Trans.). New York: Plenum Press.

Wise, R. (2010). Intergenerational relationship characteristics and grandchildren's perceptions of grandparent goal influence. *Journal of Intergenerational Relationships, 8*(1), 54–68.

Yi, C.-C., Chang, C.-F., & Chang, Y.-H. (2004). The intergenerational transmission of family values: A comparison between teenagers and parents in Taiwan. *Journal of Comparative Family Studies, 35*(4), 523–545.

Yin, R. K. (2009). *Case study research: Design and methods* (4th ed.). Thousand Oaks: Sage.

Chapter 6
A Cultural-Historical Framework for "Everyday" Research: Theorizing Development Through Visual Imagery and Dialogue

Sijin Agnes Shin Pennay

Introduction

> What really matters for development is what one does on a regular basis, with those people and objects one spends time with... what there is to be done depends on the things that are available, the people who are available, and notions about what it is that is appropriate to be done. (Tudge 2008, p. 22)

Cultural-historical researchers recognize the inherently social nature of learning and development and therefore strive to foreground the "everyday" interactions at its core while faced with a dearth of specific frameworks to make this possible. The objective of this chapter is to contribute one possible way to frame, execute, and analyze research on the conflicts and demands embedded in everyday interactions, based on a case study of two rural families in Siem Reap, Cambodia. The discussion opens with a brief look at cultural-historical theory and methodology, in particular the role of the everyday and its relevance to development. It then focuses on how this research was structured and theorized from a cultural-historical perspective. The rest of the chapter is devoted to reviewing the data collection and analysis processes that developed from the Cambodian study and culminates in the "Four R" framework that provides an overview of the transferable methodological tools and lessons learned. Given that cultural-historical research is, and should be, contextualized, the researcher is best positioned to assess when and how standard research practices should be incorporated or adapted to the research context. With cross-cultural studies in particular, open communication and a clear understanding of both the theory and methodology within the research team (including translators and co-researchers) are essential to understanding context.

S.A.S. Pennay, M.Ed., BA (✉)
Monash University, Melbourne, Australia
e-mail: agnes@pennays.com

M. Fleer and A. Ridgway (eds.), *Visual Methodologies and Digital Tools for Researching with Young Children*, International Perspectives on Early Childhood Education and Development 10, DOI 10.1007/978-3-319-01469-2_6,
© Springer International Publishing Switzerland 2014

Cultural-Historical Perspectives

Cultural-historical theory takes the position that "understanding development requires taking simultaneous consideration of activities and interactions, characteristics of the individuals involved in those activities and interactions, and the cultural setting, as developed over historical time, that gives meaning to those activities and interactions" (Fleer et al. 2009, p. 11). This perspective enables the researcher to better understand how and why needs and practices are defined as they are in a particular context, and why certain ones are prioritized over others from different perspectives and in different cultures, such that outcomes are not unfairly judged as superior versus inferior, developed versus developing, or even primitive (Freitas et al. 2009; Goncu et al. 2009; Liamputtong 2010; Tudge and Odero-Wanga 2009).

Vygotsky was critical of the simplicity of categorizing developmental levels based on single traits such as age or dentition or on linear, evolutionary standards as such methods are inadequate for understanding the complexity of development (Fleer 2010). Instead, he considered development as a dialectical process of lytic flow (or latent/stable periods), neoformations, and crises that do not necessarily have clear boundaries but enable the transition from one leading activity to another (Fleer 2010). Vygotsky argued that development is inextricably tied to the child's needs, incentives, and motives (Vygotsky 1966) and that play in particular provides an ideal forum for this development, asserting that "play continually creates demands on the child to act against immediate impulse, i.e., to act on the line of greatest resistance… the essential attribute of play is a rule which has become an affect…. Therefore, a child's greatest achievements are possible in play – achievements which tomorrow will become his average level of real action and his morality" (Vygotsky 1966, p. 14). He refuted simplistic claims that play was how children spent their time, as he observed that "in play, action is subordinated to meaning, but in real life, of course, action dominates over meaning" (Vygotsky 1966, p. 15). Elkonin also highlighted the importance of play by arguing that the evolution of play was driven by the evolution of society in general and its consequences, namely, the changing role of children as productive members of that society. In his own words, role play's "appearance is associated not with the operation of certain internal, innate, instinctive energy, but rather with well-defined social conditions of the child's life in society" (Elkonin, as quoted in Fleer 2010, p. 109).

More recent and no less significant is Hedegaards's cultural-historical model, which provides a comprehensive framework for understanding the numerous factors at play; it is discussed in greater detail in Chap. 1. As Chaiklin and Hedegaard (2009) assert, "a central tenet of the cultural-historical perspective is that psychological development is a consequence of participation in historically-formed societal practices, arising through engaged actions in relation to the demands and conditions of the practices" (p. 184). Culture will inevitably influence the types of activities and interactions that are available and encouraged (Tudge and Odero-Wanga 2009). For example, children in the Majority World often make their toys and generate their own learning opportunities, while globally there is greater pressure to provide children with objects and scenarios created explicitly to stimulate their learning (Tudge and Odero-Wanga 2009). As Tudge (2008) observes with Kenyan children, the "type of play in which the children engaged is primarily with household objects or natural objects" (p. 48) that they find on their own and with which they create their own games. Nsamenang thus questions whether people from the Majority World "neglect the needs of their infants and toddlers for stimulation, interaction, and affection, or these needs have been exaggerated by child development specialists [and advocates] who mistake Anglo-American ideologies of the second half of the twentieth century as the universal requirements of human infants" (LeVine, as quoted in Nsamenang 2009, p. 30). The failure of so many well-intended but ill-conceived early childhood education projects and policies (Croft 2002; Penn 2008) further illustrate how mainstream Western theories "do not take into account variations in childhood and thus lead to ethnocentric characterization of children of the non-Western world" (Goncu et al. 2009, p. 67).

Yet, Hedegaard's notable contribution is her focus on children's participation in everyday practices at the institutional level since "cultural values of what constitutes a good life and appropriate development are reflected in institutional practices" (Chaiklin and Hedegaard 2009, p. 113). In particular, movement from one institution to another often creates opportunities for development as demands and expectations change, and it is critical to enable children to recognize and apply the various knowledges and capabilities across different settings (Fleer 2010). She cites the case of the toddler Louise and her eating habits when she enters preschool, from the geographical grazing she was used to at home as compared to the fixed point eating she had to adopt in the classroom. This example highlights the importance of Hedegaard and Chaiklin's double move concept (Fleer 2010) – being mindful of the "everyday context" and the "concepts" in teaching. Children often tend to separate what is learned at school from everything else, and as Fleer argues, "when everyday learning and schooled learning are kept separate children do not gain insights into how different forms of learning are connected" (2010, p. 14).

Indeed, recognizing without judgment how children from different societies, unsurprisingly, engage in different practices across and within institutions can create alternatives to "placing children 'in storage'" (Suransky, as quoted in Nimmo 2008, p. 3). Nimmo (2008) highlights Canella and Viruru (1997)'s argument that the "play/work dichotomy that dominates western thinking about early childhood education (in which play is good and work is bad) needs to be reconceptualized in light of what we know about the diverse experiences of children in differing social and cultural contexts" (p. 4). He asserts that direct engagement with adults in various meaningful activities and access to real-life community relationships positively impacts children's identity, confidence, and general well-being. Williams-Kennedy reaches a similar conclusion for Australian aboriginal communities (2009), as does Mbebeb (2009) in the African context: "the philosophy is training for life and not necessarily training for a job, which later on translates into a variety of occupational options and entrepreneurial behaviors for learners" (p. 31).

Application in Research

As Anning et al. (2009) assert, cultural-historical theory "offers one way of addressing the limitations that our profession has inherited because it specifically deals with *context*" (p. 4, emphasis added). Yet, while there is little debate that "context matters" (Crossley and Jarvis, as quoted in Yang 2011, p. 395), it is unclear that context can be clearly defined or understood, especially in cross-cultural research. Yang (2011) argues against the inconsistent and contradictory use of the concept and states that a "clear operational definition of cultural context is badly needed" (p. 396). He also draws attention to the problematic simplification of the emic-etic debate as the "insider-outsider dichotomy is arbitrary and inappropriate and an insider's advantage is often taken-for-granted" (p. 401). The backgrounds of the researcher, the participants, and the translator, if one is involved, all impact the research dynamics, and it should not be assumed that an emic view is necessarily accurate or ideal (Park 2011; Yang 2011). In their review of effective cross-cultural research, Sullivan and Cottone (2010) take the position that "mixed-culture research teams and the active participation of cultural informants in cross-cultural studies are recognized as a strength and significant benefit" (p. 359). When language becomes another aspect of research, an "open dialogue between the researcher and the translator is a critical reflexive practice that helps the research team to better understand how each person's social location affects her or his way of knowing" (Wong and Poon 2010, p. 153).

Context is especially important in understanding children's development through the research process. The noble intention of many interpretivist researchers of capturing the child's "voice" is not without its pitfalls, including the well-intentioned but inaccurate translation and representation of that voice as in "ethnographic ventriloquism" (Geertz, as quoted in Fleer and Quinones 2009). As Fleer and Quinones express succinctly, research should be structured "so that *the voice of the child is not just heard, but understood*" (2009, p. 90). A study that focuses solely on the child fails to capture the important and influential interactions that she experiences as part of a family, institution, and greater society and that impact her development. In contrast, true cultural-historical research acknowledges "the individual child in the study design, and at the same time acknowledging that the child is an active participant in a collective community" (Fleer and Quinones 2009, p. 90).

In light of these challenges, a dialectic-interactive methodology, developed on the principles of cultural-historical theory, "focuses on children's motives, projects, intentional actions and interpretation" (Hedegaard et al. 2008, p. 5) while considering the context of institutional practices as well as societal values and norms. The researcher is not the proverbial "fly on the wall" but a communication partner who can ask leading questions (and perhaps even answer them depending on the situation) and has her own research intentions. Validity is defined by how well she is able to capture and interpret the different perspectives of participants in their everyday practices. Hedegaard (2008) makes a clear distinction between the writing and interpretation of protocols, not only in the timing and location of when they take place (immediate after research/on location vs. later on/off-site) but also in the focus and nature of the generated material (description of concrete observations vs. formulation of conceptual relations). She also describes three types of interpretation to be used in analyzing the data: commonsense interpretation that identifies and validates observations in a given setting; situated practice interpretation that identifies common motives, conflicts, and interactions across activity settings and observations; and thematic interpretation that transcends the other types of interpretation "to find meaningful patterns in relations to the research aim" (Hedegaard 2008, p. 61).

The Study

The contributions of cultural-historical scholars discussed above provided a strong foundation on which to build a theoretical approach relevant to my own research in collaboration with the Temple Garden Foundation. TGF is a UK-based nonprofit organization supporting sustainable development in two Siem Reap provincial communes through infrastructure, healthcare, and education initiatives.

Structure

My primary aim was to explore the question of what and how children learn in their everyday practices at the interpersonal level in one TGF village by observing and enquiring about how children spend their time and what they like to do. I was particularly interested in the network of relationships within and among families, the school community, and the village community and sought answers to the following sub-questions:

For the children

  - How do you spend time with your family?
  - What do you mostly do and enjoy?
  - What is important in your life?

For the adults

  - What knowledge and practices are important for children's learning and development in your family? Community?
  - How are these practices shared and taught?

Researching the "everyday" necessarily entails an emersion into the daily existence of participants, continuously observing their interactions and activities without expectation of one great event but with constant vigilance about the potential greatness within small ones. Hedegaard and Fleer's Children's Everyday Life

Table 6.1 Daily activities in children's lives

Category	Activity	Location
Morning	Waking up	Family 1 home
	Getting dressed	Village roads
	Eating breakfast	
	Playing	
	Walking to school	
School	Doing class activities	Classrooms in community center
	Break	or makeshift space in private
	Walking home	home
After school	Eating lunch	Family 1 home
	Napping or resting	
	Bathing	
	Playing	
Evening	Bathing	Family 1 home
	Eating dinner	
	Going to bed	

Across Different Institutions project was an essential reference on how to structure my own study and had many parallels to what was observed and analyzed with the two participant families. In this research, the daily routine of participating Cambodian village children was divided into four time-related categories (Table 6.1), which also coincided with the video footage and the categories of analysis. This chapter refers to findings from the seven members of Family 1 (mother, father, five children ranging from 10 months to 9 years at the time of research), grandparents, and neighbors.

It should be noted that in addition to the daily routines above, the children and their families also participated in a concluding group session that provided an iterative aspect to research based on a dialectic-interactive framework. Meeting with both families (along with more than a few curious neighbors and villagers) not only added another interesting dimension to the dynamic of questions and answers but also provided an opportunity to clarify and deepen our understanding of our previous sessions together.

Theory

By no means are these questions and structure original, as there are numerous studies conducted by constructionist scholars that consider societal factors and interpersonal relationships in the context of children's development, Hedegaard and Fleer's research in particular. However, any research on people and relationships in order to answer such questions is, by its very nature, unique. Darlaston-Jones rightly argues that "it is as a result of the conversation between that *particular* respondent and that *particular* researcher that resulted in the co-construction of meaning that emerged" (2007, p. 23). As such, it is imperative that the researcher, and most certainly the cultural-historical researcher, critically and honestly considers her role, identity, and expectations in the research process.

There is a need to "accept and value the role of the subjective rather than the objective" (Darlaston-Jones 2007, p. 21). It is unnatural, unnecessary, and virtually impossible to separate a researcher's own personal identity from the research in this type of engagement with participants. In this project, my status as a fellow Asian, albeit a North Asian, westernized pregnant female "expert" likely sent a number of conflicting signals that influenced the research. Positivist critics may argue against the potential biases created by not making our "cultural selves invisible" (Subedi 2006, p. 584), but I believe that any research involving people and relationships needs to go beyond oversimplified questions of accountability, ethics, and the antiseptic practice of deceptive labeling such as "objectivity" and "science." Fundamentally, it is a matter of human civility; beyond language, culture, age, gender, or socioeconomic status, an honest and open interaction will result in richer dialogue, a more meaningful connection, and ultimately access to the "real" information that researchers seek, especially in qualitative research where the boundaries are more flexible. As Alcoff asserts, "we should strive to create wherever possible the conditions for dialogue and the practice of speaking with and to rather than speaking for others" (1991, p. 23). One note of caution, however, halfie researchers in particular should take care to exercise reflexivity that avoids "self-serving 'empty autobiographical gestures'" (Subedi 2006, p. 575) and "vanity ethnography," as "their 'in-between' status requires that they be more accountable to how they have researched and written about the people with whom they affiliate" (p. 574). Here I adopt Abu-Lughod (1991)'s definition of halfie as someone "whose national or cultural identity is mixed by virtue of migration, overseas education, parentage" (as quoted in Subedi 2006, p. 573) and include myself in this category.

Data Collection

How and what data is collected inevitably determines the strength of analysis, and therefore it is critical that the researcher is fully aware of which tools and processes will be used in the limited time at the site. In a cultural-historical study of the "everyday," the researcher becomes a part of the participants' landscape for a period of time, sometimes quietly observing from the sidelines and at other times directly interacting with them. The approach, therefore, needs to be flexible enough to accommodate both these roles and capture as much data as possible. In the TGF study, three elements contributed to effective data collection: an informal interview style, use of video and still cameras, and the involvement of other assistants. They are discussed in greater detail and then summarized in Table 6.2.

Table 6.2 Key elements of data collection

Key element	Objectives	Possible approaches
Informal interview/ conversational exchange	Demystify the intrusion Establish rapport Be conscious of expectations and respond accordingly	Draw parallels through personal anecdotes (i.e., as parents, wives/ husbands, similar industries)
		Be flexible (prepare snacks, allow children to play while participating)
		Provide affirmation or advice; bring small gifts/donations as a "thank you" gesture once research is complete
Still/video camera	Capture interactions, not just people in isolation Make eye contact for the still camera portrait shots Be mindful of participants' self-awareness on camera	Point the video camera at children engaged in activity with others or their reactions while watching others
		Share footage already taken through the laptop or printed photos and film participants again
Field support	Establish rapport Ensure data collection consistency among researcher/support Simultaneously capture multiple perspectives Be aware of "lost in translation" moments	Make a connection through personal stories, eating together
		Explain the theory and methodology, not just the method
		Focus filming on individuals while support member films the whole scene; focus on the dialogue/ activity while support focuses on participants' reactions
		If necessary, question the translator for more details or offer an alternative translation

Informal Interview Style

My predominant means of engagement with participants was the informal interview or a conversational question and answer exchange. The first session with each family began with an introduction of the project and myself as an individual, to demystify the intrusion they would experience over the course of the research. I addressed adults both individually and collectively about their everyday practices and values regarding their children as individuals and as a group, rephrasing questions as necessary when things seemed to get lost in translation or simply misunderstood. In the subsequent sessions, this form of interaction increasingly enabled us to establish rapport by providing the flexibility to talk about what interested both parties at that moment. It was also a natural forum to reveal personal anecdotes so that we could relate to each other as fellow parents, wives, and the other roles we play in our lives. There were several instances where I drew parallels between our lives, for example, the juggling of motherhood and pregnancy or the similar use of fermented

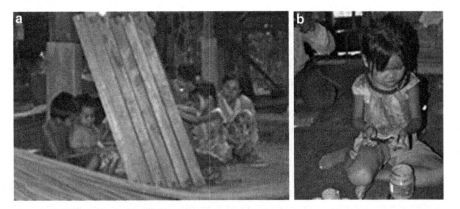

Fig. 6.1 (a) Spontaneous group play. (b) Child making snacks

fish pastes in Cambodian and Korean cooking. As Liamputtong (2010) observes, there is a need to "use methods that empower the participants and avoid power hierarchies that can occur in a research-researched relationship" (p. 232) especially with indigenous communities.

As for the children, capturing their perspectives directly was more difficult as there was limited time to become better acquainted as well as the added challenge of communicating through a translator. Much of the data was gleaned from open-ended questions addressed to the adults regarding the children and observing the children's reactions to the responses and to what was going on around them. This type of approach made it possible to capture the data I was looking for without forcing the children to give artificial responses, as they emerged as participants at their own pace and increasingly became more natural with time and without pressure. This is particularly important with children as they may not want to engage the researcher due to shyness about talking to a stranger (and a foreigner at that) or societal expectations that children do not speak out when among adults. They can also lose interest rather quickly, a challenge that Monk identifies and overcomes by using snacks and activities in Chap. 6. In the Cambodian research, the children began the first session by sitting silently next to their parents, resisting the adults' verbal and physical encouragement to answer questions or engage in play with the researcher. In subsequent sessions, however, they resumed their natural behavior and immersed themselves in elaborate, self-generated group play, weaving in and out of the adults' periphery (Fig. 6.1a). Notably, one child demonstrated a new skill in front of a large group by shyly but happily assisting me to make peanut butter snacks for the group session and distribute them (Fig. 6.1b) after trying them only the day before. The research strategy here is to create opportunities for children to emerge as their natural (or potential natural) selves with a lateral, not hovering, focus on them, yet reserving the ability to put them in the spotlight when the opportunity arises.

It should be noted that this informal conversational exchange can be enhanced by some form of feedback from the researcher to the participants. There is an expectation, especially in non-mainstream or marginalized communities, to receive some affirmation, validation, or guidance in return for participation in the research. Having intruded into their space as an "expert," the researcher is in some sense obligated to provide this. For example, the group session on the second day was intended to be an expanded, collective form of the informal conversational exchange, although in actuality a good portion of the time was spent with me talking about my observations, rephrasing questions, and providing examples in order to draw out responses. In retrospect, this is not surprising as a group session with an education researcher may have created the impression of greater formality, especially in a hierarchical Asian culture that values education highly. Quinones also discusses the complexities of participants' expectations toward the teacher-expert-researcher in Chap. 9, and her choice to embrace the role as it helped to gain the trust of the children. In this research, it was interesting to find that some responses were contrary to those given during the non-group sessions, some had evolved to reflect a deeper understanding of the original question, and that others remained completely unchanged. Regardless, it was evident that the participants' interest and enthusiasm about the research were stimulated by the video and photographic images of themselves, which helped them to contextualize my questions and the subsequent discussions that followed. It was also clear that they appreciated my support and validation of their existing cultural knowledge (farming, local biology, storytelling, music) vis-à-vis academic knowledge.

Use of Video and Still Cameras

Fortunately for researchers of the "everyday," technology today makes it considerably easier to capture, store, and access the information crucial to understanding learning and development from a cultural-historical perspective. The ability to digitally record events and later revisit them as many times as needed empowers researchers to discover significant findings from what may have been initially considered to be minutiae or not perceived at all. The challenge may be that too much data can become overwhelming and contradictory, or that the data collection itself becomes research without purpose. When used purposefully, however, technology proves to be a powerful ally in conducting serious research. The key point is that the camera needs to capture what children are doing in interactions and not just in isolation. It is unnatural and often impossible to avoid other children or individuals, especially in communal societies where the individual forms her identity as a part of a larger entity such as the family. Children are inevitably linked to their environment as well, as is the baby in Fig. 6.2a, who is a regular sleeping fixture in the center of activity. As such, I followed Fleer (2008)'s instruction that "the researcher points the videocamera at the children as they participate in everyday practices,

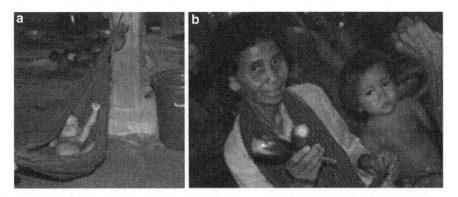

Fig. 6.2 (**a**) Baby in his environment. (**b**) Making eye contact

including their relations with others" (p. 106). This generally meant capturing the whole family as a group since the children usually sat among the adults as our interactions took place; I would focus on an individual child or groups of children when they were engaged in a particular activity or practice. I would also focus on adults when they were responding to a particular question, although the video would still capture other adults and children in the background.

The use of a digital camera also enabled me to take portraits of each participant and quickly freeze a notable activity or interaction in the moment. Portrait shots capture a sense of eye contact and help to jog one's memory regarding interactions and observations when revisiting the data after the event (Fig. 6.2b). They also can be used to make a photo album as a gift for the researched families once the research is complete. Both tools enabled me to reinforce the iterative dimension of my research methodology by providing concrete and immediate visual data I could share with them during the group session from my laptop.

Field Support

In general, the logistical support provided by research assistants proves highly useful in the field. The intrusion of research is distracting in itself, so if support is discrete and kept to a minimum, there is also the benefit of having another reference point to reconfirm facts and discuss after the research visit. I was faced with the double challenge of a very limited time frame and the need for translation, so TGF provided my visit with three local staff members. I initially thought that it would be less distracting if it were just the translator and me engaging the participants, but I soon discovered that we were a novel distraction regardless of how many people were in our group. Having two other TGF staff with us also meant that I had greater flexibility to take photographs and more actively interact with the participants, albeit via a translator, while one of them was filming. It should be acknowledged that there were instances where the assistant filmed at a distance so the translator's comments were not captured or where I probably would have focused on another person or activity; these pros and cons are also observed by Fleer (2008).

What is essential with co-researchers and translators is a critical examination of how these partnerships impact the research. Cross-cultural research in particular involves every member's interpretation of reality, from the interactions they select to film to the questions they choose to ask. In this sense, "a lack of understanding of the epistemological framework of the research by any member of the research team, including the translator, will negatively affect the quality and outcome of the research" (Wong and Poon 2010, p. 156). As mentioned above, what and how interactions were filmed may not have been consistent among the assistants, so it is helpful to discuss the theory and methodology behind the research and not just the methods, to minimize inconsistencies. Moreover, translation is "not a neutral technique of replacing words of one language with words of another language… [but] involves assigning meanings to words in both languages and is mediated by power relations and social contexts" (Wong and Poon 2010, p. 152). During my research, there were "lost in translation" moments where I definitely felt a lot more was expressed than what was told to me, not only because of the sheer number of words but also because I sensed from her body language and tone of voice that the translator (who was also the program director) made a judgment about what was important or relevant. While it is impossible to avoid this entirely, "it is crucial to make a serious attempt to be sensitive to the role language similarities and differences (between researchers and research participants) play in the research process" (Sullivan and Cottone 2010, p. 359).

Data Analysis

Research data was analyzed from a cultural-historical perspective referring to Hedegaard and Fleer's (2008) dialectic-interactive methodology and their three levels of interpretation. For my unit of analysis, I chose what I refer to as an interaction, redefined here as an interpersonal exchange between two or more people that ranges from a simple, spontaneous instance to a more regular, longer everyday practice. An interaction defined in this way best addresses the multifaceted nature of my research question as compared to a particular person or routine, which may limit my perspective to one dimension or overlook a seemingly mundane moment. I then identified three types of interactions: child/child interactions, child/adult interactions, and adult/adult interactions:

- Children – among siblings or friends
- Children and adult family members, neighbors, and research group members
- Adults – among family, neighbors, and research group members

Commonsense Level

At the commonsense level of interpretation, I captured my observations and initial impressions as much as possible on site in the form of field notes. I then reviewed the video footage and photographs as soon as possible after each session to add to these notes, usually just a few hours after the event. The last group session added another dimension to this process by enabling me to experience the iterative aspect of my research and to contribute a second round of observations and insights. Over the following days and weeks, I reviewed the video footage and photographs to build upon these notes, discussing and confirming with participating TGF staff as necessary. These field notes included specific episodes with the corresponding timing in the video and thus became a kind of video transcript as well, although I did not transcribe word for word any of the videos in their entirety. Nearly all of the dialogue is in Khmer, and I did not consider it necessary or appropriate to do so for the scope of this research. I also included my impressions of and experiences with TGF staff as our intensive time together was an inseparable part of the research process. This field note cum transcript became a critical one-stop reference point throughout the data collection and analysis, and included below are two excerpts.

Excerpt 1: Day 1 Family 1

P (the translator) then reads the explanatory statement to them as well as the consent form. While the families have been selected beforehand and prompted about us, due to the timing of the selection by the village chiefs/team leader, this was the first time they were hearing this. We read them out loud and then request that each family member tell us their name and age so that we can label the consent form for them to stamp (they are illiterate and this is typically what they do for official documents). The father initially cannot remember the children's full names (nor his official name for that matter) and goes into the house to bring an official document. The mother seems slightly embarrassed (only slightly though) and annoyed by this and tells us the children's names. There is some difficulty in mapping out how they are all related but eventually this is worked out (the translator is somewhat exasperated by how they change their answers – this proves to be a continuing issue over the next 2 days).

Excerpt 2: Group session

(24:00) Despite the very limited time filming and watching the clips, I ask if this interaction has made them think differently about how they interact with their own children. He responds by saying that he wishes he had more things to provide the children to learn (books, pencils, and other material goods), and P stops to tell me that she thinks he is not responding exactly to what she thinks I am asking. She thinks that he is answering in this way as he is expecting that we will provide something – I ask her to continue and tell me anyway what he is saying. Here is another instance where her opinions/perceptions influence the translation. I tell him that those things are important but even more so is encouragement through words and actions, and if their going to school is important to them, it is important that they find out what they are learning and learn it themselves, support them. I share my observation that while the mother is busy with the five children, the father is very supportive and he laughs sheepishly, perhaps embarrassed by my acknowledgement.

Table 6.3 Excerpt of matrix of demands, conflicts, imitation, and modeling

Setting	Child/child	Child/adult	Adult/adult
Day 2 Early Morning Family 1	Second child is very mothering toward fourth on walk to school, keeping her away from traffic First child very affectionate toward baby brother Children know not to go too close to the edge of house interior, as no walls Third child plays with insects she collected overnight, which the family will eat	Mother trusts an older neighboring child to carry infant downstairs Child can climb up to house by herself but mom carries her down on her back Children are shy but want to try my peanut butter snack so they overcome fear of interaction Mother pulls down daughter's skirt when seated	Grandmother makes comment about breakfast not being ready; translator and I initially have different opinions on what she meant

Situated Practice Level

At the next situated practice level of interpretation, I began to identify interactions across all time-related categories (morning, school, after school, evening) and settings (Kindergarten Class 1 and 2, Family 1 home, Family 2 home, group session) to create a matrix, an excerpt of which is included in Table 6.3. These interactions encapsulated any or all of the following:

– Adults and children's demands on themselves and on each other
– Conflicts in interactions between/among participants and/or researchers
– Children's imitation and modeling; parents' imitation and modeling of grandparents/peers

I revisited each setting from the matrix and drilled down into greater detail, as in the extract of the analysis of Family 1 below.

Extract of Analysis

Demands and Conflicts

The Family 1 children face demands typical of rural communities, mainly a kind of independence required for walking unaccompanied to and from school and knowing not to get too close to open railings. The mother expects that the children wash their hands before meals and that the girls maintain their propriety by pulling their skirts over their legs when seated. These parents also prioritize

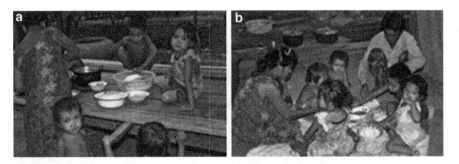

Fig. 6.3 (**a**) Breakfast at the table. (**b**) Dinner on the ground

meals together as a family, as shown in Fig. 6.3a, b. The father wants his son to attend school and confesses to offering him some pocket money as an incentive sometimes, although he himself thinks this is not the best way to handle this. Yet generally it appears that the parents, especially given their quiet and relatively gentle nature, do not place any major demands or pressures on the children, nor do the children misbehave grossly toward them or others. When I tried to engage the children with questions, gestures, and games, the parents encouraged them to respond but soon dropped it.

I sensed that the children themselves felt conflicted about interacting with me, as they were curious yet apprehensive about this stranger with her unusual language, gadgets, and food. At one point, a group of neighboring children engaged in a spontaneous activity of stacking broken tiles, and the third child was watching in interest but not bold enough to join, as were her two sisters who were also nearby. When I offered them some pieces and drew pictures in the dirt to engage them, they appeared interested and receptive but too shy to respond beyond smiling. The neighboring grandmother then approached and tried three times to encourage them to play, physically pulling them to the ground or moving their arms, but the children resisted this forced interaction and merely watched their baby brother, who began to play with the tiles on his own. It was only after these adult demands ended that the conflict was resolved for the girls, and they quietly started to play with the tiles themselves.

Modeling and Imitation

Besides the obvious instances of farming and cooking games played by the children, younger ones also takes cues from older siblings and friends regarding appropriate behavior. Three and four year olds exhibited extraordinary patience in school where they typically have to sit in one place for an extended period of time while the teacher instructs from the front of the classroom (Fig. 6.4a). Another example of imitation and modeling that stood out for me was the nurturing behavior and attitude

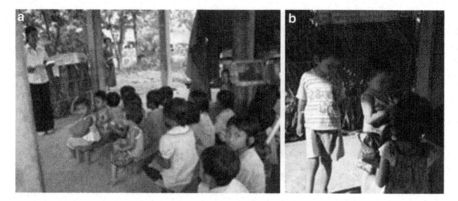

Fig. 6.4 (**a**) Ages 3–7 sitting quietly. (**b**) Caring older siblings

of the older children toward their younger siblings. As mentioned previously, the father is an active caregiver and seemingly very gentle; he does not spank his children and neither did his father, who is also very fond of his grandchildren and spanked his own son only once because he refused to go to school. The first child is noticeably affectionate toward his baby brother, spontaneously hugging or kissing him, and patient with his other siblings. In one instance, two of his sisters sat directly in front of him at the meal table although he was seated first; without a word, he got up and sat down on the other side and waited patiently to start. The second child is also tolerant toward her younger siblings, ignoring her little sister when she pulls her hair or goads her otherwise. She is particularly mothering toward the fourth child when no adults are around, holding her hand or shoulder on the walk to school and consoling her when she gets upset at school (Fig. 6.4b). She even offers her sister her own biscuit when the little one drops hers on the ground, then tries to take away the dirty one although without success.

Thematic Level

Interpretation at the commonsense level and the situated practice level as discussed above then enabled me to identify overarching themes and ultimately formulate one possible way of theorizing the cycle of how conflicts and demands within interactions give rise to the formation of new demands. Each theme was introduced in a logical sequence that would eventually lead to my model discussion and supported by the relevant findings and literature. For example, the importance of everyday interactions and its impact on development was one theme that was covered at this level of analysis. This was supported by the findings: children walk to school unaccompanied and take genuine care of siblings from a young age; even games such as insect collecting or sour-leaf picking actually contribute to the household food provision. It is argued that children are expected to do this and accomplish these tasks quite naturally because of their everyday societal conditions, in stark contrast to the assessment of children's "development" through star charts for putting away toys in other parts of the world. Parallels are drawn to the literature of researchers such as Tudge and Odero-Wanga (2009), who assert that "the culture within which these activities and interactions take place clearly plays a central role in influencing the types of activities and interactions that are available to the young of that culture, and influences which of them the children are encouraged to participate in (or discouraged from)" (p. 147). To strengthen the argument, exceptions and variances are also examined, in this case the differences in older-younger sibling dynamics: the caregiver-baby relationship in Family 1 versus the peer relationship in Family 2 despite a similar age difference. This is in part attributed to the attitudes and expectations of the Family 2 parents, who are both keenly aware of their older son's weaker physical state compared to their daughter's hardy, energetic nature and are quite attentive to his needs.

Detailed discussions of each theme pave the way for the introduction of a new model at the end of the thematic level analysis. In essence, the cyclical demand formation model (Pennay 2010) explains development as a cyclical process of transformation where demands are reinforced, internalized, and eventually modeled as new demands within interactions. It relies on the premises of Hedegaard's cultural-historical theory, which recognizes that value positions at the institutional level of family or school are affected by the cultures and traditions of greater society, and that children at the individual level can exert influence on the institutions they are a part of. It also builds upon Hedegaard and Fleer's (2008) point that demands can lead to the modeling of demands, by closely examining this process in the interactions children experience both directly and indirectly.

The Four R Framework

Cultural-historical scholarship involves a certain degree of subjectivity that does not necessarily detract from the validity or accuracy of research but does require a conscientious awareness of the factors that can influence it. Liamputtong (2010) argues that qualitative research by definition focuses on the social world and therefore relies heavily on participants' words and stories, with the aim to "capture lived experiences of the social world and the meanings people give these experiences from their own perspective" (Corti and Thompson 2004, p. 326, as quoted in Liamputtong 2010). It is also heavily dependent on the researcher's ability to interpret what the participants choose to share and why. Based on lessons learned from the Cambodian study, the Four R framework is an overview of how cross-cultural research should take place from a cultural-historical perspective. It identifies four, equally critical factors – rapport, respect, reliability, and reflexivity – that continually impact the research as well as each other, thereby exerting even more influence on the research outcome. They are represented by the four connected boxes

Fig. 6.5 The Four R
framework

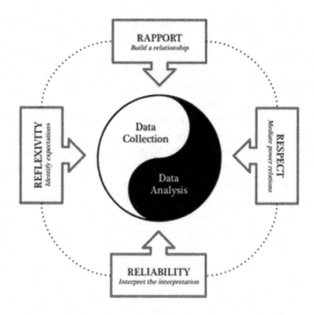

encircling and pointing to the data process in Fig. 6.5. The framework also recognizes
that data collection and data analysis are neither separate nor linear but instead are
dynamic parts of a whole that influence each other to varying degrees at various
points in time. This interplay is fittingly represented by the yin and yang symbol in
Asian philosophy, which also embodies the concepts of complementarity, contraction
and expansion, balance, and interdependence.

Rapport

As discussed earlier in the chapter, building good rapport with both participants and
co-researchers is an essential part of research. This is especially true when there are
cultural gaps that need to be bridged and thus a real need for sparking a personal
connection, in order to unlock the wealth of information that may not be accessible
otherwise. Relationship building necessitates a give and take dynamic, a reciprocal
exchange where participants share their lives and the researcher also provides something of value. This can be in the form of information, such as personal anecdotes
about parallel experiences; parenting was common ground with the participants,
while the translator and I discussed thesis writing for a master's degree, which she
was considering at the time. It can also be tangible objects such as donations or
gifts, especially in poor, rural communities where there is a real need. This should

not be misinterpreted as bribery as they are simply tokens of appreciation, keeping in mind that only appropriate items should be used. In this study, I had several boxes of donated used toys, clothes, and educational items for TGF to distribute as needed; for the participant families, I bought new coloring pencils, books, and small ice box coolers to be used at home and on the fields. All of these items were distributed after the onsite data collection was completed.

Respect

Good rapport alone is not enough to ensure good research, as power dynamics need to be recognized and addressed. In this research, there were many dichotomies to consider: researcher vs. participant, adult vs. child, urban vs. rural, developed vs. developing, educated vs. uneducated (in the academic sense), "teacher" vs. student. Discussing parallel experiences also helps the researcher, co-researchers, and participants to meet on level ground, as does living them. One memorable night, the research team and I ended up eating leftover rice that had been attacked by ants because we were too hungry and it was too late to cook more; left unspoken was the fact that it would have been very costly for them to simply throw away. I realized in that moment how disrespectful it would be not to eat and how wasteful we are in the "developed" world; so by eating it and not making it a cultural and socioeconomic issue, it did not become one. Lastly, body language is important, and effort should be made to engage at eye level and at a close but respectful distance; I took cues from the villagers about when to stand, sit, or squat on the ground and eventually felt comfortable enough to gauge on my own.

Reliability

As mentioned earlier, there were moments when the translator, in her role as TGF program director and perhaps also as an educated member of Cambodian society, made judgments about the rural participants' comments and decisions. Field support members made their own decisions about what and when to film even within the guideline parameters, thereby impacting what video footage was actually collected. In turn, I needed to make my own judgments about which instances were acceptable and which warranted questioning, and fortunately our relationship had been strengthened enough by then for me to be able to disagree and request alternative translations and footage without seeming offensive or disrespectful. Reliable data can only result from a collection and analysis process that has been challenged and revisited from various angles, and it is the responsibility of the main researcher to interpret the various interpretations and synthesize a cohesive yet nuanced analysis of the data (Table 6.4).

Table 6.4 Summary structure for interpretation and analysis

Level of analysis	Objectives	Tools of analysis
Common sense	Capture responses, impressions – the spoken and unspoken	Field notes Video transcript
	Verify and validate observations	Co-researchers
Situated practice	Identify common motives, conflictions	Matrix of demands, conflicts, imitation, modeling (Table 6.3)
	Match images to explanations	Drill down analysis per setting
Thematic	Identify meaningful patterns leading to research aim	Conclusive themes that support the argument
	Conceptualize understanding of observations and analyses	Theoretical model of phenomenon

Reflexivity

The researcher must also be aware of her expectations and how they influence the participants and the process, especially in what may be considered non-mainstream societies. Interactions with the Other often "privilege[s] the expert knowledge of the researcher and does not consider community-based knowledge, which has been part of a people's ways of being and knowing for generations" (Subedi 2006, p. 587). My own epistemological leanings toward this transformative perspective made me particularly sensitive to capturing this knowledge, and I had to acknowledge that my engagement with participants would be affected as a consequence. Prior to visiting the research site, I anticipated that knowledge about culture, tradition, and the environment would be found there even in this present age when academic knowledge is prioritized and alternative knowledges are undervalued. Therefore, when I felt that adults participants were giving answers they thought I wanted to hear (i.e., prioritizing academics), I found myself probing further and in different ways to uncover what other skills they valued for their children. This is precisely the kind of judgment call cultural-historical scholars must make in seeking out what they believe to be the true answers, in the face of criticism that such approaches are not sufficiently "objective." At the same time, they must avoid being overly sensitive and thus overcompensating for what they believe to be an unjust representation of the Other.

Conclusion

The objective of this chapter was to provide a framework for conducting cultural-historical research on the "everyday," with guidelines on how to structure the data collection and analysis. Only a constant vigilance and commitment to cultural-historical theory throughout the research process can ensure that data is captured, analyzed, and ultimately understood with cultural-historical integrity. As such, researching people and relationships from this perspective requires the researcher to strategically embrace subjectivity and leverage its ability to capture what supposedly "objective" methodologies cannot. It must also recognize that "people and practices are never seen in isolation but in the context of complex webs of social relations and institutions" (Macdonald et al. 2002, p. 144). This applies not only to research participants but also to the research team, especially one with multiple cultures and languages that can bring both richness and complexity to the research process. These two ideas are the pillars of conducting research on the "everyday" that do not preclude the possibility of upholding the methodological rigor necessary for valid cultural-historical research.

Acknowledgments Professor Marilyn Fleer provided invaluable guidance on my unpublished master's thesis, from which this chapter was born. The research also could not have been possible without the Temple Garden Foundation and the two brave families who opened their homes and hearts to a stranger and her video camera.

References

Abu-Lughod, L. (1991). Writing against culture. In R. Fox (Ed.), *Recapturing anthropology: Working in the present*. Santa Fe: School of American Research Press.

Alcoff, L. (1991). The problem of speaking for others. *Cultural Critique, 20*, 5–32.

Anning, A., Cullen, J., & Fleer, M. (2009). Research contexts across cultures. In A. Anning, J. Cullen, & M. Fleer (Eds.), *Early childhood education: Society & culture* (pp. 1–24). London: Sage.

Canella, G., & Viruru, R. (1997). Privileging child-centered, play-based instruction. In G. Canella (Ed.), *Deconstructing early childhood education: Social justice and revolution*. New York: Peter Lang.

Chaiklin, S., & Hedegaard, M. (2009). Radical-local teaching and learning: A cultural-historical perspective on education and children's development. In M. Fleer, M. Hedegaard, & J. Tudge (Eds.), *Childhood studies and the impact of globalization: Policies and practices at global and local levels* (pp. 182–201). New York: Routledge.

Corti, L., & Thompson, P. (2004). Secondary analysis of archived data. In C. Seale, G. Gobo, J. F. Gubrium, & D. Silverman (Eds.), *Qualitative research practice* (pp. 327–343). London: Sage Publications.

Croft, A. (2002). Singing under a tree: Does oral culture help lower primary teachers be learner-centred? *International Journal of Educational Development, 22*(3–4), 321–337.

Darlaston-Jones, D. (2007). Making connections: The relationship between epistemology and research methods. *The Australian Community Psychologist, 19*(1), 19–27.

Fleer, M. (2008). Using digital video observations and computer technologies in a cultural-historical approach. In M. Hedegaard & M. Fleer (Eds.), *Studying children: A cultural-historical approach* (pp. 104–117). Maidenhead/New York: Open University Press.

Fleer, M. (2010). *Early learning and development*. Melbourne: Cambridge University Press.

Fleer, M., & Quinones, G. (2009). Constructing childhood: Global–local policies and practices. In M. Fleer, M. Hedegaard, & J. Tudge (Eds.), *Childhood studies and the impact of globalization: Policies and practices at global and local levels* (pp. 86–107). New York: Routledge.

Fleer, M., Hedegaard, M., & Tudge, J. (2009). Constructing childhood: Global–local policies and practices. In M. Fleer, M. Hedegaard, & J. Tudge (Eds.), *Childhood studies and the impact of globalization: Policies and practices at global and local levels* (pp. 1–20). New York: Routledge.

Freitas, L., Shelton, T., & Sperb, T. (2009). Conceptions of early childhood care and education in Brazil. In M. Fleer, M. Hedegaard, & J. Tudge (Eds.), *Childhood studies and the impact of globalization: Policies and practices at global and local levels* (pp. 279–291). New York: Routledge.

Goncu, A., Ozer, S., & Ahioglu, N. (2009). Childhood in Turkey: Social class and gender differences in schooling, labor and play. In M. Fleer, M. Hedegaard, & J. Tudge (Eds.), *Childhood studies and the impact of globalization: Policies and practices at global and local levels* (pp. 67–85). New York: Routledge.

Hedegaard, M. (2008). Principles for interpreting research protocols. In M. Hedegaard, M. Fleer, J. Bang, & P. Hviid (Eds.), *Studying children: A cultural-historical approach* (pp. 46–64). New York: Open University Press.

Hedegaard, M., & Fleer, M. (2008). Family practices and how children are positioned as active agents. In M. Fleer, M. Hedegaard, & J. Tudge (Eds.), *Childhood studies and the impact of globalization: Policies and practices at global and local levels* (pp. 86–107). New York: Routledge.

Hedegaard, M., Fleer, M., Bang, J., & Hviid, P. (2008). *Studying children: A cultural-historical approach*. New York: Open University Press.

Liamputtong, P. (2010). Cross-cultural research and qualitative inquiry. *Turkish Online Journal of Qualitative Inquiry., 1*(1), 16–29.

Macdonald, D., Kirk, D., Metzler, M., Nilges, L., Schempp, P., & Wright, J. (2002). It's all very well, in theory: Theoretical perspectives and their applications in contemporary pedagogical research. *Quest, 54*(2), 133–156.

Mbebeb, F. (2009). Priming entrepreneurial mindsets through socialization in family occupations. *International Journal of Early Childhood, 41*(2), 23–34.

Nimmo, J. (2008). Young children's access to *real life*: An examination of the growing boundaries between children in child care and adults in the community. *Contemporary Issues in Early Childhood., 9*(1), 3–13.

Nsamenang, A. (2009). Cultures in early childhood care and education. In M. Fleer, M. Hedegaard, & J. Tudge (Eds.), *Childhood studies and the impact of globalization: Policies and practices at global and local levels* (pp. 23–45). New York: Routledge.

Park, J. (2011). Metamorphosis of Confucian Heritage Culture and the possibility of an Asian education research methodology. *Comparative Education, 47*(3), 381–393.

Penn, H. (2008). Working on the impossible: Early childhood policies in Namibia. *Childhood, 15*(3), 379–395.

Pennay, S. (2010). *Everyday interactions in a rural Cambodian community: An exploration through imagery and dialogue.* Unpublished masters thesis, Monash University, Melbourne.

Subedi, B. (2006). Theorizing a halfie researcher's identity in transnational fieldwork. *International Journal of Qualitative Studies in Education, 19*(5), 573–593.

Sullivan, C., & Cottone, R. (2010). Emergent characteristics of effective cross-cultural research: A review of the literature. *Journal of Counseling and Development, 88*, 357–362.

Tudge, J. (2008). *The everyday lives of young children: Culture, class & childrearing in diverse societies*. New York: Cambridge University Press.

Tudge, J., & Odero-Wanga, D. (2009). A cultural-ecological perspective on early childhood among the Luo of Kisumu, Kenya. In M. Fleer, M. Hedegaard, & J. Tudge (Eds.), *Childhood studies and the impact of globalization: Policies and practices at global and local levels* (pp. 142–160). New York: Routledge.

Vygotsky, L. S. (1966). Play and its role in the mental development of the child. *Voprosy Psikhologii, 12*(6), 62–76.

Williams-Kennedy, D. (2009). Building bridges between literacies. In A. Anning, J. Cullen, & M. Fleer (Eds.), *Early childhood education: Society & culture* (pp. 91–102). London: Sage.

Wong, J., & Poon, M. (2010). Bringing translation out of the shadows: Translation as an issue in methodological significance in cross-cultural qualitative research. *Journal of Transcultural Nursing, 21*(2), 151–158.

Yang, R. (2011). Educational research in Confucian cultural contexts: Reflections on methodology. *Comparative Education, 47*(3), 395–405.

Chapter 7
A Visual and Tactile Path: Affective Positioning of Researcher Using a Cultural-Historical Visual Methodology

Gloria Quiñones

Introduction

The aim of this chapter is to discuss how the researcher is positioned when studying everyday life of children in a Mexican rural community. The cultural-historical concept of *positioning* is defined as the place children have through relating with others in the different social situations and experiences in life (Bozhovich 2009) explored in this chapter. This concept is theorised as *affective positioning* where the research participants give a role to the researcher, an important place in their lives and relate to the researcher affectively.

This chapter considers how the researcher has many different *zones of sense* (Vygotsky 1987; Gonzalez Rey 2002) created through verbal exchange and implicit subjective senses in which intellectual and affective psychological elements act in unity. Visual video methodologies used to capture the moment of *affective positioning* created in the relationship with the participants and in different *perezhivanie* moments (Vygotsky 1994).

The research orientations, decisions and choices about interactions are unpacked. While the research process becomes a complex endeavour, there is little evidence *how visual methodologies allow the capture of the emotions of the participants and researcher*. The role of the video camera as a methodological tool discussed in how it allows capture of different dialogues and emotions that the participants have towards the researcher. The researcher filmed the everyday life of Mayra in the kindergarten and in her family home.

Emotions are lived and relived throughout all the stages of the research process. This chapter explores how can emotions be captured and *how can the field research data be presented visually. While these are captured, what role does the researcher*

G. Quiñones, M.Ed. EC, B.A. (✉)
Faculty of Education, Monash University, Melbourne, Australia
e-mail: gloria.quinones@monash.edu

M. Fleer and A. Ridgway (eds.), *Visual Methodologies and Digital Tools for Researching with Young Children*, International Perspectives on Early Childhood Education and Development 10, DOI 10.1007/978-3-319-01469-2_7, © Springer International Publishing Switzerland 2014

have? The researcher must consider his/her role while interacting with participants and must make choices and take actions that lead to obtaining data to answer the research question. The researcher takes not only a *visual path* with the participants but a *tactile and sensorial one where emotions flourish*. The researcher and participant emotions are important – while the research unfolds, as the researcher becomes more familiar with the community and as she steps into the everyday life of his/her participants.

A Visual and Tactile Path

Child rearing is like researching, steps are taken and it is a complex endeavour. Vygotsky (1997) writes that child rearing is never a simple process but an 'organic transition… rearing must exert itself every time whenever it had been following a smooth road before, that it must take a leap where it seems that it could limit itself to step. The primary merit of the new research is specifically a complex picture where formerly we saw a simple one' (p. 226–227). This is also the case when new research methodologies are introduced. Visual methodologies offer a new and complex way of researching and can offer a complex picture. They also offer not only a visual path to understanding and seeing the child but also a tactile, affectionate and perceptual path where not only the 'eye' is needed but an affectionate sense and touch from the researcher.

Visual methodologies can be useful when a child has a hearing or visual impairment. Through the creation of new cultural methods and techniques, the child can understand different forms of communicating. For example, for a child with a hearing impairment, their ability to understand speech can be achieved by learning how to read lips 'reading lips, that is, replacing speech sounds with visual images, the movement of the mouth and lips' (p. 227). For children with visual impairment, visual writing is replaced by tactile writing where children can touch letters 'a system of signs just as writing can be diverted from the visual path to the tactile path' (p. 227) such as the creation of the Braille system. Through these new systems, children are able to communicate with others in different ways such as gestures and movement. These examples are given to understand how new methods are created to understand signs and symbolic language which can be verbal but non-verbal. This can also be the case when researchers are trying to understand different forms of communication such as how affect and children is communicated non-verbally in different cultural communities such as Mexican communities.

Visual images are able to translate emotional and affective moments in the research process. The researcher's journey through a visual to tactile path is discussed in this chapter. The researcher chose a visual path using video methodologies to capture and analyse visually experiences and practices. In this research journey, the visual and tactile path related to what the researcher's 'eye'

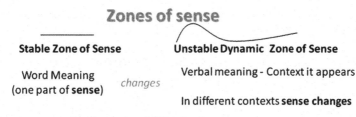

Fig. 7.1 Vygotsky's interpretation of zone of sense citing Paulhan's work (1987, p. 222)

could see (visual path) but also the emotional relationship (tactile and affective path) between participants.

Methodological choices and orientations are discussed in the different moments of the research process. The theoretical underpinnings are discussed in the next section; this chapter questions *how can cultural-historical researchers understand affect and sense, and how does this relate to their role as researcher?*

Intellectual and Affective Senses

Throughout his writings, Vygotsky alerts researchers to understand the unity of the whole, such as the unity of the human being with their social environment. One of Vygotsky's methodological problems was the search for unity between intellect and affect through the concept of *zones of senses.*

Intellect and affect contain affective forces such as motives, needs, interests, tendencies and incentives (Vygotsky 1987). In every idea, the individual holds an affective attitude that transformed into dynamic movements. Through the concept of emotion, affect and thinking in a dynamic system, children and adults experience different social situations in their everyday lives.

Meaning depends on the context in which it appears, and *sense* changes according to the context in which it is located (Vygotsky 1987). Through speech, there are explicit words spoken that give a *stable zone of sense* while *unstable dynamic zone of sense* relate to implicit verbal meanings. In different contexts, sense and verbal meanings change, and this is what Vygotsky called *intellectual and affective senses.* In drawing upon Paulhan, Vygotsky illustrates the *zone of sense* shown in Fig. 7.1.

Vygotsky (1987) gives an example on how in the fable of the ant and the grass-hopper, the grasshopper says to the ant 'go to dance' and the way this word has different *zones of sense*, meanings that are explicit and implicit. The *stable zone of sense* can mean literally 'go and dance' such as dance as an action. However, in a different context these words can have an *unstable dynamic zone of sense* in which there are hidden intentions of have fun or go away.

Vygotsky explains that in order to understand others' thinking, it is important to understand individual motivations and affections, and these can be possible through an understanding of *stable and unstable dynamic zones of sense* in which individual senses the whole context. This is important to understand because *sensing* goes beyond verbal meaning; it means that the *dynamic zones of sense* can contain non-verbal language, like gaze and gestures, and meaning depends on the social situation and context the individual has in their own meaning creation through *subjective sensing*.

Sense is a very dynamic concept that involves emotions and symbolic expressions which becomes an expression of the subject through his/her own subjectivities (Gonzalez Rey 2002, 2008). The concept of *sense* allows researchers to work and reformulate categories like personality and emotions as a system of *sense* rather than as an internal structure and is part of a complex representation of mental functions. Emotions are 'an element of *sense* that acquires a subjective expression' (Gonzalez Rey 2008, p. 145).

Experience-*ing* Everyday Life: Vivencia

The cultural-historical concept of *perezhivanie* theorised by Vygotsky (1994) was used to understand the influences that the social environment has on children's development and learning. Through the concept of *perezhivanie vivencia* (in Spanish), Vygotsky investigated the changing relationships between the social environment and the child's complex dynamic system of affects, feelings and emotions. In the heart of this concept was how 'affect' shapes people, situations, events and conflicts they live. Further, children in their everyday lives have different *positions* that allow them to express the different meanings, affective attitudes and their sense of their world.

The concept of *perezhivanie* allows for an understanding of how children and adults are able to make sense of their lives through their interactions and how they are affected by a specific intense, emotional and dramatic experience. New relationships are established when new situations give different meaning and senses. The *perezhivanie vivencia* is being – living and unfolding, becoming. The child is able to affectively perceive and interpret emotions and in a situation lived with others and in relationship with others:

> Experiences, once they have taken place and formed a complex system of feelings, affects, and moods, begin to take on significance for people in and of themselves. (Bozhovich 2009, p. 74)

Experiences contain a complex system of *feelings, affect and moods that are significant for people*. The experience transforms into a goal and leads to new needs into a special and unique form of the subject's life (Bozhovich 2009). As Vygotsky identified experience, this concept was the 'central nexus in the children's mental development' (Bozhovich 2009, p. 70). Intellect and affect contains a dynamic system of desires, wishes, needs and impulses. Consequently, this also determines the formation of personality, on how the child relates to their real everyday life.

Affective Positioning

The concept of *children's position in life* is explained by Bozhovich as a 'place that children occupy within the system of social relationships available to them and their own internal position in life' (p. 75). Adults assign a mental internal image of children and space or place where they imagine who children are or will become. This is determined in specific situations children are living.

Bozhovich (2009) gives the example of 'school success', a particular situation children are assigned a role, a position or a place. The meaning of what 'school success' is defined by families and schools. Children have attitudes towards school success; this directly relates to the child's learning, and vice versa, parents have particular attitudes towards children in *assigning* their children academic success in their lives and to their performance in school life. The system of relationships (parents, teachers and peers), which the child is surrounded by, brings to the child demands. For example, if a family values academic ability, the child will be assigned demands and pressures to do well at school. Adults and children are able to mentally and emotionally *place and position* an image or role of who they are (and others) in a specific situation. The place children occupy through interacting with others is in a dynamic relationship.

The relationships between demands, needs and the *positioning* of children are important concepts to understand as they determine a child's affective *emotional experiences*. Bozhovich explains that 'in order to understand the nature of the effect the environment has on children, first and foremost, the place that they occupy within that environment must be examined' (p. 80). It is important to understand 'the system of demands' (p. 83) that the social environment places to children.

This chapter argues how the concept of *affective positioning* also involves the researcher as he/she is studying the everyday life of children. Participants determine the role of the researcher in the community researched, and in turn, this role can be *affectively* determined. Children and adults are able to position and place a role in the life of the researcher, and on the other hand, the participants have a role and position assigned by the researcher. The concepts of affective positioning theorise through using Bozhovich concept of position in life. *Affective positioning* refers to the *affective emotional experiences* that someone occupies in the social environment, such as *perezhivanie* where a critical and intense moment in life shapes the child's learning and development.

The research participants, such as adults and children, are able to assign a role, place and position to the researcher and have demands and expectations of the researcher. The researcher becomes part of the system of relationships. Depending on the nature of the research, the researcher will have or may not have an impact in the lives of the children he/she is researching.

Role of the Researcher

In sociocultural research, Rogoff (2011) reflects on her role in a Mayan community in Guatemala. She writes how the community positions her as a teacher, she recounts:

> As people saw my interest in children's learning and child development, the identity most commonly ascribed to me was "teacher:" I always tried to clarify that I was trying to learn about children, and that I was not teaching the children but learning from them. But there was not a local category of "psychological researcher" at that time, in the eyes of most Pedranos, I remained a teacher. (p. 38)

This quote presents the complex role the researcher has with the participants in how they *ascribed* a position in the community. In this Guatemalan community, the role of the researcher did not exist nor did it have any meaning to the community. Therefore, the researcher was positioned as a teacher.

Hedegaard (2008) acknowledges the importance of being aware of the researcher's role. She explains how important it is to keep in mind the researcher's own participation and her aim when researching activity settings because the researcher becomes a member of the community, but not a partner in the activities. The role of the researcher becomes a 'balancing act' (p. 204) between situations of authority and position of trust in relating with children. For example, in a school setting, the researcher needs to balance when or not to intervene while observing children, for example, when the child needs help. The role of the researcher becomes a 'balancing act because the children become aware that the researcher does not have the authority of the caregivers' (Hedegaard 2008, p. 204). Some examples of this 'balancing act' given on how the researcher cannot tell children not to do something as the teacher decides on important decision, as she is the authority in class.

When researching, it is important to consider who the research participants are and how they are positioned in the wider context. How the children are positioned and how the researcher becomes aware of this is important for making decisions about how the researcher might act and what to observe, when to stop the video camera or when to intervene. The *affective positioning* of the researcher needs to consider when in the research site and when filming. In the next section, an example of the *affective positioning* of the researcher is presented to illustrate the visual and tactile path taken by the researcher when researching in a Mexican community.

Research in a Mexican Community

This research took place in a rural community in the state of Nuevo Leon, Mexico. The researcher was familiar with the *ejido* before the research took place. *Ejido* means a communal piece of land used for agricultural purposes, which is shared with others such as sharing water and land. Although, in the present time this no longer happens, historically the name *ejido* remains part of this community. In the past, these communities' survival was dependent on agriculture. The researcher

Fig. 7.2 'Ejido' state
of Nuevo Leon, Mexico
(Photo taken by Mayra,
5 years old)

knew this community for about 10 years before she researched the everyday life of Mayra (Fig. 7.2).

The children who attend the community kindergarten invited to participate in the project. Four children attended the kindergarten. Mayra's family was interested in participating in the project. Gina, Mayra's mother, informed the researcher through a community birthday party her interest in being part of the research. The family consisted of Mayra, five and a half years old; her brother Jake, 8 years old; stepfather; Gina; and two uncles that lived in close proximity to Mayra's home. A total of 10 h of video observations of family everyday life were gathered, while for the kindergarten, six visits were video recorded and around 30 h of video recordings taken.

The researcher also interacted informally with Mayra and her family while living in the community. The researcher was living in the community for a period of a month, which brought informal interactions. While walking around the community to visit a family member, the researcher greeted and stopped to talk to Mayra and her family. For example, the researcher saw Mayra riding her bike around the community. Children, families and other members of the community referred to the researcher mainly as *teacher*. Similar to Rogoff (2011), the researcher explained how she was not a *teacher* but a researcher discussed later in the chapter.

'Visual Vivencias' from a Visual to Tactile Research Path

Visual methodologies provide a detailed way to document practices in the learning sciences (Derry et al. 2010). Video as a research tool allows different philosophical orientations and therefore conveys complex challenges such as selection of what is recorded and videotaped, editing and analysis and reporting about the data gathering (Derry et al. 2010; Goldman 2007).

Fig. 7.3 Researcher's
camera position

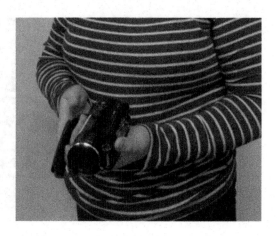

However, video research is considered as a context rather than as a method (Goldman 2007). It is important to consider how participants' perspectives are represented, what actions taken and how the research will affect others in the study (Goldman 2007).

The different points of viewing or perspectives are important to capture when video researching. Goldman (2007) points out how being there in the research context is important when video recording. The researcher needs to pay attention to participants and to locate the reader/viewer.

Researchers following cultural-historical theory focus on capturing the wholeness of the different perspectives such as kindergarten and family practices through video recording observation of these. Through video observations, different perspectives can be captured, and interpretations can be done in an 'iterative way' (Fleer 2008, p. 116) and the data can be seen many times for ongoing interpretation and analysis.

'Visual Vivencias' as a methodological tool captures children's moments of intense emotion and intellect and affect. Vivencia is a critical moment of children's learning and development. The experience the child is participating with others and the affective relationships all influence children learning and development. Vygotsky (1994) explains this affective relationship and attitude when the child is in a specific situation with others. Adding to these, the child makes sense not only by what he/she is able to think but a moving force in development where the child is emotionally and affectively sensing and perceiving the *ambience* – the qualities and what encompasses the environment.

Through this conceptualisation, 'Visual Vivencias' enables the researcher to capture the social environment. Through video recordings, it is possible to capture emotions and affects, symbolic language and how children relate with others. This is presented in *visual mobile images* (see Fig. 7.3).

Visual Vivencias is also an analytical tool where *perezhivanie vivencias* can be analysed in the *visual mobile images* in different alive 'momentitos' of emotionally intense and charged living experiences. The different subjective configurations of symbolic verbal and non-verbal (facial gestures, expressions and embodiment), voice and affections are represented visually as shown on the images and narratives below (see Fig. 7.7) (Quiñones and Fleer 2011). Even though the researcher does not appear in the film, voice and conversations are captured. Through this visual methodology, emotions, feelings and senses in different forms are captured even though these emotions might not be available for the 'eye' in the moment of filming. The researcher and the video camera are in dynamic unity. The position of the camera needs consideration as this allows for the capturing of important moments of interaction between participants.

In Fig. 7.3, the researcher positions the camera above the waist so she can interact with participants. Traditional approaches to filming position the camera over the eye. The position 'above the waist' allows the research to talk and make visual contact with participants. The camera should also allow movement. However, there are moments where the camera still allows the researcher to have more intense interaction with participants. The unity of intellect and affect allows rethinking the role of the research just filming (visual path) but accounting for the researcher's emotions (tactile path) which the researcher experienced in this community.

Findings

Researcher as a Teacher

Once the video observations have been downloaded through computer programs (such as Window Media Player), visual mobile images of important moments can be captured. For example, in Figs. 7.4 and 7.5, the researcher made two decisions. First, in the moment of interaction, the researcher decided to take the role of teacher and left the camera in a still position. Because in this rural community the researcher

Figs. 7.4 and 7.5 Researcher's role as the 'maestra'

positioned as 'la maestra' the teacher, in the classroom the researcher expected to enter into activities associated with teaching (Hedegaard 2008). In this situation, the researcher invited children to read a book to children at the end of the day.

In this community, the researcher was called a teacher, but this also brought expectations of acting as one. The role of the researcher needs to understand in the specific context. Even though the teacher did not say to the researcher that she should be a teacher, the researcher had to *sense* the teacher's intentions and expectations. This sensing involved reading the implicit non-verbal and vernal language and the *hidden intentions* that were part of the *unstable dynamic zone of sense* the researcher was located. This moment of *sensing* related to reading a story. The researcher positioned the camera to capture the story telling moment.

The researcher took this role because it contributed to children trusting the researcher, to not only intellectual connecting to children but emotionally. The researcher *subjectively sensed* how children were interested in having someone else reading them a book. The researcher's *sensing* was an important moment she had to think and feel in the moment and make a choice. The teacher implicitly communicated this through assuming the researcher was a teacher and her familiarity with the practice of reading a book. Other researchers might choose not to be involved in activities not related to researching, but through *subjective senses*; the researcher chooses this opportunity to emotionally and affectively connect with children through this activity.

Bozhovich (2009) explained how for children it is important to understand their environment and the place they received in a system of relationships. The researcher was a new person in the system of relationships for these four children. The activity of storytelling at the end of the day provided a close and comfortable space where the researcher could interact with children. The researcher has to be aware of the cultural context he or she is video observing and *sense* what others expect from her, not only intellectually but also affectively about the choices taken in the research field. *Sense* is very subjective and very dynamic through words, and verbal and non-verbal meanings remain important when sensing what children and the teacher intend the researcher to do. These intentions communicated in this community implicitly and non-verbally through gaze and expressions. In this community, it was important to understand the *hidden intentions* of being a teacher. The following *visual mobile images* show the researcher as a teacher.

The researcher spent a period of 20 min telling stories to children. The video camera positioned in front of the activity. The decisions made were to capture the whole activity. The second image shows a 'close-up' where affective gaze and gestures can be perceived such as close attention from the children.

The role of the researcher is very dynamic, it is not only about recording everyday life (visual path), but the researcher is in the everyday life of children not only as a spectator but also as a participant and member of the community. The researcher was encouraged to be teacher and to act as one. The *visual mobile images* make possible to analyse the role of the researcher visually and perceive the tactile path, how the images can be affectively perceived and *subjectively sensed* by the researcher and the reader.

Researcher as a Friend

During the everyday interactions the researcher had in Mayra's family, it can be seen how the entire family member have an *affective relationship* towards the researcher and how the researcher was able to build this *affective relationship*. In the *visual mobile image* below, Mayra's mother, Gina, was washing clothes, and Mayra needed help from the researcher to watch a DVD. While the researcher was not aware of the impact, she had in the community, through analysing the video tapes and transcribing the conversations a *new zone of sense* and awareness of her role unfolded. The researcher could see a close affective interaction with Mayra and close gaze that could tell more than words; see Fig. 7.6.

It can be seen how the research process took a visual to a tactile path where the researcher was not only capturing visually everyday life but also capturing an affective relationship with the participants. The dynamic relationship that the camera played in this allowed the researcher to be aware of these experiences, this not only happened after the video recordings but in the moment. This image shows how the video camera allowed to capture an intimate moment with Mayra where emotions and affect can be seen through their *miradas – gaze.*

The visual to the tactile path is seen through a dialogue with Mayra's uncle who is blind. He was present in three of the four visits made to Mayra's home. He expressed how the researcher was *affectively positioned* in the family. He was not able to see the researcher, but he was able to *sense* the relationship between Gina (Mayra's mother) and Mayra with the researcher. The video observation captures the following dialogue.

> Uncle: *no maestra usted es de nosotros de aqui... usted es de nosotros...(silencio)*
> *Usted no cree pero aquí se le aprecia a toda la gente ya ve ya se hallo con Gina es mi sobrina... y Mayra la quiere mucho bastante...*
> *Conocemos mucha gente que no vienen en plan de trabajo verdad conocemos gente y nos hacemos amigos y yo tengo amistades de 15 años no he tenido disgustos si yo me doy mi lugar se dé a respetar y nos cuidamos unos a otros la amistad no se acaba es para toda*

Fig. 7.6 An affective relationship with Mayra

la vida no es para un día eso como usted está con Gina por su trabajo tiene que irse un día puede volver usted no sabe ni nosotros sabemos cuándo va a volver pero cuando vuelva y si estamos vivos la volvemos a tratar igual porque somos amigos somos amigos...

    Uncle: no teacher you are one of us... you are one of us... (silence)

    You don't believe it but here we appreciate (value, respect, love) you and all the people, you see, you [*hallo* expression] relate, feel comfortable, with Gina my niece... and Mayra loves you very much...

    ... we know a lot of people who come planning to work that we know, we know people and we become friends and I have friends of 15 years and I haven't had any problems, if I make myself respect and we take care of each other, the friendship never ends, it's forever it's not just for one day, it's like you, you are with Gina because of your work, but because of your work you have to go and one day you might come and we don't know when you are coming back and we don't know, but when you come back and if we are alive, we might see each other and we will relate the same, because we are friends, we are friends...

When this dialogue was captured, Mayra, Gina and the researcher were present. This was one of the last visits, and this was a goodbye moment in the research. In this moment of dialogue, the researcher listens to what her participants have to say. The researcher remained silent as she made *sense* of what these words meant. As time passed, the researcher analysed and transcribed this dialogue, and there is a *new zone of sense*, a new visual to a tactile path taken. In this tactile path, the researcher is able to understand her impact and how she related to her participants and how the uncle, as a participant, is able to take a tactile path.

It is important that the researcher considers the cultural community she or he participates in the research. As Bozhovich (2009) explains, experiences have a complex system of feeling and affect that are significant for people. It is important to recognise how emotions and affect might play in the research process. This moment becomes an intense moment because through verbal words, *stable zones of sense* are spoken. However, *unstable dynamic zones* of sense are present in this cultural context. These *dynamic zones of senses* are intense to the participants and to the research. In different moments, while capturing a dialogue she is in a *stable zone of sense*, listening to verbal meanings and letting silence speak for itself – sensing what this might mean. In another moment, through analysing the dialogue, an *unstable zone* is present: complex words and verbal meanings contain intense affects and emotions that are experienced by everyone.

The *zone of sense* is not only interpreting verbal meaning. It is also about interpreting intentions and motivations of the participants – *sensing* beyond verbal meaning and imagining the place the researcher occupied at the moment she was in the field, as this emotional experience is revisited and relived.

Researcher's Role in a *Perezhivanie Vivencia*

The following example discusses an *affective moment* of the research process – during video capturing visual vivencias and after analysing the video. First, the researcher is not only a participant but she is in a *perezhivanie* – living and experiencing an intense and dramatic – moment in the life of Mayra. Through analysing the research material, the researcher is able to make *sense* of the events through analysing her role in how the events unfold. The following table shows the video research material in visual forms where the influence of the researcher is seen as Mayra exchanges gaze with the researcher. Mayra's and the researcher's different emotions are communicated and expressed and visually presented. Non-verbal communication is a cultural practice seen in many Mexican and Mayan indigenous communities (Rogoff 2003).

The research example takes place in the afternoon. The researcher arrives to the household for an afternoon visit that takes place for 2 h. The family has the television turn on and Gina is cooking soup. Mayra wants to eat cereal and Gina is not letting this happen. While the space is small, the researcher manages to capture Mayra and the conversations taking place. However, unsure of what will happen next, the researcher's voice and conversation is captured. Through *visual mobile images* captured by the camera, the research captures Mayra's emotional expression in relation to this *perezhivanie* and the role of the researcher participating in this situation.

'Visual Vivencias' allow capturing a moment of emotional and affective intensity in the everyday life of the child. In these minutes of interaction, the video camera follows Mayra and captures the dialogues surrounding this *perezhivanie*. Mayra has to learn that there is only soup available and she will not have nuggets to eat.

Gina, Mayra, her brother and the researcher's perspectives are captured in the next example. The researcher is not only a participant in the *perezhivanie* but is able to sense when or not to intervene and when to listen and be silent, she is affectively touched by the event. Through interacting, the researcher is not fully aware that this moment is an important event that will influence Mayra's learning.

The role of the researcher is to record everyday life and how this influences children's learning and development. The researcher had different choices to make while video recording this event. At first, the researcher films the everyday life of Mayra. Then, through analysing this situation, the researcher is aware that this situation is a *perezhivanie*. Vygotsky (1994) explains how children have different *affective relationships* to their social environment and that there are affective forces, motives and intentions in children towards their social environment. Mayra has a strong motive and intention in this situation; she did not want to eat soup. As the researcher was recording these, she also interacted and was affected by this experience. This only comes to realisation through analysing the video observation and taking *visual mobile images* of the experience.

Mayra's affects communicated through non-verbal communication to all the participants, her mother and the researcher. Mayra exchanges gaze with the researcher seeking for help. The researcher is able to have a wholeness view of the situation through accounting the different perspectives of the event – while acting and through analysing, filming affective intonations of everyone's voice (Figs. 7.7 and 7.8).

Figs. 7.7 and 7.8 Mayra's 'gaze' family and researcher 'no quiero sopa'

Mayra: I don't want to eat, I don't want souuuup, *yo no quiero comer, yo no quiero sopaaaa* **(high voice emphasis on sopa)! Makes a small jump. Mayra moves her head and then her feet on floor and with her voice she pauses sooopaaa!**

Mayra: I don't like sopa! *no me gusta la sopa!* **And turns around, looks at the researcher and goes outside.**

Gina: (laughs) what an ugly girl! *que fea nina!*

Researcher goes outside and talks to Mayra.

Researcher: they are not going to give you choco crispies (cereal) [changes voice] soup nice soup... *oye no te van a dar choco crispies, sopa sopita..*

Mayra moves outside and the researcher moves with her.

Mayra: but I don't want soup, *pero no quiero sopa* **(in a calm tone)**
Researcher: the soup smells very nice, *huele bien rica la sopa* (Fig. 7.9)
Mayra: yes but I don't like soup, *si pero no me gusta la sopa.*
Gina: yes you like soup Mayra *si te gusta la sopa Mayra* (Figs. 7.10 and 7.11).

Mayra moves upwards and backwards almost like dancing and her shoe almost scratching the floor and a shhh sound can be heard.

Gina tells the researcher: It's because I was going to cook nuggets but there aren't any *es que iba a hacer unos nuggets pero no hay.* **Only fish [nuggets]** *solo de pescado.*

Mayra's emotional expressions are captured visually. Visual methodologies such as 'Visual Vivencias' allow the reader to see beyond the images and to be able to imagine the event.

In this analysis, the researcher makes *sense* of the *affective relationship* she has towards the *perezhivanie* event and to Mayra. The researcher is empathetic when the *perezhivanie* becomes more intense and dramatic. She tells Mayra how nice the

Fig. 7.9 Mayra moves outside as the situation becomes more intense and exchanges gaze with researcher

Figs. 7.10 and 7.11 Mayra's emotional expressions

soup smells to show empathy towards her mother's wishes. There are pauses and silences where the researcher does not interact, and Gina and Mayra continue with their discussion. This form of communication forms part of a family practice where Gina is able to communicate with Mayra even so that she is not physically present. For Mayra, she manages her emotions through moving outside the 'intense space' and continues insisting and negotiating. This negotiation continues for the next 5 min, and there is no more intervention from the researcher. After a period of 20 min, Mayra is able to eat soup and learn how soup is the only meal she is going to eat. This is an important moment in Mayra's learning and development, which the video camera is able to capture. The video observations in the form of *visual mobile images* allow the research process to analyse the role of emotions in Mayra's lives and the researcher role in *this perezhivanie.*

The researcher takes a *tactile path – through sensing the perezhivanie event*. The researcher is able to perceive emotional changes in Mayra while she leaves the space she is in with her mother and the space she is in outside being freely, able to express her emotions to everyone. The camera films this *visual path* and the expressions, emotions and verbal meanings. However, it is the *tactile and sensing path* the researcher brings to the event, being empathetically towards Mayra and Gina.

Visual and Tactile Affective Path Interrelated in the Researcher's Role

The researcher's role can contain many dilemmas. As the researcher becomes more involved in the community as a member and through affective relations and roles given to her. The researcher *senses – sensing* as an active member who has emotions and thinking merges a visual and a tactile affective path (see Fig. 7.12).

The researcher has two paths to take a *visual* that consists of capturing and recording the events and through planning how the data are generated. However, this *visual path* intertwines with a *tactile affective path* through relating, being with emotions and becoming part (affectively positioned) in the everyday life of her participants. Through *subjectively sensing*, the researcher made her own complex interpretations of what she feels about the participants and how the participants' emotions and affection towards the researcher made her feel welcome. Through the examples shown in visual forms and through dialogues, the researcher using video methodologies is always an active person who has emotions, which are part of the research. Emotions are complex to define. In each cultural community the researchers becomes aware of them through interpreting feelings and emotions of the participants. For example, the researcher felt welcome in the community and made interpretations through gestures, gaze and verbal meanings of participants. These provides the researcher with different *dynamic zones of sensing*.

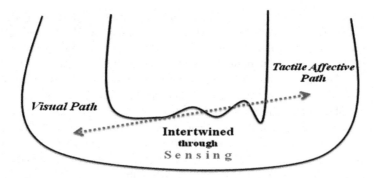

Fig. 7.12 Path taken by the researcher using visual methodologies

In a different moment, the researcher takes a tactile path – through living the experience, *affected and touched* by the experience. However, why is it important for the researcher to be taking a *tactile path* and be *affected* by field research experiences? Because it creates a trusting relationship with participants and a more authentic research experience. The role of the researcher is dynamic, at once, she is a teacher, in another moment she is a friend to Mayra and to her family. None of these had implications with the data gathering and answering the research question. As the researcher spends time with the participants, it cannot only be as a 'researcher'. The researcher's role is *subjectively sensed* by the researcher and the participant who are making meaning of what it means to their lives. It has a subjective component because the researcher and participants are able interpret and reinterpret each time, each moment, in each interaction.

In the last three examples, the reader is able to make their own interpretations. The visual data in the form of *visual mobile images* allow making and remaking subjective interpretations. In this chapter, different examples visually presented examine the role of the researcher. In this cultural community, it was important that the researcher was an active participant in the generation of data. The researcher was flexible to be in all these roles. These dynamic roles enriched the trust of the participants and the community, which in the future she will remain a friend and a teacher.

The methodological tool of 'Visual Vivencias' allows to film, be a participant and analyse the data through reliving moments in time. *Visual mobile images* are never static; they allow making new interpretations of the data. In this chapter, the data certainly 'touched' the researcher. I hope that the reader will be able to 'see' more of what the eye can offer and perceive the emotions in the images and dialogue. The role of the researcher needs consideration in what it means in each cultural community. Through participating *affectively* and understanding the *affective positioning*, the researcher unpacks what it means to be more than a participant in the research field.

Acknowledgements I would like to thank Prof. Barbara Kramler and authors of this book for their discussions and contribution to this chapter. I extend my gratitude to Prof. Marilyn Fleer and Dr. Avis Ridgway for their comments to this chapter and shared experiences in the field. Muchas gracias to my participants, Mayra and family, for welcoming me to their everyday life and for letting me be a friend, a teacher and a researcher.

References

Bozhovich, L. I. (2009). The social situation of child development. *Journal of Russian and East European Psychology, 47*(4), 59–86.

Derry, S. J., Pea, D. R., Barron, B., Engle, R. A., Erickson, F., Goldman, R., Hall, R., Koschmann, T., Lemke, J. L., Sherin, G. M., & Sherin, L. B. (2010). Conducting video research in the learning sciences: Guidance on selection, analysis, technology, and ethics. *The Journal of the Learning Sciences, 19*, 3–53.

Fleer, M. (2008). Using digital video observations and computer technologies in a cultural–historical approach. In M. Hedegaard & M. Fleer (Eds.), *Studying children: A cultural-historical approach* (pp. 104–117). London: Open University Press.

Goldman, R. (2007). Video representations and the perceptivity framework: Epistemology, ethnography, evaluation, and ethics. In R. Goldman, R. Pea, B. Barron, & S. J. Derry (Eds.), *Video research in the learning sciences* (illustrated edition.). New York: Routledge.

González Rey, F. (2002). *Sujeto y Subjetividad. Una aproximación histórico cultural*. México: International Thomson Editores.

González Rey, F. (2008). Subject, subjectivity, and development in cultural-historical psychology in the transformation of learning. In B. V. Oers, W. Wardekker, E. Elbers, & R. Van Der Ver (Eds.), *Advances in cultural-historical theory* (pp. 137–154). Cambridge: Cambridge University Press.

Hedegaard, M. (2008). A cultural–historical theory of children's development. In M. Hedegaard & M. Fleer (Eds.), *Studying children: A cultural-historical approach* (pp. 10–29). London: Open University Press.

Quiñones, G., & Fleer, M. (2011). "Visual vivencias": A cultural-historical tool for understanding the lived experiences of young children's everyday lives. In E. Johansson & J. White (Eds.), *Educational research with our youngest: Voices of infants and toddlers*. Netherlands: Springer.

Rogoff, B. (2003). *The nature of human development*. Oxford: Oxford University Press.

Rogoff, B. (2011). *Developing destinies: A Mayan midwife and town*. Oxford: University Press.

Vygotsky, L. S. (1987). *Pensamieno y lenguaje*. Barcelona: Paidos.

Vygotsky, L. S. (1994). The problem of environment. In R. Van der Veer & J. Valsiner (Eds.), *The Vygotsky reader* (pp. 338–354). Oxford: Blackwell Publishers.

Vygotsky, L. S. (1997). Problems of the theory and history of psychology. In J. Wollock & R.W. Rieber (Eds.), *The collected works of L. S. Vygotsky* (Vol. 3). New York: Plenum Publishers.

Chapter 8
Refocusing the Lens on Development: Towards Genetic Research Methodology

Nikolai Veresov

"Attacks" on Statistics: A New Tendency?

New times bring new questions and perspectives. A tendency towards increasing dissatisfaction with pure statistical quantitative methods in psychological research (Gelo et al. 2008; Mey 2010; Molenaar 2004; Lamiell 1995; Shames 1990) strongly manifests itself. Although this tendency does not dominate in the realm of mainstream psychology, today it demonstrates itself so clearly that it could not be neglected or underestimated. I agree that the lack of critical inquiry into statistical methods is an example of a "symptom" of what Michell (2000) has described as the "pathology of science" within psychology. Measuring psychological attributes (such as intellectual abilities or personal traits) without ever having studied whether these traits are quantitative in the first place and thus whether they are subject to quantitative measurement leads to a situation where psychological attributes are measured through quantitative instruments even though the question "Is that attribute quantitative?" (Michell 2000, p. 648) has not been answered and in fact is rarely asked.

Simultaneously, as we see rising pleas for rethinking methodological issues, we find various attempts at the re-conceptualisation of these challenging matters on new methodological bases and theoretical frameworks. Some of these attempts look like prospective answers to this "pathology" (Michell 1997, 1999; Toomela 2007, 2010; Valsiner 2009; Rosenbaum and Valsiner 2011; Westerman and Yanchar 2011).[1]

Recent decades in psychological research have provided thousands of ways to statistically predict one psychological variable by way of another. At the same time,

---

[1] An example of such debate could be found in recently published issue of *Theory & Psychology* Journal (2011), 21(2).

N. Veresov, Ph.D. (✉)
Faculty of Education, Monash University, Melbourne, Australia
e-mail: nikolai.veresov@monash.edu

M. Fleer and A. Ridgway (eds.), *Visual Methodologies and Digital Tools for Researching with Young Children*, International Perspectives on Early Childhood Education and Development 10, DOI 10.1007/978-3-319-01469-2_8,
© Springer International Publishing Switzerland 2014

many essential questions have not yet been asked because of limited methodological thinking. Limited methodological thinking is the result of lack of knowledge and vice versa.

> We still find "objective" scores without knowing how many different psychological mechanisms may underlie the same score. We do not know how psychological aspect of experimental conditions may have contributed to study results. Study of fragments gives very little to understanding of a human person as a whole... Statistical probabilistic prediction has become an end goal of studies even though most of the thinking and insight should begin where the science of mainstream psychology seems to end now. (Toomela 2007, p. 18)

In some sense, psychology can be viewed as a "Puritan science"—where the question is often "what is the right method to use?" rather than "what research questions are worth asking, and how are methods to be derived accordingly?" (Valsiner 2009, p. 4).

> Psychologists' "measure" some psychological characteristics—ironically, the "measurement" of various psychological features of human beings—personality, etc.—is seen as a contribution to science, while the phenomena—temporary, never to repeat themselves—acts of conduct are let to escape the sieve of psychology's research instruments. A "standardized method" collects answers from respondents that are immediately de-contextualized—hence losing their psychological specificity. Seemingly such methods "gather facts"—but that is precisely a problem. In general terms—psychology lacks a clear understanding of what a fact is— how it is created, and how solidly it stands within the ocean of alternative interpretations. (Valsiner 2009, p. 5)

Toomela (2010) continues in this respect:

> Already Vygotsky...suggested that it is much more meaningful to answer the right question even approximately than to answer the wrong question exactly. For instance, we can ask a question: Which statistical data analysis procedure gives the best way for interpreting data? This question is asked in modern psychology, and, as a result, increasingly complex and sophisticated data analysis procedures are invented. But all these sophisticated new data analysis tools may turn out to be useless if the statistical data analysis itself is inappropriate for understanding the phenomena studied. The first question should be, whether statistical data analysis is appropriate for data interpretation at all. (Toomela 2010, p. 9)

Thus, we see that despite obvious strengths of statistical methods their fundamental weaknesses gradually became the target of methodological reshaping. These discussions today are more and more concentrating on the topic of the fundamental limits of statistics as a research method.

The Limits of Quantitative Methods: Claim for Quality?

More and more researchers today support the position that statistical methods have essential limits since these methods (1) do not reflect the dynamic character of the process under study and (2) they are very limited in describing the processes in their wholeness (Anderson 1998; Dawson et al. 2006; Marecek 2011; Smith et al. 1995; Westerman 2006). Speaking about these limits, Valsiner (2009) pointed out that there are three major domains of oversight in psychology which are

(1) eliminating the dynamic flow of the phenomena in the data, (2) eliminating of the hierarchical order (part-whole relations) in the transformation of the phenomena into data and (3) eliminating the immediate context of the phenomenon in its transformation into data.

Even more, according to Toomela, the problem is that statistical data analysis cannot in principle answer the two basic questions that are related to validity: (1) Does the attribute supposedly measured by a test really exist? (2) Do variations in the attribute causally produce variations in the outcomes of measurement procedure? (Toomela 2010, p. 1). On the other hand, as Sato (Sato et al. 2007) has noted, one of the defining features of contemporary psychological methodology is to depict a person as a mixture of many relatively independent "variables". "Ironically speaking, human beings are viewed as if they were determined by precisely those variables in which psychologists have interest" (Sato et al. 2007, p. 53). The real task—that of constructing a psychology that is universal while being culture inclusive and generalising while being based on careful empirical analyses of individual cases (Molenaar 2004)—suffers (Valsiner 2009, p. 2).

"Dissatisfaction tendency", which characterises the state of affairs in methodological debates, becomes a crucial and seemingly unavoidable problem with respect to *developmental psychology*. What are the methods for studying the *development* of a certain system in its dynamics and wholeness? It seems that studies in the field of early childhood should not remain indifferent to this new trend towards searching for a new methodology. Even more, findings in the field of child development might bring new solutions or, at least, may open new perspectives.

So what about developmental psychology and early childhood studies? Is there any research strategy or method in this field which, compared to existing methods, (1) is able to reflect and to explain the dynamic character of the process under study, (2) is able to describe the processes in their wholeness and complexity and (3) can be applied to developmental psychology, providing a kind of fruitful combination of quantitative and qualitative approaches? This list of requirements is so formidable that it makes a positive answer nearly impossible. However, there is one method that, in my opinion, does meet these requirements. This method is the "experimental-genetic method" developed within the cultural-historical psychological theory by Lev Vygotsky.

Cultural-Historical Theory and Experimental-Genetic Method: Vygotsky's Contribution

CHT as a Theory of Development

Cultural-historical theory (CHT) provides a kind of efficient experimental method of analysis of mental development. This method, I believe, is able to "refocus the lens" of experimental psychology on development.

For Vygotsky, descriptive explanatory models and principles based on empirical methods of investigation should be replaced by explanatory models and principles (Vygotsky 1997, p. 298). Instead of merely describing the stages of development, psychological theory should find ways to explain development. Vygotsky's claim and basic principle was: "To understand the mental function means to restore both theoretically and experimentally the whole process of its development in phylo- and ontogenesis" (Luria and Vygotsky 1992).On the other hand, Vygotsky's theory and method was a kind of attempt towards overcoming the one-sidedness which dominated in "traditional" approaches to development dominating within the "classical" psychology in those times.

> The one-sidedness and erroneousness of the traditional view …on higher mental functions consist primarily and mainly in an inability to look at these facts as facts of historical development, in the one-sided consideration of them as natural processes and formations, in merging and not distinguishing the natural and the cultural, the essential and the historical, the biological and the social in the mental development…; in short—in an incorrect basic understanding of the nature of the phenomena being studied…Putting it more simply, with this state of the matter, the very process of development of complex and higher forms of behaviour remained unexplained and unrealised methodologically. (Vygotsky 1997, p. 2)

The cultural-historical theory is a developmental theory since it takes *the very process of mental development as its subject matter.* Development is not a simple change, growth or maturation (Vygotsky 1998, p. 189). Moreover,

> …development is not simply a function which can be determined entirely by X units of heredity and Y units of environment. It is an historical complex, which at any stage reflects its past content. In other words, the artificial separation of heredity and environment points us in a fallacious direction; it obscures the fact that development is an uninterrupted process which feeds upon itself; that it is not a puppet which can be controlled by jerking two strings. (Vygotsky 1993, p. 253)

Development is always a very complex and contradictory process, but, first of all, it is a dialectical process of *qualitative change.* To overcome the one-sidedness of "classical" psychology means to create a kind of theory and methods which are able to investigate the *process* of development both theoretically and experimentally in its whole complexity and dynamics. By the word "complexity" I mean that the process of mental development is a complex process of the qualitative reorganisation of a certain system, which includes several essential aspects.

These aspects will be discussed later in this chapter, yet what is important to mention here is that Vygotsky's theory is not just a number of several concepts and principles. What makes CHT unique is that every concept refers to a certain aspect/ aspects of the complex process of development of the higher mental functions. The role, place and interrelationships of all the concepts within the theory become clear in terms of the origins and development of the higher mental functions. Therefore, CHT provides a system of interconnected instruments for the theoretical analysis of the process of development in its wholeness and complexity. In other words, paraphrasing Vygotsky's own words, CHT provides the correct basic understanding of the nature of the phenomena being studied and allows the very process of the development of complex and higher forms of behaviour to be explained and realised methodologically.

However, a theory, even a highly developed one, without the experimental method is nothing but just words. Theory without an experiment is a voluntary play of mind; an experiment without a theory is a knife without a handle. The researcher needs not only concepts as theoretical instruments of analysis, the researcher needs an appropriate experimental method, for which he/she needs adequate experimental instruments.

CHT is a theory that provides a system of concepts as theoretical instruments for investigating the complex process of mental development and at the same time gives the experimental instruments for the investigation of the process of development. It provides a new, "nonclassical" type of experimental method, which is called the *experimental-genetic method*.

Experimental-Genetic Method: Main Traits

The first trait of the experimental-genetic method is that it is targeted *not* on results but on the analysis of the process of development.

When the analysis of things is replaced by analysis of process, then the basic problem becomes the genetic restoration of all the instances of development of the given process. Accordingly, the principal task of analysis is restoring the process to its initial stage or, in other words, converting a thing into a process. This kind of experiment attempts to dissolve every congealed and petrified psychological form and to convert it into a moving, flowing flood of separate instances that replace one another.

> In short, the problem of such an analysis can be reduced to taking each higher form of behavior not as a thing, but as a process and putting it in motion so as to proceed not from a thing and its parts, but from a process to its separate instances. (Vygotsky 1997, p. 68)

The second general feature of the method consists in opposing descriptive and explanatory tasks in genetical analysis. According to Vygotsky, there are two types of analysis—phenomenological (descriptive) and conditional-genetic. The essential difference between the two is that

> ...phenomenological... analysis takes a given phenomenon as it is in its external manifestation and proceeds from the naive assumption that there is a coincidence between the external appearance or manifestation of matter and the real, actual, causal-dynamic connection that underlies it. Conditional-genetic analysis proceeds from disclosing real connections that are hidden behind the external manifestation of any process. The latter analysis asks about origination and disappearance, about reasons and conditions, and about all those real relations that are the basis of any phenomenon. (Vygotsky 1997, p. 69)

The necessity of opposing these two ways of analysis becomes obvious since very often two phenotypic common or similar processes may seem to be causally-dynamically extremely different and conversely—two processes that are extremely close from the causal-dynamic aspect may seem different from the phenotypic aspect.

Thus, the basis for the phenotypic point of view is a combining of processes that is based on external resemblance or similarities.

> Actually ... two actions may proceed similarly from the external aspect, but may differ profoundly from each other in genesis, in essence, and in their nature. In such cases, special means of scientific analysis are required to disclose the internal differences that lie behind external similarity. In such cases, scientific analysis is also required, that is, knowing how to disclose the internal essence that lies behind the external appearance of the process, its nature, its genesis... A phenomenon is defined not on the basis of its external appearance, but on the basis of its real origin.
>
> The whole difficulty of scientific analysis consists in that the essence of things, that is, their true, real relation, does not coincide directly with the form of their external manifestations; for this reason, processes must be analyzed, and through analysis, the true relation that lies at the base of these processes, behind the external form of their manifestation, must be disclosed. (Vygotsky 1997, p. 70)

At the same time, genetical (causal-dynamic) analysis does not neglect or eliminate the phenomenological aspect:

> ...in psychology, the explanation itself becomes possible to the extent that the new point of view does not ignore external manifestations of things, does not limit itself exclusively to genetic considerations, but of necessity includes both scientific explanation and external manifestations and the traits of the process being studied ... In this way, analysis does not limit itself to only the genetic point of view, but of necessity considers the given process as a certain circle of possibilities that only with a certain complex of conditions or in a certain situation results in the formation of a certain phenotype. Thus, the new point of view does not eliminate, does not put aside the explanation of phenotypic features of the process, but places them in a subordinate position with respect to their actual genesis. (Vygotsky 1997, p. 71)

The experimental-genetic method of analysis was designed to investigate the process of mental development (1) in its dynamic and (2) in its complexity. Furthermore, this method was based on understanding development as a complex process of qualitative change. And finally, this method provided a causal (genetic), not descriptive (phenomenological), analysis of the phenomena under study.

How are all these theoretical matters related to the topic of this volume, i.e. to (1) early childhood and (2) methodological issues connected to the efficient use of digital visual tools as an experimental technique?

It is important and absolutely necessary to say that the experimental-genetic method was created in (and for) the experimental investigation of development in early childhood and therefore is strictly connected with this age period. The majority of Vygotsky's experiments described in his articles and books were done with children. However, the fundamental task of experiments was neither to describe changes or differences in development related to age nor to detect specific psychological characteristics of different ages. The general approach was to reveal the *general laws of mental development* which lay behind the external manifestations of changes. Early childhood is the most appropriate age to investigate this, since at this time higher mental functions are in the process of development. Thus, studies in child development are able to produce results which are important for general psychology, since they bring to bear on the experiment grounds for reconsidering general psychological ideas and principles. This shows the fundamental difference between applying the experimental-genetic method, compared to classical experimental methods, in relation to the area of early childhood studies.

As already noted in Fleer (Chap. 1, this volume), to do a nonclassical "Vygotskian" experiment is not the same as to do the experiment based on classical methods. Accordingly, requirements for organisation, design and conducting the "Vygotskian experiment" differ from those which are based on classical methods. This approach brings the possibility for reconsidering the role and the place of video recording in experimental studies. Yet, before arguing the place of visual tools, it makes sense to undertake a brief survey of the requirements for the organisation of the kind of concrete experimental study that follows from the principles of genetic research methodology.

Principles of Genetic Research Methodology

What does it mean to organise, arrange, conduct and control an experimental study of a child development according to the experimental-genetic method? What does it mean to do a nonclassical "Vygotskian experiment" in research practice? Such questions might look strange and even paradoxical since experimental-genetic method nowadays is widely presented in developmental studies of early childhood all over the world (Bodrova and Leong 2001; Fleer 2010; Connery et al. 2010; Kravtsov and Kravtsova 2009).[2] However, Vygotsky's "nonclassical psychology" obviously requires a "nonclassical" genetic research methodology. Theoretical ideas of CHT still need to be connected with research practices. Theoretical and experimental research instruments should be harmonised on the basis of "nonclassical" research methodology.

What Is Vygotsky's Genetic Research Methodology?

Figure 8.1 presents the general model of Vygotsky's genetic research methodology. It consists of two interconnected components. On one hand, it includes the system of theoretical concepts. What is important is that these concepts are not unclear arbitrary combinations of abstract ideas and considerations. On the contrary, they reflect all the main aspects of the subject matter of cultural-historical theory, i.e. they theoretically explain the basic features of the process of mental development (its source, the character, moving forces, direction, main features and results). In other words, they are the system of theoretical instruments (tools) for the study of mental development in its dynamics and complexity. The cultural-historical theory (CHT) is the system of *theoretical tools* of analysis of mental development.

---

[2] For more details, see this volume Chaps. 5, 3, and 7 of Monk, Li, and Quinones.

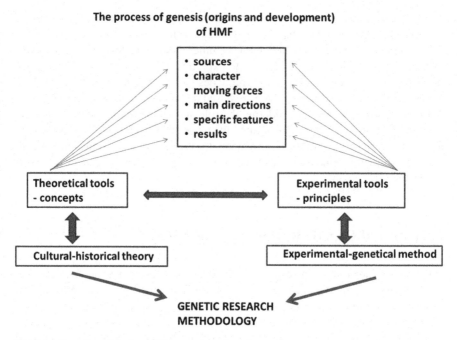

Fig. 8.1 General model of genetic research methodology

On the other hand, genetic research methodology is not limited by theoretical concepts only; it includes the "experimental-genetic method". This method involves several principles which create a system of *experimental tools* for the study of development. What is essential is that the principles of the experimental-genetic method strictly and directly follow from concepts of CHT in such a way that it makes it possible to study the process of development both theoretically and experimentally. Each principle of the experimental-genetical method directly follows from the appropriate theoretical concept, and, therefore, theoretical instruments and experimental instruments together create a unity as the main components of this concrete research strategy. Both the theory and method create the unity which I define as "Vygotsky's genetic research methodology". Unfortunately, Vygotsky's scientific legacy does not contain a description of these principles, for many years they were not even clearly formulated in Vygotsky's school. However, they can be "unpacked" and derived from descriptions of various experimental studies presented in Vygotsky's writings. I undertook such an analysis and formulated principles of genetic research methodology (Veresov 2010a, b).

To create a coherent strategy for the concrete experimental study, the researcher has to answer two questions: "What to study?" and "How to study?" The answer to the first question which sounds like "I am going to study development" is too general. The answer to the "what" question should include two aspects: (1) what exact psychological process of function is he/she going to study in a course of experiment and (2) which aspect(s) of the process of development of this exact psychological function is the researcher going to analyse.

To answer the "how" question means that the researcher, according to his/her answers to "what" questions, selects those theoretical concepts which reflect the selected aspects of development. This creates the theoretical framework of the study. Finally, the researcher selects those principles of the experimental-genetic method which correspond to the theoretical concepts and follow from them. As a result, the researcher becomes equipped with all sufficient theoretical and experimental tools of analysis, i.e. the coherent research strategy for the concrete experimental study.

Genetic Research Methodology in Action

Probably the best way of presenting principles of genetic research methodology is to show them "in action". For this purpose, the following section of the chapter begins with the example of Vygotsky's experimental study. Then I describe each of all five principles of genetic research methodology in their connections with the theoretical concepts of CHT in order to show how principles (experimental "instruments") correspond to concepts of CHT (theoretical "instruments").

Figure 8.2 presents an example taken from Vygotsky's description of the concrete experimental study of memory (Vygotsky 1997, pp. 180–182). This two-page description clearly reflects all five principles of genetic research methodology. It produces an impression of the observation which was recorded and then presented in written form in such a way that it emphasises the most important aspects of the process under experimental study. The right column (Descriptions) presents quotations of Vygotsky's text and the left column reflects the principles of genetic research methodology.

Vygotsky's experimental study of memory in child is an example of "nonclassical" genetic research methodology in action. The research task was to compare the two types of memory. Yet the study was not to compare the external manifestations; it was focused on the process of development as the transition from non-mediated to mediated higher mental process, i.e. the process of active creation of qualitatively new mental structures through social interaction. Because of this, the experimental study of a single mental function (memory) uncovers the general fundamental mechanisms and regularities of development of *every* higher mental function.

Principles	Descriptions
Buds of development	In our studies, we tried to compare directly the two types of memory, the two methods of remembering, and to elucidate by comparative analysis the elementary composition of both operations, their structures and genesis.
Category	In experiments, we asked a child to memorize a series of words (for the most part nouns, names of concrete objects). We used standard procedures such as are used in studies of memory in experimental psychology except that we tried to make it clear to the child that it would be impossible to remember the whole series in the given order.
Ideal and real form	Then we introduced a new method of memorizing: we gave the child a number of cards either of separate pictures of the concrete objects or geometric figures, lines, dotted lines, etc. We added this auxiliary material in different series in various ways. Sometimes it was presented simply with the hint: "Perhaps these cards will help you remember?" but with no explanation as to how they would help. In other cases, we gave a short instruction (we explained to the child that he must try in some way to connect the words he was to memorize with corresponding cards) and we even gave a demonstration.
Developmental tools	The child did make a transition from natural, innate remembering to mediated or mnemotechnical remembering. The whole character of his operation changed instantly; every assigned word now elicited reference to a picture. The child established a connection between the word and the picture, then moved on to the next word, etc. The studies showed that even at preschool age, the child is capable of mastering the operation of using auxiliary pictures for memorizing and applying them correctly. Whoever observed the direct transition from the natural method of remembering to the mnemotechnical cannot help but have the impression that he has seen a seemingly experimentally elicited change from innate to cultural memory. The process of remembering was restructured instantly in such a way that remembering any given word was accomplished through the picture that played the role of a sign. If in natural remembering a certain connection is made between two points, mnemotechnical remembering introduces a certain new, initially neutral stimulus-card that plays the role of a mnemotechnical sign and directs the course of nerve connections along a new path replacing one nerve connection with two new connections. The whole advantage of identifying the nerve connection lies in that we master a new way of remembering and can subsequently recall the appropriate connection as we wish when we need it.
Sustainable results	In a great majority of cases, the child begins to create completely new structures and does not renew the old. For example, when the child remembers the word "theater" with the aid of a picture of a crab at the shore, he creates a special auxiliary structure. "The crab is looking at the stones on the bottom, it is beautiful, for him it is a theater." The child undoubtedly compares the "crab" and the "theater" for the first time. He created this structure exactly for remembering. Thus, in selecting the picture of a camel for the word "death," the child recalls a story which contained both these elements. The situation is entirely different when the child must remember a given word with the help of a given picture, when he is not permitted to make a choice, and when recalling is actually impossible. Then the child begins to create new structures actively and this is the basis of the process of mastering memory. For this reason, from the psychological aspect, in such experiments it is not memory that is studied but the active creation of structures.

Fig. 8.2 Principles of genetic research methodology in action: experimental study of memory (Vygotsky 1997, pp. 180–182)

Principles of Genetic Research Methodology in Their Relation to Concepts of CHT[3]

The experimental-genetic method is the method of the *artificial reconstruction of the process of development* in its complexity from the very beginning, from the "buds" of development to its "fruits". However, to select the appropriate theoretical and experimental tools is the most difficult part of refocusing the lens on development. I therefore will try to present five basic principles of the experimental-genetic method (experimental instruments) in their interrelation with of concepts of CHT (theoretical instruments).

Principle of "Buds of Development"

The principle of "buds" follows from two important theoretical positions which reflect *the character* of mental development. First, the process of mental development,

> ...is not confined to the scheme "more-less," but is characterized primarily and specifically by the presence of qualitative neoformations that are subject to their own rhythm and require a special measure each time. It is not correct to assume that all development is exhausted by the growth of these basic, elementary functions which are the prerequisites for higher aspects of the personality. (Vygotsky 1998, p. 190)

Second, mental development is not a linear, homogenous process. Simultaneously, there are different levels of development of different psychological processes and functions in the child. At each age there are functions which are already matured (developed) and there are functions that are in a process of maturation. So there is always a complex nexus of (1) functions that have not yet developed but are in the process of development, (2) functions that will develop but are currently in an embryonic state and (3) developed functions. Metaphorically, they could be defined as "buds", "flowers" and "fruits" of development (Vygotsky 1935, p. 41). So, the first question "What psychological process am I going to investigate in my experimental study?" should be followed by the question "Which stage of development is the process/function under study in?" To put it simply, the "experimental development" (development in specially created conditions) should take place within the "zone of proximal development" (ZPD).[4]

The principle of "buds of development" means that the experimental study should begin with revealing that the function under study is on its "bud" (embryonic) stage and is not yet developed. It does not make any sense to organise the process of

---

[3] Because of limited space of the chapter, I will describe these principles in brief form with special emphasis on the topic of this volume.

[4] According to Vygotsky's concept "...the zone of proximal development defines those functions that have not yet matured but are in the process of maturation, functions that will mature tomorrow but are currently in an embryonic state." (Vygotsky 1935, p. 42)

development of certain functions in a psychological laboratory in a situation when this function is already developed, when the function under study is in the "fruit" stage. On the other hand, it makes no sense to organise the development of a function which does not yet exist in child's mind. The principle of "buds of development" helps the researcher to avoid these extreme poles.

The Principle of Interaction of Ideal and Real Forms

This principle follows from the idea that in contrast to traditional psychology, which describes the development of human mind as a process influenced by two main groups of factors (biological and social), the cultural-historical theory defines social environment not just as a factor but as a source of development.

> The social environment is the source for the appearance of all specific human properties of the personality gradually acquired by the child or the source of social development of the child which is concluded in the process of actual interaction of «ideal» and present forms. (Vygotsky 1998, p. 203)

This quotation encloses two theoretical concepts, related to development: the social environment and the interaction of ideal and present forms. Two following examples illustrate their developmental content. The first example is that of the origins of the pointing gesture in child. This example, Vygotsky wrote, shows the essence of the process of cultural development expressed in a purely logical form (Vygotsky 1997, p. 105). In the beginning, the pointing gesture of a child is merely an unsuccessful grasping movement aimed at an object. When the mother comes to the aid of the child and comprehends his movement as a pointing gesture, the situation essentially changes. The child's unsuccessful grasping movement gives rise to a reaction not from the object but from another person. The original meaning of this unsuccessful grasping movement is thus imparted by others. And only afterwards the child himself begins to treat this movement as a pointing gesture. Here, the function of the movement itself changes: from a movement directed towards an object it becomes a movement directed towards another person, a means of communication; the grasping is transformed into a pointing. Thus, the pointing gesture first begins to indicate by movement that which is understood by others and only later becomes a pointing gesture for the child himself.

The second example illustrates the interaction of "ideal" and "real" forms:

> We have a child who has only just begun to speak and he pronounces single words... The child speaks in one word phrases, but his mother talks to him in language which is already grammatically and syntactically formed and which has a large vocabulary, even though it is being toned down for the child's benefit. All the same, she speaks using the fully perfected form of speech. Let us agree to call this developed form, which is supposed to make its appearance at the end of the child's development, the final or ideal form—ideal in the sense that it acts as a model for that which should be achieved at the end of the developmental period; and final in the sense that it represents what the child is supposed to attain at the end of his development. And let us call the child's form of speech the primary or rudimentary form. (Vygotsky 1994, p. 348)

Speaking generally, every cultural form of behaviour might become an ideal form for the child. The grasping movement is a kind of primary form which, from the beginning, interacts with the "ideal" form (the mother's comprehension of the movement as a pointing gesture), and this creates the moving force for grasping to transform into pointing. In both examples, social interaction as a source of development exists as a process of interaction of the ideal and real forms. The development of any higher mental function in child is impossible without the interaction of the ideal and real form. The grasping movement never becomes the pointing gesture without an adult. There is no speech development without communication. We can say exactly the same about the development of thinking, logical memory and voluntary attention.

There is no development if there is no interaction between the ideal and real forms. From this follows the principle of interaction of real (natural) and ideal (cultural) forms. This principle means that in the course of experimental study, both forms should be detected and presented. It also means that the higher "ideal form" must be present in the beginning of the experiment. And, finally, tools and means of interaction between these forms should be specially created and involved in the experimental procedure.

Principle of Category (Collision, Dramatic Event)

The principle follows from two interconnected theoretical positions. The first is expressed in the following requirement for the experimental study:

> Processes must be analyzed, and through analysis, the true relation that lies at the base of these processes, behind the external form of their manifestation, must be disclosed. (Vygotsky 1997, p. 70)

The keywords here are "the true relation". Yet, what does it mean to disclose the "true relation", and what kind of relation is this "true relation"? The general genetic law of cultural development gives the answer. Here is the formulation of the general genetic law:

> …every function in the cultural development of the child appears on the stage twice, in two planes, first, the social, then the psychological, first between the people as an intermental category, then within the child as a intramental category…Genetically, social relations, real relations of people, stand behind all the higher mental functions and their relations. (Vygotsky 1997, p. 106)

According to the law, every function appears firstly on the social plane, among people. However, social relations are not the "area", not the field and not the "level" where mental functions appear—the social relations themselves become human individual functions.

> …every higher mental function was external because it was social before it became an internal strictly mental function; it was formerly a social relation between two people. (Vygotsky 1997, p. 105)

However, does it mean that every social relation can become a mental function? There is a clear notion of what type or relation can become a mental function. I mean in particular the word "category".[5] One of the meanings of the word "категория" is a collision, contradiction, dramatical event.

> Genetically, social relations, real relations of people, stand behind all the higher functions and their relations. From this, one of the basic principles is …of experimental unfolding of a higher mental process into the drama that occurs among people. (Vygotsky 1997, p. 106)

So, intermental, original, social forms of higher mental functions are not ordinary social relations between two individuals. This is a social relation that appears as a category, i.e. as an emotionally coloured and experienced collision, the contradiction between two people, the dramatical event, a drama between two individuals. Being emotionally and mentally experienced as social drama (on the social plane), it later becomes the individual intra-psychological category. So, according to Vygotsky's approach, the dramatical social relation—a category—is the true relation that lies at the base of mental processes and which must be disclosed.

Such emotionally experienced collisions can bring radical changes to the individual's mind and therefore can be a sort of act of development of mental functions—the individual becomes different, she becomes higher and above her own behaviour. Without internal drama, an internal category, such mental changes are hardly possible. Dramatic character development, development through contradictory events (acts of development) and category (dramatic collision)—this was Vygotsky's formulation and emphasis.

The principle of category means that the concrete experimental study should begin with the category (dramatic event, collision) the child should experience (as in Quinones, Chap. 7, this volume). The experimenter has to construct a category, i.e. intermental plane of higher mental function. This collision should be artificially created. The dramatic event is the primary form in which the higher mental function appears as a social relation before it becomes an internal higher mental function.

Principle of Developmental Tools

This principle is strictly connected with the concept of sign mediation, which is rightfully considered as one of the core ideas in cultural-historical theory. Even more, for many experts this concept is a kind of distinguishing feature of CHT. In Vygotsky's writings, we could find various examples of sign mediations such as knots for memory, drawing straws in case of two equal stimuli and many others. He even listed a number of examples of systems of cultural signs: "language; various systems of counting; mnemonic techniques; algebraic symbol systems; works of art; writing; schemes, diagrams, maps and mechanical drawings; all sorts of conventional signs and so on" (Vygotsky 1981, p. 137).

---

[5] Категория (Vygotsky 1983, p. 145).

However, signs and mediation were known and had been studied in psychology long before cultural-historical theory. Vygotsky's specific approach to signs and mediation was essentially new; cultural signs and mediation were analysed from the point of view of their role and place in the process of mental development. In other words, CHT explores the genetical approach to sign mediation. The cultural sign (or system of signs) is seen as a developmental tool.

The development of the human mind is not a biological but rather a cultural-social process. The transition from the biological to the social path of development is the central link in the process of development, a cardinal turning point in the history of the child's behaviour (Vygotsky 1999, p. 20). The psychological essence of the sociocultural path of development is that

> the basic and most general activity of man that differentiates man from animals in the first place, from the aspect of psychology, is signification, that is, creation and use of signs. Signification is the creation and use of signs, that is, artificial signals. (Vygotsky 1997, p. 55)

Therefore, sign and sign mediation obtain an extraordinarily important role in mental development. *Reorganisation* and *transition* are two important aspects of the process of development that the concept of sign and the principle of sign mediation are related to.

First, cultural signs and sign mediation are essential for the process of qualitative reorganisation of the psychological functions in a course of development:

> The sign as a tool reorganizes the whole structure of psychological functions. It forms a structural centre, which determines the composition of the functions and the relative importance of each separate process. The inclusion in any process of a sign remodels the whole structure of psychological operations. (Vygotsky 1929, p. 421)

Every new structure of mental functioning is the result of its remodelling, the product of sign inclusion. Using Vygotsky's terminology, a new structure is a "fruit of development". However, Vygotsky's methodology is not focused on "fruits"; it is directed on the analysis of the process of development, i.e. the transition "from buds to fruits". This leads to second aspect of the process of development the concept of sign is related to, i.e. the aspect of *transition*.

Mental development as a process is a "transition from direct, innate, natural forms and methods of behaviour to mediated, artificial mental functions" (Vygotsky 1998, p. 168). The sign (or system of signs) originally exists as an external tool, and later it becomes a tool of internal mediating activity. What is important is that the sign (external tool of activity) should not be given by experimenter to the child directly. The processes of active searching and finding a sign, as well as the transformation of the whole unit and the transition from direct connections to indirect (mediated) connections, were the focus of Vygotsky's experimental studies of the origins of mediating activity.

So, the principle of developmental tools means that during the experimental study of development the experimenter should have a set of tools (signs) that the child should discover, create and master in the course of experimental study. The design of the experimental settings should somehow lead the child to discovering the signs as external tools of solving problems and tasks given to the child. On the other hand, the experimental study should include special procedures supplying the process of transition from direct to mediated actions.

Principle of Sustainable Results

This principle of experimental-genetic method reflects the results of development. Continuing Vygotsky's metaphor, we could say that the results are "fruits" of development. However, these "fruits" are of very special nature. The result of development is not just new functions that appeared as outcomes at the end. Results of development are not new higher mental functions only, they are "qualitative neoformations" (Vygotsky 1998, p. 189). "Neoformation" is a result of reorganisation of whole system of functions, a new type of *construction* of child's consciousness and mental functions (Vygotsky 1998, p. 190). This new type of construction is the result of qualitative reorganisation of the whole system. Actually,

> Higher mental functions are not built up as a second story over elementary processes, but are new psychological systems that include a complex merging of elementary functions that will be included in the new system, and themselves begin to act according to new laws; each higher mental function is, thus, a unit of a higher order determined basically by a unique combination of a series of more elementary functions in the new whole. (Vygotsky 1999, p. 43)

Thus, not a new function, even a new higher mental function, but a qualitatively new structure of functions characterises the result of development.

The principle of sustainable results in relation to experimental investigation of the process of development means that the results of the experimental study must not simply be statistically valid changes but a new quality. Therefore, an experimenter has to have enough supplementary means to investigate what type of changes happened during the experimental study to make sure that the changes reflect the new system (new structure) that appeared.

I presented these five principles one by one separately from each other because my task is to show their relations with main aspects of the process of development and their connections with the main concepts of CHT. In fact, they all are interconnected and, in some sense, define and complement each other, representing a kind of unity of experimental requirements and tools.

Visual Methods Within Cultural-Historical Theoretical and Experimental Framework

The theme of this book is the discussion of various aspects of the use of visual tools within a cultural-historical theoretical framework. Therefore, it makes sense to return to the questions "What to study?" and "How to study?" from this particular perspective. Nowadays, it is nearly impossible to imagine an experiment in the field of early childhood without video recording. General questions "What to study?" and "How to study?" obtain concrete meaning—"What to capture/record?" and "How to analyse the video-data obtained?" Actually, the answers depend on the selection of particular fragments/episodes from the tons of video-data which the researcher considers important to be taken for the analysis.

However, cultural-historical theory as "nonclassical theory" requires a nonclassical approach to experiment, i.e. genetic research methodology. The use of video devices as a tool within the genetic research methodology is of a different character. Video recording as an experimental tool obtains an essentially new status. This new character depends upon the general task—how to use video devices in the experimental study of the process of *development in its dynamic and complexity*.

Two interconnected aspects are of primary importance here. First, the experimental-genetic method is the method which artificially elicits and creates a genetic process of mental development in specially created laboratory conditions. Here, as I already mentioned, the process of development occurs in front of the researcher's eyes. In other words, in this kind of experimental conditions the process of development becomes visible and observable. Therefore, it becomes video recordable.

I completely agree with the opinion that

> Digital video observations provide detailed accounts of how, in everyday life, cultural development is shaped by and shapes the social situations that the child finds themselves. Digital video analysis allows these cultural interactions to be examined and re-examined, in ways which include the researcher and the researched, the material world, and the past events that are active in the moment. (Fleer, Introduction to this volume)

However, principles of genetic research methodology might help to convert this rather general claim into concrete experimental strategy. The question of "What to record/capture?" becomes a derivative of other two: "The development of which mental function is under study?" and "Which particular aspect/aspects of development are under study?" Principles of genetic research methodology give answers to these questions. They are tools of "refocusing the lens" on development.

Second, in such experimental settings, video recording is not just a kind of registration (objective observation) of what happens with the subject during the experiment. In contrast to classical experiments, when an experimenter excludes him/herself from the process in order to escape any kind of influence, the nonclassical approach presupposes an active role of the researcher. The position of a researcher can be described in what Hedegaard defines as "the doubleness of the researcher" (Hedegaard 2008). There are two roles of the researcher: an active participant during the experiment, when the researcher actively interacts with the participants, and the role of an investigator in the analysis of the video-data obtained.

Experimental-genetic method transforms the general idea of "doubleness" into concrete experimental requirements. Principles of genetic research methodology open the way to the comprehension of which interactions of a researcher with participants during the experiment are the most important from a developmental perspective. The experimental-genetic method does not exclude but requires special types of interactions between the researcher and participants; one of the researcher's most important tasks is to create developmental interactive situations during the process. In this type of experiment, the video recording becomes a recording of specially organised processes of higher mental processes first appearing between people as social relations and then reappearing within the child as intramental functions. Video recording here is, first, the recording of interactions, real relations of people (experimenter and the participant) which, according to Vygotsky, stand behind all the higher mental functions and, second, their internalisation, i.e. the process of socio-genesis and the process of becoming higher mental functions.

Another side of "researcher doubleness" is the analysis of the video-data obtained. What is important and what is not in video-data? Which fragments/episodes/segments from the data should be selected for the analysis, which fragments should not be missed or excluded? Here, again we can see principles of genetic research methodology in action. The essence of experimental-genetic method is to "dissolve every congealed and petrified psychological form and to convert it into a moving, flowing flood of separate instances that replace one another" (Vygotsky 1997, p. 68). What Vygotsky defines as "separate instances of flowing flood" or "nod points of development" are reflected in the principles of genetic research methodology. The example of an experimental study of memory presented in Fig. 8.2 illustrates this clearly.

Principles of genetic research methodology do not only reflect the main aspects of the complex process of development; they refocus the researcher's lens on development by asking the question "Which particular aspect/aspects of development are under study?" Accordingly, the researcher decides which fragments/episodes of video materials are important and should be analysed. Obviously, these fragments are mostly those that show the "nod points".

The "nonclassical" genetic research methodology creates the basis for organisation and conducting the experimental study of development. On the other hand, genetic research methodology brings to the fore the task of reconsidering the place and role of visual tools and devices. Digital video tools are becoming tools of recording and analysing the process of development and therefore obtain an exclusively important role as sources for the analysis of its dynamics and complexity.

Conclusions

In this chapter, I have discussed some issues concerning the experimental-genetic method, as a method of experimental study of mental development in early childhood. This method as a part of Vygotsky's "nonclassical" psychological theory might to some degree be considered as an efficient solution to what Michell (2000) has described as the "pathology of science" within psychology. Experimental-genetic method overcomes the limits of "classical" experimental methods, especially in developmental psychology, since it is able (1) to reflect and to explain the dynamic character of the processes under study and (2) to investigate the processes in their wholeness and complexity from genetic, developmental perspective.

The general model of genetic research methodology was offered in this chapter. This methodology represents the system of interconnected theoretical and experimental research instruments/tools for refocusing the researcher's lens on development by making visible processes that are ordinarily hidden beneath the surface, namely, changes in behaviour. In this chapter, principles of genetic research methodology were described and examined from the point of view of how they reflect main aspects of developmental as a complex process of the qualitative reorganisation of mental functions.

Genetic research methodology brings to the top of the agenda the question of the possible reconsideration of the place and role of the use of digital video tools within the cultural-historical theoretical framework. Experimental study based on principles of genetic research methodology makes the very process of development through social interactions visible. Therefore, video recording the process obtains an exclusively important role and place. Consequently, methods of video recording and the analysis of obtained video-data gradually become efficient research methods in experimental studies in early childhood development in various sociocultural contexts. This opens new perspectives and possibilities. I believe this book is a step forward on this direction in search for a nonclassical methodology for nonclassical psychology.

Acknowledgements Kajaani Research Consortium and Centre for Developmental Learning and Teaching (Kajaani, Finland) provided funds and equipment which made this study possible. I am grateful to my colleagues Pentti Hakkarainen and Milda Bredikyte (Finland), Marilyn Fleer and her team (Australia), Vera Tsybulia, Ludmila Obukhova and Tatiana Akhutina (Russia), Myra Barrs (the United Kingdom), Katarina Rodina (Norway), Jaan Valsiner and Mohamed Elhammoumi (USA), Laure Kloetzer (France) and Michalis Kontopodis (the Netherlands) for valuable discussions and critical feedbacks. I thank Aili Helenius (Finland) and Ana Marjanovic-Shane (USA) for providing video-data and fruitful discussions. I thank all participants and professors of ISCAR Summer University for Ph.D. students (2011) for their interest and support. I address special thanks to Steve Gabosch (USA) for his suggestions on improving this text and making my English understandable.

References

Anderson, J. (1998). Embracing uncertainty: the interface of Bayesian statistics and cognitive psychology. *Conservation Ecology, 2*(1), 2. http://www.consecol.org/vol2/iss1/art2/. Accessed 26 May 2012.

Bodrova, E., & Leong, D. J. (2001). *Tools of the mind: A case study of implementing the Vygotskian approach in American early childhood and primary classrooms* (Innodata monographs – 7). Geneva: UNESCO, International Bureau of Education.

Connery, M. C., John-Steiner, V. P., & Marjanovic-Shane, A. (2010). *Vygotsky and creativity: A cultural-historical approach to play, meaning making, and the arts*. New York: Peter Lang Publishing.

Dawson, T. L., Fischer, K. W., & Stein, Z. (2006). Reconsidering quantitative and qualitative research approaches: A cognitive developmental perspective. *New Ideas in Psychology, 24*, 229–239.

Fleer, M. (2010). *Early learning and development: Cultural-historical concepts in play*. New York: Cambridge University Press.

Gelo, O., Braakmann, D., & Benetka, G. (2008). Quantitative and qualitative research: Beyond the debate. *Integrative Psychological & Behavioral Science, 42*(3), 266–290.

Hedegaard, H. (2008). The role of the researcher. In M. Hedegaard & M. Fleer (Eds.), *Studying children: A cultural-historical approach* (pp. 202–207). London: Open University Press.

Kravtsov, G. G., & Kravtsova, E. E. (2009). Cultural-historical psychology in the practice of education. In M. Fleer, M. Hedegaard, & J. Tudge (Eds.), *Childhood studies and the impact of globalization: Policies and practices at global and local levels* (World Yearbook of Education, pp. 202–212). New York: Routledge.

Lamiell, J. T. (1995). Rethinking the role of quantitative methods in psychology. In J. Smith, R. Harré, & L. van Langenhove (Eds.), *Rethinking methods in psychology* (pp. 143–161). London: Sage.

Luria, A., & Vygotsky, L. (1992). *Ape, primitive man, and child: Essays in the history of behavior.* New York: Harvester Wheatsheaf.

Marecek, J. (2011). Numbers and interpretations: What is at stake in our ways of knowing? *Theory & Psychology, 21*, 220–240.

Mey, G. (2010). Qualitative developmental psychology. In A. Toomela & J. Valsiner (Eds.), *Methodological thinking in psychology: 60 years gone astray?* (pp. 209–230). Charlotte: IAP.

Michell, J. (1997). Quantitative science and the definition of measurement in psychology. *British Journal of Psychology, 88*, 355–383.

Michell, J. (1999). *Measurement in psychology.* Cambridge: Cambridge University Press.

Michell, J. (2000). Normal science, pathological science and psychometrics. *Theory & Psychology, 10*, 639–667.

Molenaar, P. C. M. (2004). A manifesto on psychology as idiographic science: Bringing the person back into scientific psychology, this time forever. *Measurement: Interdisciplinary Research and Perspectives, 2*, 201–218.

Rosenbaum, P., & Valsiner, J. (2011). The un-making of a method: From rating scales to the study of psychological processes. *Theory & Psychology, 21*(1), 47–65.

Sato, T., Watanabe, Y., & Omi, Y. (2007). Beyond dichotomy – Towards creative synthesis. *Integrative Psychological & Behavioral Science, 41*(1), 50–59.

Shames, M. L. (1990). On data, methods, and theory: An epistemological evaluation of psychology. *Canadian Psychology, 31*(3), 229–238.

Smith, J. A., Harré, R., & van Langenhove, L. (Eds.). (1995). *Rethinking methods in psychology.* Thousand Oaks: Sage.

Toomela, A. (2007). Culture of science: Strange history of the methodological thinking in psychology. *Integrative Psychological & Behavioral Science, 41*(1), 6–20.

Toomela, A. (2010). Modern mainstream psychology is the best? Noncumulative, historically blind, fragmented, atheoretical. In A. Toomela & J. Valsiner (Eds.), *Methodological thinking in psychology: 60 years gone astray?* (pp. 1–38). Charlotte: IAP.

Valsiner, J. (2009). Integrating psychology within the globalising world: A requiem to the post-modernist experiment with Wissenschaft. *Integrative Psychological & Behavioural Science, 43*, 1–21.

Veresov, N. (2010a). Introducing cultural-historical theory: Main concepts and principles of genetic research methodology. *Cultural-Historical Psychology, 4*, 83–90.

Veresov, N. (2010b). Forgotten methodology: Vygotsky's case. In J. Valsiner & A. Toomela (Eds.), *Methodological thinking in psychology: 60 years gone astray?* (pp. 267–295). Charlotte: IAP.

Vygotsky, L. S. (1929). The problem of the cultural development of the child. *Journal of Genetic Psychology, 36*, 421.

Vygotsky, L. S. (1935). *Umstvennoe razvitie detei v protsesse obuchenia.* Moscow: Leningrad. Gosudarstvennoe Uchebno-pedagogicheskoe izdatelstvo.

Vygotsky, L. S. (1981). The instrumental method in psychology. In J. V. Wertsch (Ed.), *The concept of activity in Soviet psychology* (pp. 134–143). Armonk: M. E. Sharpe.

Vygotsky, L. S. (1983). *Sobranie sochinenii* (Vol. 3). Moscow: Pedagogika.

Vygotsky, L. S. (1993). *The collected works of L. S. Vygotsky* (Vol. 2). New York: Plenum.

Vygotsky, L. S. (1994). The problem of the environment. In R. van der Veer & J. Valsiner (Eds.), *The Vygotsky reader* (pp. 338–355). Oxford: Blackwell.

Vygotsky, L. S. (1997). *The collected works of L. S. Vygotsky* (Vol. 4). New York: Plenum.

Vygotsky, L. S. (1998). *The collected works of L. S. Vygotsky* (Vol. 5). New York: Plenum.

Vygotsky, L. S. (1999). *The collected works of L. S. Vygotsky* (Vol. 6). New York: Plenum.

Westerman, M. A. (2006). Quantitative research as an interpretive enterprise: The mostly unacknowledged role of interpretation in research efforts and suggestions for explicitly interpretive quantitative investigations. *New Ideas in Psychology, 24*, 189–211.

Westerman, M., & Yanchar, S. (2011). Changing the terms of the debate: Quantitative methods in explicitly interpretive research. *Theory & Psychology, 21*(2), 139–154.

Part III
Ethical and Conceptual Issues
When Researching with Children
Using Digital Visual Tools

Chapter 9
Beyond Alienation: Unpacking the Methodological Issues in Visual Research with Children

Joseph Seyram Agbenyega

Introduction

Child development is interactively complex with 'no single methodology to fully explain the nature of human development and learning' (Amso and Casey 2009, p. 85). However, headway is being made in recent years through visual research methodologies and methods to understand the process of young children's development. It can be argued that visual research with children poses particular difficulties in relation to how children fully understand and contribute to the visual research data generation and interpretation process. There is also limited evidence of how visual research methods are critically attentive to methodological issues associated with *habitus, field* and *capital*. Drawing on critical social theory of Bourdieu, this chapter introduces the concept of habitus, field and forms of capital that are crucial for understanding and conducting visual research with young children. This is followed by a research example that utilised children's drawing to illustrate a Bourdieuian approach to visual data analysis.

Critical social theory which is used to inform this chapter is not a child development theory but a method of practising critical reflexivity in visual research, which enables visual researchers to dig beneath surface appearances of images, asking how interactive social systems influence child development and research data (Mills and Gale 2007). Critical reflexivity engages researchers in thinking about the self (Nagata 2006) in relation to their choices of visual tools, for example, whether to use video, digital camera, children's drawings or a combination of these. It also involves a critical engagement with the data they generate and the meanings they assign to it beyond the surface of research as an academic and technical exercise, to research as critical praxis, and applying the research findings to benefit

J.S. Agbenyega, Ph.D. (✉)
Faculty of Education, Monash University, Melbourne, Australia
e-mail: joseph.agbenyega@monash.edu

M. Fleer and A. Ridgway (eds.), *Visual Methodologies and Digital Tools for Researching with Young Children*, International Perspectives on Early Childhood Education and Development 10, DOI 10.1007/978-3-319-01469-2_9, © Springer International Publishing Switzerland 2014

the individual child, groups of children or families who are the focus of research. The arguments put forward in this chapter are intended to influence the methodological and theoretical approaches visual researchers with children employ. It is a move towards methodologies that demonstrate the value of social justice and equity in visual research.

Researchers' choice of visual methods, whether simple or complex, has serious implications for the researchers, children and their families in terms of the construction of the visual and how the visual is interpreted and consumed (Alderson and Morrow 2004; Masson 2004; Wiles et al. 2008). In particular, the chapter argues that critical reflexivity in visual research is undervalued in the current visual research climate and that its revaluing requires theoretical work on the habitus of visual researchers in order to transform their embodied structured master dispositions (habitus) towards a more socially just practice when working with children in visual research. It concludes by considering how visual research with children can become a transformed performance of rights, equity and social justice.

This chapter begins with a discussion of Bourdieu's concepts of field, capital and habitus, which assist understanding of how and why some visual research practices still constitute practices of domination and exploitation of children (Mills and Gale 2007). Bourdieu's work, which is applied here, constitutes critical reflexivity into the researcher's self, 'reproductive tendencies of educational research, society and culture, which, by extension, reproduce essentially' (Karol and Gale 2004, p. 1) dominant practices.

Taking a Critical Standpoint on Visual Research

The main contribution of Bourdieu's work to visual research is the understanding of the role that educational research plays in reproducing the theoretical and method-ological status quo, limiting certain innovative research practices (Bourdieu 1998). There is overwhelming concern by the visual research community regarding institutional and cultural regulations rendering some visual research with children difficult. For instance, stringent ethics regulations regarding the use of images in research have compelled some visual researchers to obscure faces to preserve anonymity which result in data becoming meaningless, particularly to those who are not part of the research and need to draw their own interpretations from clear images (Prosser and Loxley 2007; Wiles et al. 2008). Similar views and concerns are expressed by visual researchers in North America that institutional guidelines and fear of litigations from parents and child-right advocates are resulting in visual researchers protecting their institutions rather than the rights of participants (Gunsalus et al. 2007; Wiles et al. 2008). Taking a critical stand on child develop-ment research requires visual researchers to first and foremost serve the interest of children. It is along this line of thinking that Bourdieu's ideas of habitus, capital and field contribute to how the visual researcher can turn a critical eye on himself/herself, the visual data generation process and the tools being used. It is also important for those involved in the research with children to critically consider the contribution that the research would make to the participants' overall development, and not only to the institutional and professional fame.

In contemporary early childhood research, visual approaches are increasingly becoming sophisticated but by and large, turning into philosophical and methodological movements, and in many cases, the visual is being used as appendages for textual data (Deppeler et al. 2008). Visual researchers adopt different technological tools and approaches in their research: video, digital still cameras and children's drawings. Irrespective of which visual tools are used, visual research with children is informed by different theories. Whichever theoretical path one takes (cultural-historical, postmodern, poststructural, feminist etc.), Bourdieu 'reminds us that 'theory' should not be valued for its own sake' (Karakayali 2004, p. 352) and that reflexivity, reflectivity and critical reflexivity should be a key component of research because these enable researchers to be aware of the implications and effects of theory in relation to the social world they conjure up in their research (Bourdieu 1998).

Critical reflexivity is the awareness that emerges through the researcher attending to the visual research moment from a non-judgemental perspective. It is shifting preoccupation away from the researchers' and the participants' past and future, in order to locate oneself into the actuality of the lived experience of the participants (Bishop et al. 2004; Nagata 2006). Without critical reflexivity, visual research becomes depersonalising, objectifying and compartmentalising and treats research participants in mechanical terms, neglecting visual research as lived experience. Bourdieu is critical of what he called the 'intellectualist bias' which often arises, for example, when a visual researcher is inadequately critical of visual tools being used, the research site, the visual imagery and the 'presuppositions inscribed in the act of thinking about the world' (Bourdieu and Wacquant 1992, p. 39). Inadequate knowledge and the lack of critical reflexivity results in the failure to grasp 'the logic of practice' stemming from the choice and use of visual research methodologies and methods. Critical to Bourdieu's contribution which is relevant to this chapter is his attempt to deconstruct and reconstruct the intellectual habitus, 'a system of dispositions necessary to the constitution of the craft of the intellectualist in universality' (Bourdieu 1993, p. 271). I would argue that the visual researcher needs certain attributes in order to bring together all the interactive components of development for a holistic understanding rather than as disjointed pieces of research information. The following sections look at Bourdieu's three conceptual metaphors through which to develop the attributes for conducting visual research with children.

Habitus and Visual Research

Bourdieu defines 'habitus' as 'internalised embodied social structures' (Bourdieu 1989, p. 18) and 'cultural unconscious or mental habits or internalised master dispositions' (Bourdieu 1989 cited in Houston 2002, p. 157), which include beliefs, values, norms and attitudes. Dispositions of researchers inevitably reflect the social and institutional contexts in which they acquire them. Habitus influence the ways researchers interpret and make sense of the world. Visual research with children and families is one way researchers make sense of the world of children and families through visual data. The mental structures and dispositions from which visual researchers make choices of which method or visual technology to use, and how they make sense of the data are generated within the habitus. Habitus as embodied is visible through practice. This means the knowledge and skills the visual researcher possesses become visible through how the researcher conducts the research in the field. Therefore, the only way to determine whether the visual researcher respects children's rights and takes their contribution to knowledge seriously is not in the ways the research is designed on paper but how the data gathering, analysis and interpretation involve the children. On the one hand, perceiving children as simplistic participants and families as non-experts could lead to imposing predetermined structures on them that 'humiliate' their knowledge and experiences. On the other hand, a positive image of children would enable the visual researcher to enact visual research practices that consider children's developmental strengths and families' cultural and symbolic capital, all which add richness to the visual research data and analysis.

In the selection and use of visual research methods, researchers activate their skills taking into consideration their child participants and enter into a social world of which they are both the product and agent (Bourdieu 1989). Product because institutional regulations and the visual approach they utilise dictate how the research should be conducted; agents because they act on the visual process with their knowledge. In many instances the visual researcher's practice may constitute a situation like 'fish in water', without feeling the weight of the water (Bourdieu 1993). This means complacency on the part of visual researchers can turn them away from taking a critical view on the visual data they generate with children.

Researchers are social and academic agents endowed with habitus, inscribed in their bodies by past experiences and by virtue of their training (Houston 2002). These past experiences and training may predispose a visual researcher to think and act in particular ways. The habitus as a system of schemes of perception, appreciation and action should enable visual researchers to perform acts of practical knowledge, based on the identification and recognition of conditional and conventional stimuli to which they are predisposed to react (Mills and Gale 2007), and to generate appropriate and endlessly renewed visual strategies. This is in recognition of the fact that child development takes place in a 'structured social world full of material and symbolic artefacts such as tools and language, structured social interactions such as rituals and games, and cultural institutions such as families and religions' (Tomasello 2009, p. 207). Social institutions, family practices and the children that visual researchers study are dynamic, fluid and shifting; hence, visual research cannot restrict itself to pre-programmed and rigid set of activities but rather must be generative and transformative to answer complex child development questions. Some of these complex questions are addressed in other chapters of this volume.

Bourdieu sees habitus as potentially generating a wide collection of possible actions, at the same time enabling the individual to draw on transformative and constraining courses of action. He writes that habitus:

> is a kind of transforming machine that leads us to 'reproduce' the social conditions of our own production, but in a relatively unpredictable way, in such a way that one cannot move simply and mechanically from knowledge of the conditions of production to knowledge of the products. (Bourdieu 1993, p. 87)

Therefore, 'on the one hand, habitus is a structuring structure; that is, it is a structure that structures the social world. On the other hand, it is a structured structure; that is, it is a structure which is structured by the social world' (Ritzer 1996, p. 541).

To apply this sense to visual research means the composition of our internalised master dispositions determine the ways we select our visual methodologies. In doing a research in a particular way, we produce knowledge to structure our social world which we are part of. We are in turn affected by the knowledge we put in the public domain. This is circularity.

Capital and Visual Research

Visual research with children is not a capital-free process. Capital manifests in various forms including economic, cultural, social and symbolic. Economic capital – wealth defined in monetary terms – determines the choice of the kind of visual technology to use in a particular visual research. Cultural capital – a person's or institution's possession of recognised knowledge – influences the visual research design and fieldwork. Important also in conducting visual research are social capital, which is capital constituted by social ties, and symbolic capital, which is one's status, honour or prestige (Bourdieu 1998). These capitals govern the nature of relationships that exist in the research site when we work in participatory visual research and determine whether the research we conduct constitutes oppressive practice or acts of social justice.

Economic, symbolic, cultural and social capitals contribute to child development in many important ways including influence on everyday relations in visual research practice. Capital determines researchers' and child participants' agency, that is, their ability to strategically engage in the research and contribute to the development and conduct of the research (Webb et al. 2002). Many visual researchers involve families; however, families and children may have knowledge capital that is less valued by a particular researcher resulting in limited capacity of the participants to strategically be involved in the research process.

Unless the development of the research design and visual research tools consider the nature and extent of capitals that both the researcher and the participants bring to the research field, visual research can become a destabilising experience for families and children. This implies that the nature of the researcher's and the participants' capital turns visual research into a field of struggle. Bourdieu argues that the outcome of the struggle one engages in within an educational research field is determined by the amount and nature of capital possessed by competing actors in that given field (Webb et al. 2002). The visual researcher's position in the research field and that of the child and family with whom the visual research is concerned are informed according to Bourdieu by hierarchy of the amount of knowledge and symbolic capital the individuals possess (Wacquant 1998). Thus, there is always an issue of social justice, human rights and equity when working in participatory visual research with children and families endowed with unequal amounts of cultural capital (Bourdieu 1998).

A visual researcher may perpetuate inequality and injustice against some children and families without knowing or desiring to do so (Bourdieu 1998; Mills and Gale 2007). Child development research often positions some families as deficits, particularly children and families from disadvantaged backgrounds who struggle to receive recognition and supplement their meagre cultural, symbolic and economic capitals (Bourdieu 1997; Mills and Gale 2007). Visual researchers can use their well-designed research to accentuate various forms of capitals of such families and children by assigning them important roles in their research and not just treating them as data objects. This means recognising and authorising the contributions of their knowledge through data generation and interpretation of the visual data. This is like transforming one form of capital to another form. For example, cultural knowledge capital is being transformed to academic knowledge capital which can then be transformed into supporting families and children to improve their developmental status (Bourdieu and Passeron 1990). From this perspective, it is evident that the interrelationship between habitus and capital helps explain how cultural knowledge affects the kinds of visual research we conduct with children and families and how researchers reproduce their worlds (Webb et al. 2002).

Field and Visual Research

Bourdieu uses field as a spatial metaphor, a network of relations among the objective positions. Bourdieu's conception of field is different from positivist conceptions of field as social location, for example, social milieu, context and social background. Positivist conceptualisations fail to highlight sufficiently the conflictual character of social lived experience (Mills and Gale 2007) which characterises visual research epistemology. The concept of field denotes a social arena in which people interact, manoeuvre and struggle in pursuit of desirable development (Bourdieu 1997). Therefore, all human actions including visual research take place within social fields, which are arenas for the struggle of acquisition of knowledge, credentials and development. In visual research, both the researcher and participants occupy distinct positions within the field in which struggles or manoeuvres take place over specific knowledges or stakes and access to them. The intellectual distinction, class, prestige and social class in varying degrees define the stake of the visual researcher and participants. Therefore, as contemporary research with young children is increasingly adopting visual approaches, we need to use our research skills to minimise the struggles between theoretical research knowledge and the knowledge that families or children who are involved in our research bring to it.

Contemporary child development research that adopts visual methodology requires taking a critical stance to embrace and enact genuine equity, value children and create opportunity for a more in-depth understanding of children's learning and development (Deppeler et al. 2008). Critical visual research 'takes as one of its central projects an attempt to be discerning and attentive to those places and practices where social agency has been denied and produced' (Giroux 2011, p. 3). Therefore, visual research should not be viewed merely as data site to practise our research skill, technique or method. Without recognising the visual research as arenas of struggle, we may simply be reducing children and families with our visual methods to 'cheerful robots' (Giroux 2011, p. 3). For example, a child smiling in front of a camera or acting for a video recording can be taken for granted to mean a happy child. This may not be necessarily so. We do no good to children and families in visual research when our methods embrace instrumental rationality on the surface in which matters of justice, human rights, power and emancipation are silent. Practising critical reflexivity in visual research engages researchers in moving beyond the obvious to interrogate their choices of visual tools, the data they generate and the meanings they assign to it. This means interaction between the researcher and families, including children, should not be taken for granted when working with young children in participatory visual research. Therefore, reflexivity is important to keep the visual researcher on course throughout the research process.

Reflexivity according to Bourdieu is 'an interrogation of the three types of limitations (social position of field and of the scholastic point of view) that are constitutive of knowledge itself' (Schirato and Webb 2003, p. 539). This means the visual researchers are becoming conscious of their class, ethnicity, religion, etc., their position within the field in relation to the participants, for example, an expert or novice visual researcher, and the tendency to abstract research from context.

I argue that the extent to which researchers can produce useful knowledge on child development using the visual is through the logic of practice and conscious comprehension or reflexivity (Bourdieu 1990). In this chapter I drew on critical reflexivity and reflexivity to produce research knowledge with children using children's drawing as the visual.

Applying Bourdieu's Ideas to Generating Visual Data with Children

Visual research is innovative when it does not succumb to methodological fashion. Participatory visual research with children is based on a system of habitus that celebrates children's capital (knowledge) and invites them to be codesigners of the research process and to contribute to interpretations of the knowledge that is produced (Swart and Pettipher 2005). Involving children as codesigners of research is building a network of relations which Bourdieu refers to as field. It is essentially about respecting children's unique knowledge, cultural and symbolic capital, which accentuates child rights and promotes social justice. This process is multifaceted and complex and challenges researchers to both think and practise critical reflexivity in their research (Swart and Agbenyega 2010). I will illustrate this point with an example extended from my research with children in Ghana.

In a recent study comparing young children's perception of the kinds of disciplinary situation they experience at home and in preschool, I decided to use children's drawing as a method of inquiry and as a stimulus to encourage conversations during group discussion time. It is argued that providing opportunity to draw holds some potential for obtaining accurate and complete reports from young children (Bruck et al. 2000) because as children draw they spontaneously talk about what they are drawing. The process of drawing itself may provide relevant signposts that catalyses memory retrieval. Similarly, Gross and Hayne (1998) found that drawing is a useful research tool for young children to express their emotional experiences (Bruck et al. 2000). When children are asked to draw about events, they bring their imagination to play and the drawing itself serve as prompts that augment retrieval of past events (Butler et al. 1995). Importantly, drawing may help to minimise the suggestive influence of the adult researcher because the prompts are largely child generated rather than externally induced.

The study involved 25 children with a mean age of 5.6 years who attended the same public kindergarten and were taught by two teachers. The decision to use drawing is to make the research process flexible and open-ended so that all children, depending on their habitus (internalised dispositions), capital (intellectual capacity) and field (network of relations with their teachers), convey their lived experiences through drawing without fear of making mistakes. The first drawings were aimed at evoking children's memoirs on their lived classroom experiences. The drawings were carried out without the presence of the teachers in the classroom. The decision to allow children to draw without the presence of the teachers is to enact the logic of practice of freedom, that is, to create a flexible space where the children are free from fear and intimidation from their teachers, which is common culture of the school. In this way reflexivity on the culture has influenced the way the fieldwork was conducted.

The second drawing was based on children's lived experience at home which also took place the following day in the kindergarten without the teachers or parents. The same ideas related to the first drawing were reasons for doing the drawings without the presence of parents or teachers. My knowledge of the cultural situation in which the children experience their lives has been an added advantage to do the study in this way. This implies that in visual research with children background knowledge of the research sites, sociocultural norms (capital), social agents' dispositions (habitus) and the relational positioning of various agents (field) must be necessary considerations in the ways the research is designed and carried out. The children were given 30 min to produce their lived experiences on paper. The various drawings the children produced were not viewed in terms of their accuracy but rather in terms of the meanings they assigned to them. After the children completed their drawings on preschool and home discipline, we sat on the floor in a circle to analyse and co-produce meanings of the drawings.

Using Bourdieu's Ideas in the Visual Data Analysis

Visual data is complex data; therefore, Bourdieu suggests eclectic approach to making sense of our data. Bourdieu argues:

> All activity and knowledge … is always informed by a relationship between where the agent has been and how their history has been incorporated, on the one hand, and their context or circumstances (both in a general sense and 'of the moment'), on the other. In other words, agency is always the result of a coming together of the habitus and the specific cultural fields and contexts in which agents 'find themselves', in both senses of the expression. (Schirato and Webb 2003, p. 541)

I followed four steps in analysing the visual data. The first step involved the analyses of the position of the field in relation to the field power. This involved critically examining the drawings and the comments the children made about them to determine how the children are positioned in the field and how power is implicated in the ways they are positioned. The second step involved mapping out the objective structure of relations between the positions occupied by agents who compete for the legitimate forms of specific authority. In this process, I examined the children's routine comments and their drawings to establish how teachers, children and parents struggle for recognition and acceptability in their classroom and at home. This process was followed by the analyses of the habitus (beliefs, dispositions, values) of the agents involved in the research (Bourdieu and Wacquant 1992). I concluded the analyses by examining the forms of capital that are privileged within the field (relations).

Children's Representations of Lived Experience Through Drawing

The opportunity given to the children allowed them to freely and emotionally convey their lived experience through various drawings, the meanings which are not easily accessible to the external viewer without the children contributing to their interpretation.

The drawing above (Fig. 9.1) was produced by a girl aged 5.6 years. As the two drawings were quite similar in size, the distinction between who is the child and who is the adult was not readily apparent to the external viewer. However, the children interpretation clarified the issues associated with the drawing. The child who produced the drawing pointed to the image on the left as herself receiving corporal

Fig. 9.1 A mum hitting
the daughter with a stick
(5.6 years old)

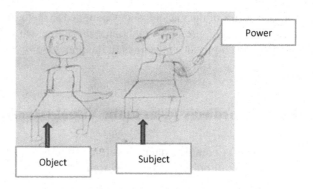

Fig. 9.2 A grandfather
slapping face of the
granddaughter
(5.7 years old)

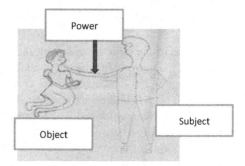

punishment from her mother because she returned late from an errand. The drawing demonstrated an object-subject relationship. A close look at the objects' face shows tears marked with pencil.

> My mother sent me to buy salt... I saw my friend... we played when I came home mother beat me with a big stick.

The visual and the child's comments are very powerful in evoking an event that symbolises the positioning of children and their parents within the field where the field power belongs to the parents. It also explains the habitus (beliefs) of the parent where corporal punishment is considered a way of correcting a child's misbehaviour. However, in child development perspective, this approach is destructive to children's emotional, behavioural and physical growth. Bourdieu argues that the formation of the habitus takes place in cultural and historical contexts. Therefore, it can be argued that the children who experience this kind of lived experience could internalise the same to develop master dispositions (habitus) that may affect their individual positionings in the future.

In terms of Fig. 9.2, a girl narrated her story about how she is frequently assaulted physically by her stepfather. During the discussions of the drawing, the child, with

Fig. 9.3 A drawing depicting a teacher who verbally abuses the children (4 years old)

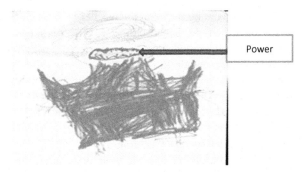

tears in her eyes, told her story of how her father abandoned her mother before she was born. The drawing illustrates lived experiences of object-subject relationship. Her reasons for the assaults include:

> If don't wash the plate he beat me...if I don't sell the water he beat me...he beat me with his hand he push me...

The story she inherited from her mother regarding her father's disappearance coupled with frequent assaults demonstrates family dynamics pregnant with emotions which have serious implications for her physical, cognitive and emotional development. This shows the complexity of Bourdieu's idea of field and how various agents within the field use a combination of their capital and habitus to enact practices. The most powerful agent here is the stepfather. The relationship as portrayed in the drawing is domineering and authoritative. For this family, it was evident from the analysis that there is extensive struggle within the field as the various agents, child, mother and stepfather, struggle for the field power and recognition (symbolic capital). It is possible that because the man is not the child's real father, issues of trust and respect may be at stake.

The third selected drawing (Fig. 9.3) was quite unique in that it was a human face but the mouth attached to it was very wide across the whole face. To the layperson, the drawing does not convey much information. As a researcher, I am likened to a layperson in this situation. I have difficulty making any sense of the drawing, and the only way to analyse and interpret it is to engage with the child who produced it to help me make sense of it. In this sense, I was drawing on the child's capital (knowledge), her feelings and beliefs (habitus) about the drawing and his relationship to it (field) in constructing meaning. When asked for interpretation, the child who drew it indicated:

> Miss Bonsua is always shouting on us (pseudonym)...if you talk she will shout keep quiet... put your mouth on the table...hey! who is still talking?

It can be argued that from the point of view of the child that their teacher was overbearing and punitive. It demonstrated the teacher's habitus as authoritative with the belief that children must be silenced to enforce discipline in class. The subordinate relationship existing between the teacher and the children brings tension and more struggles to the field. Because the field power is skewed in favour of the teacher, the children are objectified silenced and othered. I ask, how can children develop their communicative capabilities when they are often silenced in their learning? How can children develop their cognitive capacities when they are not free to express themselves? This is where Vygotsky's cultural-historical theory about child development comes to mind. Vygotsky is critical of maturational framing of children's development. He theorises that social interaction leads to continuous changes in children's thought and behaviour (Woolfolk 1998) and that the basis of development is the interaction with people and the tools that the culture provides to help form their own view of the world (Woolfolk 1998). This study has demonstrated that through children's drawing the very essential factors that impact their development can be brought to the fore.

The drawings showed that visual research in a critical paradigm gives voice to children to evoke their consciousness and tells their stories without fear. It showed a method that accentuated social justice for all children; hence, children's voices regarding their drawings were tape-recorded and played back to parents and the teachers during pickup time. The teachers and parents were also allowed to view the children's drawing for the first time. In this sense, the visual research is not only to benefit the researcher but to serve to transform the habitus of the teachers and parents for a more positive experience in early childhood education. Therefore, the next stage of the project was to organise a follow-up meeting with the teachers and parents to address discipline issues that are seriously affecting the children's rights, well-being and development. This requires an expert knowledge from the researcher to be fed into the understanding of the effects of corporal punishment and assault on children's development, hence a participatory visual research of social justice. It must be emphasised that the relationships we researchers form with children when we conduct research through visual methods are determined by our internalised dispositions, and children and families that we research with will react to us on the basis of what defines us as individual visual researchers.

The analysis proceeded with children's relationship with their drawing, where they experienced the lived experiences that they have demonstrated through their drawing and the historical and cultural circumstances that are implicated in their experiences. One important aspect of this visual research is the children's voices that accompanied their drawings. Because voice is involved in the visual research, the children's conversation was taken seriously in the analysis process in capturing aspects of the audible comments that connect to the visual elements of the participants' understanding enacted through their engagement with the drawings during data generation process. In doing this I have taken into consideration what Crossley (2000) advises:

> The comments of individuals should not be taken at face value; rather, they need to be located in wider structures of discourse and power so that their implications and ramifications can be fully understood. (p. 36)

The same view is expressed by critical researchers who use Bourdieu's ideas and that in conversational analysis researchers need to 'problematize what people say as something other than either simply a reflection of "what is going on in their heads" or a valid description of the social world' (Jenkins 2002 in Mills and Gale 2007, p. 9).

The analytical methods applied to the visual data in this research are not means to an end in themselves as Bourdieu cautions that it is not simply a question of what technique to use in research data generation and analysis and how to use it, but rather why it is used and what it will lead to (Grenfell and James 1998; Mills and Gale 2007). This suggests that the historical, ideological and political moment in which one lives should be considered seriously in addition to one's habitus, field and capital when conducting and analysing visual research data.

Conclusion

This chapter has shown that using critical theory ideas espoused by Bourdieu is a fresh effort to articulate a new critical reflexivity in new methodological movement of visual research culture in early childhood education. In this study, for example, reflexivity afforded me insight into some cultural and institutional practices that would be difficult to capture through photographs. I questioned my own habitus and knowledge about visual research whether the teachers and families in this situation would allow the children to use photographs to capture critical moments of aversive practices. How could children capture their own moments simultaneously experiencing that moment? Video is an option, but it wouldn't work for me in this situation because the teachers and parents may alter their real punitive practices, thereby defeating the purpose of the study; therefore, I opted to use drawing. The drawing approach enabled the children to connect their imagination to classroom and home discipline practices and as well felt confident to express their opinions without feeling overwhelmed and intimidated. For most of the children, their agency had been previously suppressed by their teachers and parents, and this is the first time they had had the opportunity to verbally and artistically convey their lived experiences in a holistic and confident way. The analysis of the drawings focused children's interpretations pertaining to their everyday lived experiences. It shows that the choice of visual methodology derives from habitus and capital within a given relation (field). Bourdieu argues that habitus is a 'conditioned and conditional freedom' which generates 'things to do or not to do, things to say or not to say, in relation to' research (Bourdieu 1990, p. 53). Thus, the things not to do in a sensitive research such as this one are to avoid videos or photographs. The possible things to do in this research are creating a flexible space for those who experience the situation to tell their stories boldly.

It is argued that despite the strong influence of our social and institutional structures on us, 'we are not automatons or mindless vehicles of our governing habitus' (Houston 2002, p. 157). As a visual researcher interested in social justice and equity, the choice of visual methodology must be informed by habitus loaded with passion for childhood justice, human rights and equity. I would argue that habitus acts as principles and schemes to generate and organise visual researchers' research practices in ways that enact social justice or in ways that obscure it. As representations of the world of objects, habitus can be adapted to visual research without a conscious aiming at ends or an expression of mastery of the operations necessary in order to attain the research aims. It requires critical reflexivity to constantly shift in epistemology, methodology and methods of doing research according to the demands of capital, field and habitus of both the researcher and those with whom the research is carried out (Thomas and Glenny 2005; Skrtic 1995). It means our methodological and epistemological visual approaches must show interest in the struggles of the field, cultural and institutional complexities that influence children's development and experiences in unique ways (Rogoff 2003; White et al. 2005).

Critical visual research approaches encompass co-construction and collaboration between researchers and participants (King and Horrocks 2010). These kinds of research lead to troubling one's own lived experience (Nagata 2006). In the research reported in this chapter, the children used drawings to engage the researcher and themselves in questioning issues around their everyday home and school experience. In this sense the research focus is on listening to and empowering children's marginalised voices through visual elicitation in group times (King and Horrocks 2010). This process created opportunities for participants to learn to reflect critically and learn about themselves and their everyday experiences.

Therefore, to adopt critical theory in visual research with children, the researcher must be essentially reflective and reflexive to avoid being 'methodologically formalistic' (Luke 1991, p. 21). Visual research with children and families is built on relations; therefore, in seeking a reflexive or reflective knowledge of social relations, visual researchers working with children no matter their theory should complement positivist approach of understanding children's and their families' world, tied uncritically to natural science methods of investigation with other methods of investigation. This means critical visual research must not

> follow set-piece research strategies, using formalistic methodologies intent upon gridding some pre-processed empirical data through an allegedly objective but still theory –laden hypothetical model. The results of such productions almost fail to resonate successfully with reality or more importantly, hyperreality. (Luke 1991, p. 21)

Instead our visual research approaches must be a revolutionary way of seeing and a form of knowing that employs the understanding of habitus, capital, field and reflexive reasoning to give children and families some research tools to realise new potentials for their emancipation and development (Giroux 2011; Luke 1991). Taking a critical turn on what this chapter has offered, I would like to argue that Bourdieu's lenses on critical theory and cultural-historical theoretical approaches of Vygotsky have both broadened and deepened our understanding of the nature of child development and the sources of hindrances. Although this book centres on cultural-historical approaches, the interaction between the cultural orientations of social actors and the structural environment that conditions development is a useful conceptual framework that can provide the basis for a more systematic approach to understanding the cultural roots of child development.

Finally, in doing visual research, we must adopt the goal of guiding families and children to better their lives by refining their thinking abilities and developmental sensibilities. This requires continuous new consciousness of what must be done in visual research and how to do it to accentuate child development.

References

Alderson, P., & Morrow, V. (2004). *Ethics, social research and consulting with children and young people*. Barkingside: Barnardo's.

Amso, D., & Casey, B. J. (2009). Beyond what develops when: Neuroimaging may inform how cognition changes with development. In L. S. Liben (Ed.), *Current directions in developmental psychology* (pp. 85–94). Boston: Pearson.

Bishop, S. R., Lau, M., Shapiro, S. L., Carlson, L., & Anderson, N. D. (2004). Reflexivity: A proposed operational definition. *Clinical Psychology: Science and Practice, 11*, 230–241.

Bourdieu, P. (1989). Social space and symbolic power. *Sociological Theory, 7*, 14–25.

Bourdieu, P. (1990). *In other words: Essays towards a reflexive sociology*. Stanford: Stanford University Press.

Bourdieu, P. (1993). *Sociology in question*. London: Sage.

Bourdieu, P. (1997). The forms of capital. In A. Halsey, H. Lauder, P. Brown, & A. S. Wells (Eds.), *Education: Culture, economy and society* (pp. 46–58). Oxford: Oxford University Press.

Bourdieu, P. (1998). *Practical reason: On the theory of action*. Cambridge: Polity.

Bourdieu, P., & Passeron, J. C. (1990). *Reproduction in education, society and culture* (2nd ed.). London: Sage.

Bourdieu, P., & Wacquant, L. (1992). *An invitation to reflexive sociology*. Chicago: University of Chicago Press.

Bruck, M., Melnyk, L., & Ceci, S. J. (2000). Draw it again Sam: The effect of drawing on children's suggestibility and source monitoring ability. *Journal of Experimental Child Psychology, 77*, 169–196.

Butler, S., Gross, J., & Hayne, H. (1995). The effect of drawing on memory performance in young children. *Developmental Psychology, 31*, 597–608.

Crossley, M. (2000). *Introducing narrative psychology: Self, trauma and the construction of meaning*. Buckinghamshire: Open University Press.

Deppeler, J., Moss, J., & Agbenyega, J. S. (2008). The ethical dilemma of working the visual and digital across space. In J. Moss (Ed.), *Researching education visually, digitally and spatially* (pp. 209–227). Amsterdam: Sense Publications.

Giroux, H. A. (Ed.). (2011). *On critical pedagogy*. New York: The Continuum International Publishing group.

Grenfell, M., & James, D. (1998). *Bourdieu and education: Acts of practical theory*. Bristol: Falmer.

Gross, J., & Hayne, H. (1998). Drawing facilitates children's verbal reports of emotionally laden events. *Journal of Experimental Psychology: Applied, 4*, 163–179.

Gunsalus, C. K., Bruner, E. M., Burbules, N. C., Finkin, M. D. L., Goldberg, J. P., Greenough, W. T., Miller, G. A., Pratt, M. G., Iriye, M., & Aronson, D. (2007). The Illinois white paper: Improving the system for protecting human subjects: Counteracting IRB 'mission creep. *Qualitative Inquiry, 13*, 617–649.

Houston, S. (2002). Reflecting on habitus, field and capital: Towards a culturally sensitive social work. *Journal of Social Work, 2*(2), 149–167.

Jenkins, R. (2002). *Pierre Bourdieu*. London: Routledge.

Karakayali, N. (2004). Reading Bourdieu with Adorno: The limits of critical theory and reflexive sociology. *Sociology, 38*(3), 357–368.

Karol, J., & Gale, T. (2004). *Bourdieu and sustainability: Introducing 'environmental capital'*. Melbourne: Paper presented at the AARE.

King, N., & Horrock, C. (2010). *Interviews in qualitative research*. London: Sage.

Luke, T. W. (1991). Touring hyperreality: Critical theory confronts informational society. In P. Wexler (Ed.), *Critical theory now* (pp. 1–26). Bristol: Taylor & Francis Inc.

Masson, J. (2004). The legal context. In S. Fraser, V. Lewis, S. Ding, M. Kellett, & C. Robinson (Eds.), *Doing research with children and young people*. London: Sage.

Mills, C., & Gale, T. (2007). Researching social inequalities in education: Towards a Bourdieuian methodology. *International Journal of Qualitative Studies in Education, 20*(4), 433–447.

Nagata, A. L. (2006). Cultivating researcher self-reflexivity using voice and mindful inquiry in intercultural education. *Journal of Intercultural Communication, 9*, 135–154.

Prosser, J., & Loxley, A. (2007). Enhancing the contribution of visual methods to Inclusive Education. *Journal of Research in Special Education, 7*(1), 55–67. http://dx.doi.org/10.1080/14725860601167143

Ritzer, G. (1996). *The McDonaldization of society*. Thousand Oaks: Pine Forge Press.

Rogoff, B. (2003). *The cultural nature of human development*. New York: Oxford University Press.

Schirato, T., & Webb, J. (2003). Bourdieu's concept of reflexivity as metaliteracy. *Cultural Studies, 17*(3–4), 539–553.

Skrtic, T. M. (Ed.). (1995). *Disability and democracy: Reconstructing (special) education for modernity*. New York: Teachers College Press.

Swart, E., & Agbenyega, J. S. (2010, November 29–December 2). *Developing researcher self-reflexivity and agency: A cross-cultural narrative of inclusive education research*. Paper presented at the Australian Association for Research in Education Conference in Melbourne.

Swart, E., & Pettipher, R. (2005). A framework for understanding inclusion. In E. Landsberg, D. Kruger, & N. Nel (Eds.), *Addressing barriers to learning*. Pretoria: Van Schaik.

Thomas, G., & Glenny, G. (2005). Thinking about inclusion. Whose reason? What evidence? In K. Sheehy, M. Nind, J. Rix, & K. Simmons (Eds.), *Ethics and research in inclusive education. Values into practice*. London: Routledge Falmer.

Tomasello, M. (2009). Culture and cognitive development. In L. S. Liben (Ed.), *Current directions in developmental psychology* (pp. 207–212). Boston: Pearson.

Wacquant, L. (1998). The double-edged sword of reason: The scholar's predicament and the sociologist's mission. *European Journal of Social Theory, 2–3*(Spring), 275–281.

Webb, J., Schirato, T., & Danaher, G. (2002). *Understanding Bourdieu*. London: Sage.

White, F., Hayes, B., & Livesey, D. (2005). *Developmental psychology: From infancy to adulthood*. Sydney: Pearson.

Wiles, R., Prosser, J., et al. (2008). *Visual ethics: Ethical issues in visual research*. Southampton: Economic and social Research Council.

Woolfolk, A. E. (1998). *Educational psychology* (7th ed.). Boston: Allyn and Bacon.

Chapter 10
'Baby Cam' and Participatory Research with Infants: A Case Study of Critical Reflexivity

Jennifer Sumsion, Benjamin Bradley, Tina Stratigos, and Sheena Elwick

Introduction

Bourdieu and Wacquant (1992, p. 291) advocate presenting one's research as a process of exposure: '… in which you *expose yourself*, you take risks'; a process of making public 'muddled, cloudy' thinking in all 'its fermenting confusion' (original emphasis). Yet, too often, they argue, the brush strokes – 'the touching and retouching' – are rendered indiscernible with the research revealed only in its '*finished* state'. (p. 219, original emphasis) (Sumsion in press)

In this chapter, we continue our efforts to render visible the uncertainties, risks and confusions that have been such a large part of the *Infants' Lives in Childcare* project (Sumsion et al. 2008–11). The project aims to investigate the experiences of very young children (aged up to approximately 18 months) in Australian early childhood settings – *from the 'perspectives' of the infants themselves.* Like Agbenyega (Chap. 9, this volume, pp. 153–168), and following Bourdieu and Wacquant (1992), we believe in the importance of 'reflexivity … and critical mindfulness' concerning the social worlds that we, as researchers, 'conjure up' in our research. Reflexivity, in the sense we are using it here, means cultivating the capacity 'to stand back from "the game"' (Crossley 1999, p. 451) and the immediacy of the challenges of the research. Conversely mindfulness, as we use it, refers to being

J. Sumsion, Ph.D., M.Ed., B.Ec., Dip. Ed. (✉) • T. Stratigos, B.Ed., ECE
Research Institute for Professional Practice, Learning and Education,
Charles Sturt University, Bathurst, Australia
e-mail: jsumsion@csu.edu.au; tstratigos@csu.edu.au

B. Bradley, Ph.D., MA, BA
School of Psychology, Charles Sturt University, Bathurst, Australia
e-mail: bbradley@csu.edu.au

S. Elwick, B.Ed., EC
School of Education, Charles Sturt University, Albury, Australia
e-mail: selwick@csu.edu.au

M. Fleer and A. Ridgway (eds.), *Visual Methodologies and Digital Tools*   169
for Researching with Young Children, International Perspectives on Early
Childhood Education and Development 10, DOI 10.1007/978-3-319-01469-2_10,
© Springer International Publishing Switzerland 2014

alert to and fully experiencing or 'living' those challenges – metacognitively, corporeally and ethically – in the moments they are encountered (Bishop et al. 2004; Elwick et al. in press-a). Being critically reflexive and mindful requires us to interrogate our epistemological and ontological assumptions, the theoretical and methodological resources that we employ, the practices in which we engage and the meanings that we assign. It involves looking beneath the surface, going beyond the commonly accepted, being wary of theoretical and methodological fads and attending to power relations and their effects. It also means recognising that our desires to formulate revolutionary ways of seeing (Agbenyega, Chap. 9, this volume) may blind us to the limitations of those ways of seeing and lead us, inadvertently, to reproduce the social, theoretical and methodological status quo and in doing so possibly exacerbate the inequities that we may have set out to address. We are committed, as a research team and individually, to becoming critically reflexive and mindful in all aspects of our research and to advocating for critical reflexivity and mindfulness in all research concerning young children.

Our specific purpose in this chapter is to offer a case study of critical reflexivity concerning our use of 'baby cam' (our term for small head-mounted cameras worn by infants) in the *Infants' Lives in Childcare* project. In particular, we consider the extent to which baby cam, as an example of an innovative technology for visual research, might be considered a participatory approach to researching with infants. We focus, too, on the insights it enables and/or constrains and the ethical dilemmas it can create.

The chapter proceeds in three moves. First, we contextualise our discussion by briefly outlining the *Infants' Lives in Childcare* project. Next, we introduce Rose's (2012) framework for critically examining visual methods and, inspired by Rose's framework, the heuristic device which we subsequently developed to scaffold our reflections about our use of baby cam. We then use this device to discuss some of the challenges generated by baby cam in each of Roses' three 'sites': the production of the image, the image itself and 'audience' reaction to the image. To convey a sense of the wide-ranging and complex issues that perplex and trouble us and continue to exercise our conceptual, methodological and ethical imaginations, we present our discussion in the form of a readers' theatre script.

The *Infants' Lives in Childcare* Project

The *Infants' Lives in Childcare* project set out to investigate infants' experiences in Australian centre-based and home-based early childhood education and care settings, with the hopeful and ambitious intent of developing ways of gaining insights into the 'perspectives' of the infants. A total of 14 settings (11 family day-care homes and 3 long day-care centres) in regional and rural New South Wales and Victoria[1] have participated in the project. As explained in more detail elsewhere (Goodfellow et al. 2011; Press et al. 2011; Sumsion et al. 2011), the project design has been

[1] Australian States.

informed by Clark and Moss's (2001) Mosaic approach that involves 'the bringing together of different pieces or perspectives in order to create an image of children's worlds' (Clark 2005, p. 31). We are crafting our mosaic from data from various combinations of written observational records, conversational interviews eliciting educators' and parents' perspectives, standardised measures and visual records (Goodfellow et al. 2011) for 36 'focus' infants to date, within the group context of their early childhood setting, and interpreted through multiple, diverse and continually shifting theoretical perspectives (Sumsion in press). Our visual records consist primarily of digital video data, mostly generated through tripod-mounted and hand-held cameras, but with a small amount of footage from a baby cam mounted on an infant's hat or headband. Although baby cam constitutes a very minor part of the project, it has attracted a disproportionate amount of attention. For that reason, we have made it the focus of this case study. As a scaffold for our reflections, we now turn to the framework proposed by Rose for exploring visual methods.

Rose's Framework for Exploring Visual Methods

As Rose (2012) notes, visual images can be seductive and powerful. Therefore, along with the methods used to produce them, they warrant careful and critical examination. Indeed, our experience suggests that even the *prospect* of seeing the world through infants' eyes via baby cam has wide, and possibly a kind of voyeuristic[2] or vicarious appeal, perhaps even reflecting a nostalgic desire to recapture lost memories of infancy. Such seductiveness reinforces the need for critical reflexivity on the part of researchers seeking to seize opportunities arising from advances in visual technologies. To support critical reflexivity, Rose (p. 19) proposes an analytical framework based around three 'sites' where meanings of images are constructed. She refers to 'the site of *production*, which is where an image is made; the site of the *image* itself, which is its visual content; and the site where the image encounters its spectators or users … [or] its *audiencing*' (original emphases). These sites, Rose emphasises, are interconnected, not discrete.

Moreover, within and across each site, Rose (2012) suggests, it is useful to think of three intersecting aspects or 'modalities': the technological, the compositional and the social. By technological, Rose means 'any form of apparatus designed either to be looked at or to enhance natural vision' (Mirzoeff 1999, p. 1, cited in Rose 2012, p. 20). By compositional, she means the material qualities of an image, such as its content and spatial organisation, while 'social' is her shorthand way of referring to broader social, political and/or economic 'relations, institutions and practices' surrounding an image and mediating how it is 'seen and used' (p. 20). Rose contends that many of the theoretical, methodological and ethical tensions

---

[2] Here, we draw on the sixteenth-century origins of voyeuristic as 'having a mental itching' (Oxford Dictionary of English, 2003), in this case an insatiable (non-sexual) desire 'to look in on' infants' private worlds), and Mulvey's (1975) reference to the 'looked upon' being subject to, and objectified, by curious and ultimately controlling gazes.

about visual research methods reflect disputes about the relative importance of these sites and modalities – and, we would add, their consequent implications.

We have adapted Rose's framework for use in the *Infants' Lives in Childcare* project by adding to and refining questions that she suggests may offer a useful starting point for researchers using visual methods. In the remainder of this chapter, we use our adaptation (see Table 10.1) as a heuristic device for critically reflecting on our use of baby cam as a part of our suite of devices and approaches in our admittedly contestable goal of trying to 'access' infants' perspectives and on the conceptual, methodological and ethical issues and implications that have arisen (Bradley et al. 2012; Elwick et al. in press-b). Influenced also by Pink (2007), we have tried to be alert to the interconnectivity between researchers and research participants, the visual research practices and technologies taken up and the images produced and their positioning in the specific socio-political-cultural contexts in which they are embedded. In the following section, we discuss some of the challenges we are encountering.

We link part of our discussion to a sequence of photographic 'stills' taken from synchronised video footage from a hand-held camera and baby cam footage taken by Tina (3rd author) in a family day-care home (Table 10.2) and shown simultaneously on a split screen using Studiocode™ software.[3]

The sequence features Peter who, at the time of filming, attended family day care 3 days a week and had been with Cheryl, his educator, since he was 8 weeks old. He was 9 months old when this footage was taken and on that particular day there were four other children at FDC aged between 2.9 and 4.1 years. This footage was captured by Tina on her ninth visit to the home over a period of 5 weeks. Her field notes indicate that:

> The children had been playing outside for much of the morning on this pleasant late winter day before coming inside at 12.00 for lunch. Peter sat in a high chair, slightly removed from the older children who sat at a low children's table and chairs, to Peter's left. The kitchen area from which the educator retrieved the children's lunch things was to Peter's right. During the session Peter fed himself finger food and attempted to drink water from a cup independently. Cheryl also spoon-fed Peter and helped him to drink from the cup. Peter had worn baby cam on two previous visits. On this occasion, he wore the baby cam for around 5 minutes before he reached up and tugged at it, at which point I immediately helped him to remove the camera. (24/08/10: VSS240810-9-TS)

We have selected this footage because of its 'ordinariness'; it captures an uneventful interaction between Peter and Cheryl in the daily routine of life in the family day-care setting, an interaction of the kind they would have shared many times previously. It is because of this ordinariness that the juxtaposed stills from synchronised baby cam footage and hand-held camera footage are able to render this familiar interaction strange.

In the next section we draw on our reflections on our use of baby cam, scaffolded by questions from our adaptation of Rose's (2012) framework, to construct a script for a readers' theatre. By readers' theatre, we mean a staged presentation of thematically

---

[3] Details available at http://www.studiocodegroup.com

Table 10.1 A scaffold for reflections about visual images

	Technological	Compositional	Socio-political-ethical
Site of production	What technologies were used? What were the technical reasons for using them? How were they used?	What kinds of images did these technologies make possible/impossible?	Were these technologies used for reasons other than technical? How do these technologies position the researchers and the subjects/objects of the research? Who stands to be advantaged/disadvantaged by the use of these technologies?
Site of image	What effects have these technologies had on the images produced?	Where are viewers' eyes drawn to and why? What is the vantage point? What visual effects do these images convey? What conventions do they adhere to/disrupt? Are any contradictions/juxtapositions evident? What performances do the images reflect?	What purposes do the images themselves perform? What other (than visual) effects do they achieve? Whose knowledges are deployed/excluded?
Site of 'audiencing' (where images encounter their spectators and users)	What technologies are required to view these images?	How actively do audiences engage with these images? How do differently positioned audiences interpret this image? What new meanings do these images make possible?	What do differently positioned audiences indicate that they intend to 'do' with these images? What politics might these images play to?

Adapted from Rose (2012)

Table 10.2 Contrasting views: of the infant/researcher/camera/educator

Topic	The baby's view via babycam	The adult's view via handycam
Here comes the carer		
Drink		

Food

Spoon

linked segments of text derived from several sources. Staging is simple, involving minimal props, with the performers reading from the script (Donmoyer and Yennie-Donmoyer 1995; Slade 2012).

Baby Cam: A Readers' Theatre (Script) in Three Acts

We decided to use readers' theatre – for us, an experimental form of presentation – because it evokes the inherently dialogic nature of our critical reflexivity. Accordingly, we focus on issues that have been, and continue to be, especially salient for us throughout the 4 years (at the time of writing) that we have been engaged in this project. We want to emphasise, however, that our intent is not confessional. Rather, like Johansson and White (2011), we seek to provoke discussion about ethical and efficacious ways in which researchers might gain insight into infants' experiences over and beyond what has generally been possible through more traditional methods.

The readers' theatre script that follows is constructed primarily from excerpts from email discussions in which we reflect on our use of baby cam and the opportunities for participatory research that it has opened up and constrained. We have also drawn on lines of thinking prompted by our experience of baby cam that we are pursuing in other writing about the project, as well as our responses to earlier drafts of the script. The excerpts selected portray key themes that continually resurface for us. They are arranged into three Acts, each loosely focused on one of Rose's three 'sites' and containing several scenes. We have cast ourselves as the readers and assumed our 'real life' roles in the *Infants' Lives in Childcare* project:

Jennifer: Project leader
Ben: Chief investigator
Tina: Doctoral researcher (formerly a research assistant and, in that role, charged with locating a camera suitable for use as a baby cam)
Sheena: Doctoral researcher

The script begins with a prologue that explains the genesis of baby cam.

Prologue

Mid-November and an Antipodean early summer day. Struggling desperately to shape our ideas into a competitive research proposal. Summer holidays loom, but so does the Australian Research Council's submission deadline. Concentration flags. Summer … cricket … the drone of cricket[4] commentators … gripping action replays from a camera secured to the wicket – a so-called stump-cam that provides close up views of action that would otherwise be missed. A stump-cam? How about a *baby cam*?[5] That could be just the 'wow factor' we need!

---

[4] Often considered Australia's national sport.
[5] The idea came from our colleague Sharynne McLeod.

Act 1: The Site of Production of Baby Cam Images

Author's Notes

Rose (2012) reminds us that the technologies we use in producing images determine the form of those images and also, to a large extent, contribute to their meanings and effects. As we have explained elsewhere (Sumsion et al. 2011), locating appropriate technology from which to fashion a workable baby cam required significant and time-consuming detective work and problem solving. So why did we persevere? Was it worth it? Who has gained and who, or what, might have been compromised? Such questions invite many responses. We begin by focusing on technical aspects (Scene 1) but slide quickly into ethical issues of assent, dissent and participation (Scenes 2 and 3).

Scene 1: Technical Logistics

Tina: *The technology is not quite right yet. It is still too cumbersome. Our choice of camera has been constrained by so many factors: safety for the infant (no wireless cameras as they may emit dangerous radio frequencies in close proximity to the infants' head); durability (in case it ended up being dropped on the ground or in water), quality of image produced, reliability of camera; what size camera we could reasonably hope an infant might be able to wear ...*

Sheena: *Baby cam WAS technically difficult to use at times, particularly early on. I am thinking of all the times Sandi wore the camera, only to find that the footage hadn't worked for some reason or other.*

Tina: *Finding a way for the infant to wear the camera so that we got the best approximation of their vision was tricky, particularly as we ended up using a camera that was worn on the side of the head – was the camera pointing in the right direction? Was it angled too high/too low/was it upside down?! Sometimes it would slip down if the infant was moving around a lot, such as on the see-saw. In the end, it was a compromise between something that was reasonably comfortable for the infant to wear, that was quick and easy to put on and that would give us a reasonably accurate representation of the infants' visual perspective.*

I think it may have greater potential in the future as smaller devices become available that are easier to fit and less noticeable for the infant who is wearing it and for the people around the infants. I didn't use it as much as I could have because it often seemed like an imposition, particularly if the infant appeared to be tired or just not having a good day.

Scene 2: Assent/Dissent

Jennifer: *That's the crux isn't it ... the issue of assent/dissent.*

Tina: *The infants were quite capable of tugging at or removing the camera if they didn't want to wear it and often did so. That enabled them some control over the situation and an opportunity to dissent.*

There were varying responses to baby cam from different infants and on different days. When infants didn't respond well to baby cam I think it was just that it was a strange sensation for them wearing the headband, much as very young children will often pull off sun hats.

Stage Direction

A long pause

Tina: *I know I have suggested that because they could pull the camera off they had an opportunity for dissent. But is this really meaningful dissent if, presumably, it is based* purely *upon the physical sensation of wearing the camera and not upon any understanding of what the camera is, what it does, or why it is there?*

We tried to maximise the likelihood of infants giving assent. Only using baby cam for up to 10 minutes at a time was important. And also, allowing them an opportunity to hold and explore the camera if they wanted to, to try and build some level of familiarity with it. The highchair seemed to be a good place to use it – I think because they were busy concentrating on the task of eating which distracted them away from the sensation of wearing it.

Jennifer: *That shows consideration for infants – but it also invites discussion about the ethics of distraction as a strategy for gaining assent.*

Sheena: *It's like opening a can of worms isn't it? Every point we make raises another one!*

But some infants actively seemed to like wearing the baby cam and became quite involved with the camera. Sandi is a good example. She appeared excited when she saw it, jumped up and down, reached for it and became upset when I put it away. Even on the days when she didn't appear to want to wear it, she often seemed interested in looking at it.

Tina: *I'm curious about why Sandi appeared to like the camera – what concept did she have of what it was and what it did? I wonder whether she might have enjoyed the direct interaction with Sheena or perhaps the way others treated her when she was wearing it, or just that it was something new and different that only SHE was allowed to wear?*

Sheena: *If only we could ask!*

Scene 3: Participation

Tina: *I'm going to play the devil's advocate: Why is it that we think that baby cam might be more participatory than the researcher sitting quietly in a corner of the room with a hand-held video camera? Are we kidding ourselves that it is participatory because the infant is wearing the camera, that they are responsible for recording the footage? It's not participatory in the sense that the infants presumably have no idea why the camera is on their head!*

Sheena: *Are we arguing that it is participatory because they wear it? I agree that Sandi quite possibly had no idea of why the camera was on her head, or the images it might produce – let alone how we might use these images, for instance at conferences. Although it is interesting to note that she did watch some of the baby cam footage with us (me and the educator) and appeared to recognise the images. I can't say though if she actually MADE the connection between the camera being on her head and the images she was watching – but I can't say that she DIDN'T, either. Perhaps the participatory possibilities existed more in the relations that unfolded between me and Sandi in the moments when we were using, or going to use, the camera.*

    This seems quite different to locating the participatory possibilities in a piece of technology attached to an infant's hat or headband. I'm not saying that the camera offered NO participatory possibilities; perhaps it did … by producing images that give the viewer a technologically mediated approximation of the infants' bodily view of the world – a view that would be difficult to achieve otherwise.

Tina: *If it is only participatory in that it puts us in a situation where we must interact with the infant, then I've had many situations where infants initiated interactions with me as I was using the hand-held camera.*

Sheena: *I think baby cam does perhaps offer more participatory possibilities than 'sitting quietly in a corner of the room with a hand-held video camera' because at least it REQUIRES some form of interaction between researcher and infant. Encounters between researcher and infant are important regardless of whether the camera is baby cam, hand held or tripod mounted. Like Tina, I have lots of examples where infants initiated interactions with me as I was using the tripod or hand-held camera. It is these interactions that I think are important because they have the potential to take the research into unexpected territory.*

    For example, Sandi didn't always use the camera or respond to me using a camera in ways that I expected. She put her head under water while wearing the baby cam; and, sometimes when I was filming her, she came and looked through the viewfinder with me – rather than staying on the other side of the camera as I expected her to. It is almost as if she was appropriating the technology for her own purposes. It is how we respond to these moments that is important. For me, participation is about creating space in our thoughts and actions for these moments to matter to our research. In other words, enabling a space through which something new emerges between researcher and infant; something that might differ from our own planned mode of interaction or our own planned usage of particular research techniques

    I would have some ethical concerns about using smaller cameras even if we could have found them. The smaller, more hidden and more discrete the camera, the more we'd seem to be deciding HOW infants can participate in the research. It seems to discount the value of what infants can bring to the encounter – their agencies and capacities to affect what unfolds. Is it possible that requiring them to participate by wearing a discrete camera that they have little, or no, control over might actually constrain possibilities for them to act? Would Gallagher (2005) say that it's another form of surveillance?

It also raises questions about our willingness to engage with the harder-to-recognise forms of participation that might be playing out in our research encounters. For example, the ways in which infants might participate by affecting particular embodied responses in us. It is difficult, for instance, not to react bodily to infants' expressions, their murmurs, their situations. Merleau-Ponty (1968) and Dillon (2012) say that it is not possible to halt the impact and intermingling of self and other in our human encounters. I am thinking mainly of Harry here, and the way he made me feel when he turned and looked at me when I was filming him. Although not specific to baby cam, in that one look I suddenly changed from being the 'seer' to the 'seen' and I find it very hard to discount his participation or involvement in that moment. Even though it was a subtle and perhaps not widely recognised, or easily recognisable, mode of participation, his look made me feel something: at the very least his look made me stop and question my own actions of continuing to film him. It also evoked feelings of sympathy, confusion, uncertainty, etc..... All of these things occur through difference and suggest some form of reversible relation is at play. Perhaps this could also be understood as an awakening of our ethical consciousness about our own ways of being with infants in practice. Almost as if the infants' agencies and desires decentre our own sense of self: a moment where we find ourselves confronting the need to make more deliberate choices about our actions because of the demand of the Other.[6]

Tina: *What Sheena is saying is really interesting, but, as she has pointed out, baby cam was not required for these moments to occur; they can also occur through the use of other research methods. Baby cam, however, FORCED us into having a direct encounter with the infants as we fitted it. I have to say, though, that sometimes I felt that the infants might not be comfortable with me putting the headband and t-shirt on them, particularly in the earlier visits, as this was not a role they were used to me taking. In some cases I actually asked the educator to put the t-shirt on the child for me to help alleviate any potential discomfort on the infants' part. The interactions that occurred while using the hand-held camera were generally spontaneous interactions initiated by the infant, for instance, crawling towards me and offering me a toy or reaching up to the camera. Perhaps these are more genuine participatory opportunities for the infant as they were initiated by the infant, not by me.*

Ben: *I wonder how much the idea that baby cam is more participatory is because it gives babies greater power over our actions – because a baby*

---

[6] Elwick et al. (in press-a).

can 'agree' or 'refuse' to wear it? This has less to do with the role of baby cam itself in our research and more to do with how much it has to do with giving the infant something that is very valuable to us because it can block what we want to do. For example, we could give the infant a portable light switch which could plunge the house (assuming no daylight!) into darkness whenever they pressed it. Presumably we would have to negotiate with the baby about this switch in order to do our research, as we do with baby cam. In fact, I think it's quite a good idea! Why stop at assent? Why not go for dissent? Whenever an infant didn't like something, they could plunge the room into darkness. But they would 'not like' lots of things that were not to do with research. And the same goes for their reaction to baby cam. They might throw it away/pull it off just because they were annoyed with the educator or a peer – nothing to do with the researcher or the research. AND they might just press the switch for fun.

Stage Direction

A momentary stunned silence as we digest this possibility. Some of us begin to imagine how we might incorporate such a light switch in our future research. The room then plunges into darkness!

Authors' Notes

After our 'Aha' baby cam moment described in the prologue, we searched the literature for references to research involving infants wearing cameras on their heads. Our initial investigations led us to a laboratory study conducted by Yoshida and Smith (2008) to ascertain the relationship between the camera view and the direction of the infants' gaze. Two years into our project, we became aware of the parallel development of a similar methodology to baby cam in New Zealand, where Jayne White, like us, was using split-screen technology to watch synchronised footage captured in a naturalistic early childhood setting. In White's (2011) case, footage was captured from three cameras simultaneously, including via a camera mounted on an infant's hat. Yoshida and Smith (2008) and White (2011) both used cameras operated by wireless transmitters, but, as explained more fully elsewhere (Sumsion et al. 2011), we were wary of the potential effects of radio waves in such close proximity to infants' heads and settled for the more cumbersome and larger 'lipstick style' cameras attached by a cord to a small recording device. White's study involved only one child, an 18-month-old toddler, who like 11-month-old Sandi in our project, made it clear that she wished to participate. In both cases, participation provided at least some scope for infant agency. We are less certain about what benefits, if any, infants like Peter (Table 10.2), who showed little interest in baby cam, gained from wearing it. We could find no instances in the literature of infants having access to the equivalent of the 'light switch' mooted by Ben as a means of making their consent to participate unequivocally clear!

Act 2: The Site of the Images

Authors' Notes

Here we are concerned with the visual content of the image, including its framing and composition, its vantage point and spatial perspectives, its narrative potential, and other effects that command or divert the viewer's attention (Rose 2012; Schirato and Webb 2004). Guided by the questions in Table 10.1, we are interested in the contradictions and/or juxtapositions that are evident and the purposes they perform.

Scene 1: Utility

Tina: *Although it's not so evident in this footage (Table 10.2), we still couldn't capture the infants' full range of vision even with a wide-angle lens. Baby cam can tell us about the infants' bodily perspective and where they are interested in focusing their attention but because of the technical challenges and limitations of the equipment, we can't even be sure that these were captured accurately.*

             Could we have got the same (or indeed better) information and insights from having another hand-held camera positioned behind Peter (the infant in Table 10.2) instead of him wearing baby cam? Looking at the series of matched images (Table 10.2), what do we get from the two images together that we couldn't have got from the handy cam images alone?

Jennifer: *Watching the dual footage from both cameras simultaneously on the split screen makes me feel quite queasy. I feel much less able to make sense of what I am seeing than if I'd seen the footage sequentially – but maybe I have a neurological processing problem!*

Sheena: *I prefer to watch the footage sequentially, first the tripod camera and then the baby cam. Watching them together might be helpful though when we start some fine-detailed analysis.*

Scene 2: 'Authenticity', Performance, Positioning, and Power Relations

Tina: *Is the baby cam footage a bit contrived? The adults and older children have shown a lot of interest in it. Does its highly visible nature change the way people around the infant 'perform'? Do the images reflect an element of 'Here is another camera being pointed at us! Let's give the infant something interesting to look at'? Or even, 'Let's entertain the infant in an effort to distract attention away from the sensation of wearing baby cam'?*

Sheena: *I agree. I think it might invite 'performance'. But it's not something I've particularly noticed. Often it was hard to know where the infant was even looking (often our feet or the ceiling!) or going to look next, which probably made 'performance' less likely than with tripod cameras. Polly [an educator] and I had NO idea that Sandi was going to put her face in the water bowl. There was no performance happening under the water – except perhaps by the toys in the water bowl if we use Lenz-Taguchi's (2010) ideas about non-human entities having agency! We (and I include all the educators here) were often more concerned that the technology was even working than concerned with what it was filming!*

Jennifer: *The footage of Peter and Cheryl (Table 10.2) has a naturalistic feel – I suppose because it's captured such a familiar, everyday context and event. In terms of visual organisation, though, it's a challenge to read. Are we meant to move from left to right, from Cheryl to Peter and back to Cheryl, zigzagging down the image? It seems to invite lots of questions and narratives about what is happening. In that sense it's quite powerful. Why did we place the baby cam sequence on the left-hand side? Does it position Peter as object (of Cheryl's attention) and target (of the spoon)? And Cheryl looms so large, especially in the frame she almost fills. That image really grabs viewers' attention, but what are we meant to make of that? And what did Cheryl make of it?*

Tina: *I certainly found it a bit of a shock when I saw myself on the baby cam footage. Suddenly the baby was researching ME?! I was used to being the one behind the camera, not in front of it!*

Authors' Notes

We are still developing our visual literacy capacities to read the baby cam images through the analytical frames of visual theorists such as Rose (2012). We accept that 'every act of looking and seeing is also an act of not seeing' (Schirato and Webb 2004, p. 14). Therefore, 'deciding where to look is highly political because it involves deciding where *not* to look, what to exclude from sight…' Thomas (2001, p. 4, original emphasis). Yet we have much to learn about recognising and articulating our political, as well as compositional decisions, in framing our baby cam images, and conversely in deciding what to omit (at the time of capturing the original video footage; in reducing it to manageable 'units of analysis'; and in selecting inevitably brief excerpts for presentation and representation). We also have much to learn about technical aspects, such as perspective, in baby cam image production. To what extent, for example, should we discount distortions produced by the baby cam following infants' head, rather than eye, movements and, especially with younger infants, the 'wobbliness' of their heads?

Act 3: Audience Encounters with Baby Cam Images

Authors' Notes

Initial audience reaction to baby cam footage is invariably one of shock. Some appear shocked by the radical disturbance to their accustomed spatial perspectives and the subsequent defamiliarising of the familiar (Schirato and Webb 2004); others by the effects and potential consequences and possibilities of the infant's gaze. For viewers who have been captured on baby cam footage, the shock can come from being the object of that gaze. Guided by the questions in Table 10.1, we are interested in how differently positioned audiences interpret baby cam images, the new meanings those images make possible and the shocks they engender, the new intentions they inspire and the politics surrounding the use of baby cam images.

Scene 1: On Voyeurism/Shock/Devereux

Ben: *So why DO we researchers find it a shock to see ourselves from the baby cam's viewpoint?*

   One possibility is that baby cam invites us into a space which is ethically shocking. For example, the shock of being seen from the baby's point of view is not particularly about the shock of being seen by the baby. This 'being seen' just dramatises the fact that baby cam invites us into a form of 'voyeurism' – whatever the baby is looking at (as we suggested at the start of this chapter). Yet how can a camera on a baby's headband equate to voyeurism when a voyeur is usually defined as a person who gets gratification from spying on the naked flesh, pain or sexual antics of others?

   One answer comes from film theory. In a famous article, Laura Mulvey argues that film has traditionally structured the movie camera's 'look' as active and male, while the object of the look is passive and female. For Mulvey (1975, p. 2), the narrative conventions of film create a voyeurism in which a curious and aroused (male, controlling) subject is remote from the 'undercover world of the surreptitious observation of an unknowing and unwilling victim'.

   This could be taken up in a number of ways. We could gloss the 'private world' that we are prying into as the infant's world. The infant is, after all, 'unknowing' of what we are doing when we put that headband on his/her head. Or we could widen our field of view to recognise that, here, the 'male' gaze of our tiny camera is spying on a quintessentially female world of caring for small children (all the educators in this study to date have been women). Hence perhaps the feeling that there is something voyeuristic about the vision we get through baby cam. Or we could, somewhat ingenuously, position ourselves as the 'unknowing and unwilling victim' – perhaps on the grounds that we didn't realise how much directorial power we were giving the babies when we gave them baby cam!

Sheena: *I'm not at all keen on the word voyeurism in relation to researching with infants. And I don't see a connection between voyeurism and the ethical shock that we've discussed at length in earlier conversations.*

Jennifer: *It's a confronting idea. But remember that Mulvey was writing in the 1970s, at a particular feminist moment. Rose (2012, p. 167) argues that Mulvey's work has been incredibly important in demanding that we think about 'the gendering of who sees and who is seen' but that, in many ways, it's quite dated because it assumes a patriarchal, heterosexual narrative and a binary distinction between the male bearer of the gaze and the female object of that gaze. But the notion of gaze itself, and of its power, seems potentially very productive for our project, especially as we could explore it from diverse theoretical perspectives.*

Ben: *Erm … 'dated', …. OK. Well, if we don't like voyeurism as a concept, how about this as an explanation for the 'shock' Tina describes when seeing ourselves through the 'eyes' of the baby cam … According to*

Georges Devereux (1968), a fundamental anxiety structures behavioural research, surrounding observers' wish to ward off the awareness that they are themselves observed by the subjects of their research. Unconsciously the observer knows they cannot subordinate the subject's mental life to the researcher's scheme of things. But, methodologically, researchers deny this and experimental artefacts result (Bradley 2005). Devereux (1968) called his book <u>From Anxiety to Method in the Behavioural Sciences</u> *because he believed that most of the science-like methods used in disciplines such as psychology are defences, attempts to deny or repress the anxiety of being observed and interpreted by others when one is ostensibly being a detached and invisible observer.*

In Devereux's account, this anxiety can be glossed as the researcher refusing to experience the subjective uncertainty of not knowing about others, anxiety about not having the same kind of epistemic authority that biologists have over microbes. Instead of experiencing this uncertainty, the social researcher acts out a controlling role that highlights 'those moments of research when you feel like a disinterested scientist, secure in the knowledge that by following agreed-upon methods you are a part of discovering the world in an unbiased and objective way' (Selby 1999, p. 173). Devereux challenges us to ask what would happen if behavioural scientists became more aware of the fluidity of their own often unsettling experiences of others while doing research.

In this light, the shock of seeing footage from baby cam is the shock of having our bluff called, our defences breached, by empowering the vision of the Other, in this case, the previously objectified baby. This vision is traditionally repressed by the science-like methods of behavioural research. We are shocked by baby cam because we are being forced to acknowledge that the research situation is far more symmetrical than we have been trained to imagine:

> *Time and again it becomes evident that many difficulties in behavioural science are due to the warding off and ignoring of such interactions [between observed and observer] and especially of the fact that the observation of the subject by the observer is complemented by the counter-observation of the observer by the subject. This insight forces us to abandon -- at least in a naive sense -- the notion that the basic operation in behavioural science is the observation of a subject by an observer. We must substitute for it the notion that it is the analysis of the interaction between the two, in a situation where both are at once observers to themselves and subjects to the other. (Devereux 1968, p. 275)*

Stage Direction

Ben pauses for breath ...

Sheena: *My understanding of ethics and thoughts about how we might talk about the shock of seeing oneself on film come more from Dillon (2012) who extends Merleau-Ponty's (1968) ideas about reversibility/écart. It's to do with the idea that seeing ourselves on film may bring with it a sort of*

*ethical decentering because we suddenly find ourselves looking at ourselves.
And also, possibly and more indirectly, looking at ourselves from something
akin to the baby's 'standpoint' since they were the one with the camera.*

*Using Merleau-Ponty's ideas about reversibility and Dillon's related
work on ethics, it's possible to think about the experience of seeing oneself
through the eyes of the Other. But not necessarily a human Other. Baby
cam footage can function as Other because it renders visible for the viewer
their own presence in the world. Merleau-Ponty (1968) uses the term
'reversibility' (p. 147) to point to an overlapping or reflexive relation
through 'écart' (or a moment of differentiation) (p. 124) that is present in
our living experience: to see the thing is to feel the thing seeing me; to
touch the thing is to feel the thing touching me ... although this is a simplistic explanation.*

*According to Dillon (2012), this reversible relation through difference
can provoke ethical reflection: do I see myself as I want to see myself; do I
see myself as I would want you to see me etc..? I could go on!!*

Ben: *Can I draw out a nuance from that, Sheena? If Merleau-Ponty and Dillon
are right, then whenever we look at the baby, reversibility ensures that we
feel the baby looking at us. What baby cam does is starkly confront us
with a point which both Merleau-Ponty and Dillon make: that 'I see the
Other and the Other sees me; <u>but I do not experience my being seen as
he does</u>' (Dillon 1997, p.174; my emphasis). ...Under normal conditions
we do not question what we assume about the baby's view of us. But baby
cam thrusts it in our face: baby cam challenges the veridicality of reversibility. Normally, when we look at someone else, baby or not, we <u>feel as if</u>
we see them seeing us. But baby cam proves such reversibility to be
largely imaginary ... our assumptions about the baby's viewpoint are
shown to be what Lacan would call a misrecognition. In his terms, baby
cam is a shock because it shows the shallowness of our fantasised
relationship to the baby, moving us towards the more decentred 'thirdness'
of the symbolic order, the order in which what we have been calling
'ethical reflexivity' can arise[7]*

Tina: *For my part, seeing myself on the baby cam footage really did make me think
more about what we are asking of the infant and the other children and
adults around the infant, when they participate in this kind of visual research.
It can be easy to lose sight of this when you have been in the field for quite
some time. In the footage that I recorded [by tripod or hand-held camera], it
is as if I was never there. The baby cam has allowed my presence to be
recorded, it has put me in the picture both literally and figuratively.*

*But I also wonder how much of the shock is simply about suddenly and
unexpectedly seeing yourself in the footage and the experience of seeing
yourself from the outside – What was I wearing that day? Look at my hair!*

---

[7] On Lacan, the imaginary baby and Peirce's concept of thirdness, see Bradley (1989, 2010a, b).

Similar to how we wonder, 'Is that what I really sound like?' when we hear an audio recording of ourselves.

Sheena: *So maybe some form of decentering was happening? You didn't see what you expected to see and perhaps you were vulnerable to this difference? That's where ethics as reflexivity comes in...*

Scene 3: Other Audiences and Spectators

Tina: *Family Day Care Australia[8] was quite open about wanting to get a 'good news story' about family day care into the press. They saw baby cam as the vehicle for that. If not for baby cam, there would have been no publicity.*

EVERYTIME I have presented on this study I have been asked to show baby cam footage! I find that a bit frustrating because there is a lot more to the study than baby cam. Sometimes I'd rather show other footage that better helps me make my point.

Sheena: *It probably wouldn't have the same sort of audience impact.*

Tina: *I think that a lot of the reaction that we have to baby cam is about the size of objects and spaces from their bodily perspective – it is a novel experience for us. It's interesting, but what insight does it give us to the infants' experiences? I think it can give us an idea of WHAT they are interested in looking at, but we can't know WHY that might be or what that might MEAN.*

Tina: *At conferences where I have shown baby cam footage people have wondered what it means for the infant to be in spaces – such as outside play spaces – that seem so big on the baby cam footage or to have objects, including people's faces, appear so large (Table 10.2). One person wondered whether infants might find this frightening. But this is the infant's daily experience, and there is nothing in their behaviour that would seem to indicate they are bothered by this. How are we to interpret these kinds of images?*

So I guess I'm wondering to what extent the baby cam helps us to achieve the aims of the research, both in terms of understanding what life is like for infants and responding to the methodological challenges of attempting participatory research with infants. I'm not sure what the answer is but I think we need to think about the question.

Having said all that, after using baby cam footage at the Family Day Care Australia workshop, I think that baby cam IS an engaging means of encouraging discussion about infants' experiences with educators and reminding educators about the importance of thinking about infants' physical perspectives in their practice.

[8] Family Day Care Australia and KU Children's Services were our Industry Partners. We deeply appreciate their support.

Sheena: *Maybe viewing the baby cam footage can decentre the viewer in ways that
         awaken their ethical consciousness and perhaps invoke questions, reflections
         and discussions about their own ways of being with infants in practice
         (including research practice). Put another way, perhaps it baby cam can
         foster reflexivity through difference.*

         *I am not convinced that viewing baby cam footage can tell us an awful
         lot about infants' own experiences, and I think we need to be careful about
         this point in relation to participatory research. Ultimately, WE construct
         what we call the infants' experience.*[9]

Authors' Notes

In various theoretical and every day connotations, 'gaze' has been a powerful theme
throughout Act 3. Conventionally, 'gaze' refers to 'a fixed or intent observation
performed and controlled by the viewer through the eyes' (Thomas 2001, p. 2). In
contrast, from psychoanalytic perspectives (e.g. Lacan 1977) tangentially touched
on by Ben (2nd author) and phenomenological perspectives (e.g. Dillon 2012;
Merleau-Ponty 1968) as described by Sheena (4th author), gaze has a strong element of reciprocity. In other words, as Thomas (2001, p. 2) argues, rather than
implying 'a powerful and controlling spectator', there is 'no simple dichotomy
between seeing and being seen but unstable roles that conflict and overlap'. Other
theoretical and practice-based understandings and perspectives offer different conceptualisations of gaze. In our view, the diversity of ways of conceptualising gaze
opens up an array of potentially productive methodological and interpretive possibilities that are yet to be fully explored by researchers, practitioners and others with
an interest in infants' experiences.

Conclusion

In this chapter, we heed Bourdieu and Wacquant's (1992) exhortation to reveal the
endemic uncertainties, tensions and challenges of research that so often go unacknowledged. While we have focused on our use of baby cam in the *Infants' Lives in
Childcare* project, the chapter contributes to broader discussions about ethical
tensions in methodological innovation (Nind et al. 2012). These tensions are likely
to be accentuated, we believe, by the seductiveness and affordances of emerging
visual technologies such as baby cam. Our experience of baby cam leads us to
strongly endorse warnings about the dangers of 'uncritical romanticisation' (Phillips
and Shaw 2011, p. 610) of innovatory methodologies and technologies. We would
like to think that this chapter might serve as reminder of the importance of
attending to, and retaining a degree of scepticism towards, the rhetoric and promises

---

[9] For elaboration, see Elwick et al. (in press-b).

that so often accompany innovative research technologies, and especially, it seems, visual technologies.

Accordingly, we conclude with the general observation that the use of technological apparatus has a rhetorical force in science and research which is independent of its practical utility. To most people, the cultural impact of sending men to the moon far outweighed the geological discoveries the trip has afforded. It was a paramount *coup de theatre* for modern science. As Buzz Aldrin (1969) said in a broadcast during the historic voyage of Apollo XI, 'We feel this [first moon-landing] stands as a symbol of the insatiable curiosity of all mankind to explore the unknown'. Likewise, the age of 'brass instruments' in psychology is widely seen to have had more to do with showing that psychology had found a way to conform to the 'techno-scientific' ideal of the physical sciences than in producing earth-shattering research findings (Coon 1993).

We are not equating our baby cam innovation with major scientific breakthroughs! Rather, we are suggesting that one way of understanding others' responses to baby cam is that it too has a certain rhetorical force: it neatly dramatises the key motivation underpinning our research project, that is, to understand how infants and toddlers experience early childhood settings. The *practical utility* of baby cam as a research methodology has turned out to be something quite different from what rhetorically it appears to offer: direct line of *sight into the baby's world.* It is its *ethical utility*, we believe, that warrants continuing consideration.

Acknowledgements The *Infants' Lives in Childcare* project was funded by the Australian Research Council (LP0883913), Family Day Care Australia and KU Children's Services. We also deeply appreciate the contributions of our fellow researchers: Linda Harrison, Sharynne McLeod, Frances Press, Joy Goodfellow and Sandra Cheeseman. We are indebted, too, to the children, educators and parents who participated in the project.

References

Aldrin, E. E. (1969). Broadcast from Apollo XI. In *Eyes turned skyward: Apollo moon missions.* http://www.spacequotations.com/apollo.html. Accessed 31 Aug 2012.

Bishop, S. R., Lau, M., Shapiro, S., Carlson, L., Anderson, N. D., Carmody, J., et al. (2004). Mindfulness: A proposed operational definition. *Clinical Psychology: Science and Practice, 11*(3), 230–241. doi:10.1093/clipsy.bph077.

Bourdieu, P., & Wacquant, L. J. D. (1992). *An invitation to reflexive sociology.* Chicago: The University of Chicago Press.

Bourdieu, P. (1998). *Practical reason: On the theory of action.* Cambridge: Polity.

Bradley, B. S. (1989). *Visions of infancy: A critical introduction to child psychology.* Cambridge: Polity Press.

Bradley, B. S. (2005). *Psychology and experience.* Cambridge: Cambridge University Press.

Bradley, B. S. (2010a). Jealousy in infant-peer trios: From narcissism to culture. In S. Hart & M. Legerstee (Eds.), *Handbook of jealousy: Theories, principles and multidisciplinary approaches* (pp. 192–234). Hoboken: Wiley-Blackwell.

Bradley, B. S. (2010b). Experiencing symbols. In B. Wagoner (Ed.), *Symbolic transformations: Toward an interdisciplinary science of symbols* (pp. 93–119). London: Routledge.

Bradley, B., Sumsion, J., Stratigos, T., & Elwick, S. (2012). Baby events: Assembling descriptions of infants in family day care. *Contemporary Issues in Early Childhood, 13*(2), 141–153.

Clark, A. (2005). Ways of seeing: Using the Mosaic approach to listen to young children's perspectives. In A. Clark, A. T. Kjørholt, & P. Moss (Eds.), *Beyond listening: Children's perspectives on early childhood services* (pp. 29–49). Bristol: Policy Press.

Clark, A., & Moss, P. (2001). *Listening to young children: The Mosaic approach.* London: Joseph Rowntree Foundation.

Coon, D. J. (1993). Standardizing the subject: Experimental psychologists, introspection and the quest for a technoscientific ideal. *Technology & Culture, 34,* 757–783.

Crossley, N. (1999). Book reviews: Pierre Bourdieu, practical reason: On the theory of action, Cambridge: Polity, 1998. *Sociology, 33*(2), 451–452. doi:10.1177/s0038038599210279.

Devereux, G. (1968). *From anxiety to method in the behavioural sciences.* The Hague: Mouton.

Dillon, M. C. (1997). *Merleau-Ponty's ontology.* Evanston: Northwestern University Press.

Dillon, M. C. (2012). *The ontology of becoming and the ethics of particularity.* Athens: Ohio University Press.

Donmoyer, R., & Yennie-Donmoyer, J. (1995). Data as drama: Reflections on the use of readers theater as a mode of qualitative data display. *Qualitative Inquiry, 1*(4), 402–428. doi:10.1177/107780049500100403.

Elwick, S., Bradley, B., & Sumsion, J. (in press-a). Creating space for infants to influence ECEC practice: The encounter, écart, reversibility and ethical reflection. *Educational Philosophy and Theory,* 1–13. doi:10.1080/00131857.2013.780231.

Elwick, S., Bradley, B., & Sumsion, J. (in press-b). Infants as others: Uncertainties, difficulties and (im)possibilities in researching infants' lives. *International Journal of Qualitative Studies in Education,* 1–18. doi:10.1080/09518398.2012.737043.

Goodfellow, J., Elwick, S., Stratigos, T., Sumsion, J., Press, F., Harrison, L., et al. (2011). Infants' lives in childcare: Crafting research evidence. *The First Years Ngā Tau Tuatahi Journal of Infant Toddler Education, 13*(2), 43–48.

Johansson, E., & White, E. J. (Eds.). (2011). *Educational research with our youngest: Voices of infants and toddlers.* Dordrecht: Springer.

Lacan, J. (1977). *The four fundamental concepts of psychoanalysis* (A. Sheridan, Trans.). London: Hogarth Press.

Lenz Taguchi, H. (2010). *Going beyond the theory/divide in early childhood education.* New York: Routledge.

Merleau-Ponty, M. (1968). *The visible and the invisible* (A. Lingis, Trans.). Evanston: Northwestern University Press.

Mirzoeff, N. (1999). *An introduction to visual culture.* London: Routledge.

Mulvey, L. (1975). Visual pleasure and narrative cinema. *Screen, 16*(3), 6–18. doi:10.1093/screen/16.3.6.

Nind, M., Wiles, R., Bengry-Howell, A., & Crow, G. (2012). Methodological innovation and research ethics: Forces in tension or forces in harmony? *Qualitative Research.* doi:10.1177/1468794112455042.

Phillips, C., & Shaw, I. (2011). Innovation and the practice of social work research. *British Journal of Social Work, 41*(4), 609–624. doi:10.1093/bjsw/bcr072.

Pink, S. (2007). *Doing visual ethnography.* London: Sage.

Press, F., Bradley, B. S., Goodfellow, J., Harrison, L. J., McLeod, S., Sumsion, J., et al. (2011). Listening to infants about what life is like in childcare: A mosaic approach. I. In S. Roulstone & S. McLeod (Eds.), *Listening to children and young people with speech, language and communication needs* (pp. 241–250). London: J&R Press.

Rose, J. (2012). Dilemmas of inter-professional collaboration: Can they be resolved? *Children & Society, 25*(2), 151–163. doi:10.1111/j.1099-0860.2009.00268.x.

Schirato, T., & Webb, J. (2004). *Reading the visual.* Crows Nest: Allen & Unwin.

Selby, J. M. (1999). Cross-cultural research in health psychology: Illustrations from Australia. In M. Murray & K. Chamberlain (Eds.), *Qualitative health psychology: Theories and methods* (pp. 164–180). London: Sage.

Slade, B. (2012). From high skill to high school. *Qualitative Inquiry, 18*(5), 401–413. doi:10.1177/1077800412439526.

Sumsion, J. (in press). Opening up possibilities through team research: Investigating infants' experiences of early childhood education and care. *Qualitative Research.* doi:10.1177/1468794112468471

Sumsion, J., Harrison, L., Press, F., McLeod, S., Bradley, B., & Goodfellow, J. (2008–11). What is life like for babies and toddlers in childcare? Understanding the 'lived experience' of infants through innovative mosaic methodology. *Australian Research Council Linkage Project* LP0883913.

Sumsion, J., Harrison, L., Press, F., McLeod, S., Goodfellow, J., & Bradley, B. (2011). Researching infants' experiences of early childhood education and care. In D. Harcourt, B. Perry, & T. Waller (Eds.), *Researching young children's perspectives: Debating the ethics and dilemmas of educational research with children* (pp. 113–127). Milton Park/New York: Routledge.

Thomas, J. (2001). Introduction. In J. Thomas (Ed.), *Reading images.* Basingstoke: Palgrave.

White, E. J. (2011). 'Seeing' the toddler: Voices or voiceless? In E. Johansson & E. J. White (Eds.), *Educational research with our youngest: Voices of infants and toddlers* (pp. 63–85). Dordrecht: Springer.

Yoshida, H., & Smith, L. B. (2008). What's in view for toddlers? Using a head camera to study visual experience. *Infancy, 13*(3), 229–248. doi:10.1080/15250000802004437.

Chapter 11
Ethics in Researching Young Children's Play in Preschool

Hanne Værum Sørensen

Introduction

An individual never has anything to do with another person unless they personally care about that person's life. It need only be very little, a passing attitude, an engagement, one either gets to wither, or awakes, an association one develops or emphasizes. But it can also be shockingly much, so it is simply up to the individual person, whether the others person's life succeeds or not.[1] (Løgstrup 1956)

As Løgstrup[2] wrote about the ethical demand, we, as human beings, shape the conditions for the development of other human beings and thereby determine how another human being's life will be. Whether she or he will be successful or fail. He also wrote: "We are always holding a piece of another person's life in our hands, and therefore we have a responsibility to act ethically in relation to the other person regardless who the other person is." Many years earlier Kant[3] wrote that we as human beings must always act in a way that we want can be made to a general law: "Do unto others as you want them do unto you" (Kant 1797 cited in Hjort 2010, p.14). And Bayer (2010) writes: "ethics basically is about behaving properly." But what does it mean to do to others as one would want them to do to one self and what does it mean to behave properly? And how does a researcher know that she in this very moment is holding a piece of a young child's life in her hand? This is something that should be reflected and discussed when researchers engage themselves in human science and especially science where children are involved as focus in the research.

---

[1] Translation Dereck E. W. Chatterton, University of Copenhagen.

[2] Knud Erik Løgstrup, Danish philosopher (1905–1981).

[3] Immanuel Kant, German philosopher (1724–1804).

H.V. Sørensen, Ph.D. (✉)
VIA University College Pædagoguddannelsen,
Peter Sabroes Gade 14, DK 8000, Aarhus C, Denmark
e-mail: hsor@viauc.dk

M. Fleer and A. Ridgway (eds.), *Visual Methodologies and Digital Tools for Researching with Young Children*, International Perspectives on Early Childhood Education and Development 10, DOI 10.1007/978-3-319-01469-2_11,
© Springer International Publishing Switzerland 2014

Fig. 11.1 Did you tape me?

Conducting empirical cultural-historical research always involves interaction and relation with the subjects studied, and, therefore, ethical issues should be part of the methodological considerations in all phases of a research project. Not the least when the research is on children (Sørensen 2012). The researcher is part of the social situation she wants to observe. Investigating children's life affords sensitivity and respect of children's rights to privacy also when the children attend a public institution and even if their parents and the pedagogues have given their acceptance to the research activity (Robert-Holmes 2005). Acceptance from parents and pedagogues are given on behalf of the children but the researcher has to negotiate with the children by acting with respect and so to speak earn the children's acceptance to participate and observe in the situation where and when the research is conducted. The convention on the rights of the child (UNESCO 1989) also encourages those who work and research with young children to listen to the voices of children.

The topic in this chapter is a discussion of the considerations a researcher must do in the research of young children's play in preschool when she is using video. Examples from the project "Young children's physical activities in preschools" are applied to illustrate the ethical and methodological reflections. And the researcher on behalf of her research makes guidelines on how to deal with ethics and children in research (Fig. 11.1). The context of the research and the pedagogical ethics is preschools in Denmark, but consideration on ethics is relevant in child care institutions anywhere.

Visual Technologies in Research

By using visual technology several researchers have described how their studies of human beings are technically, analytically, and interpretively done, and thereby they have made significant and valuable contributions of scientific knowledge on people's lifestyles and conditions in foreign societies (Mead 1963 cited in Flick 2002) and on children's life and perspectives in school, kindergarten, and families (Fleer 2008; Fleer et al. 2006; Goldman and McDermott 2007; Quiñones, Chap. 7, this volume).

Building on this scientific ground, modern video technology affords different possibilities of researching the everyday life in preschool. Video data can support the researcher's memory (Rønholt et al. 2003) and the understanding of the social process of learning and development (Fleer 2008). Conducting video observations the researcher can follow some focus children and document their competences and the demands they meet from their environment, i.e., the pedagogues and get insight in the participants perspective on the everyday practice they are part of (Fleer 2008). Using video observation the researcher can document children's interactions and intentions in real-life situation by catching minor actions, movements, and expressions that would not have caught the observer's attention in the social situation of research (Goldman and McDermott 2007; Rønholt et al. 2003). Through analyses of video data, the researcher can observe the topic of the research, i.e., young children's physical activities and interactions (Schutz 2005).

Over the last 20 years, video research has done much progress and video equipment has become familiar in most people's life, so it is not so strange to be observed and videotaped any more (Flick 2002). But video must, according to Flick, be seen as a contextual enrichment of statements and activities. Video observation could be a main part of the data collection together with ethical considerations, as I will unfold further in this chapter.

Ethics in Research of Children

Recent research build on the Nuremberg Code (1949) that states "the absolute necessity for voluntary consent of research subjects and the necessity of allowing research subjects to withdraw from the research at any stage of the process" (Greg and Taylor 1999 cited in Robert-Holmes 2005). When the researched subjects are adults, the researcher can give written information, give the subjects a phone number to call if they have questions, ask them to come to a meeting, or give them a name of a home page to look for further information. Adults can confirm by signing a paper that they are well informed and know they can withdraw from the project at any time if they want to. But when the researched subjects are children, the parents must accept on their behalf but as an ethical researcher it is not enough, there is a need for ensuring that the children accept their own participation in the research. So a very relevant question to ask is: How can a researcher get an informed permission from the children? And how can a researcher detect if a child feel uncomfortable in the situation? How does the researcher know if a child wants to withdraw from the research? The permission has to be negotiated in relation to the specific child and in the specific situation.

The Nuremberg Code also stresses the qualifications of the researcher: The experiments in human science should be conducted only by scientifically qualified persons. The highest degree of skill and care should be required through all stages of the experiment of those who conduct or engage in the experiment. The Nuremberg Code also stresses that during the course of the experiment, the researcher must be prepared to terminate the experiment at any stage, if she has probably cause to believe, that a continuation of the experiment is likely to result in a negative outcome for the experimental subject (Nuremberg Code 1949).

Hammersley and Atkinson (2010, p.209) points out five headings of ethical issues in human science: informed consent, privacy, harm, exploitation, and consequences for further research. Again, different questions can be asked: Is an informed consent from parents or pedagogues enough when the research is on young children? And what is privacy in a public institution where a large group of children live their daily life together in limited space? Even if a research does not cost any physical harm, how can a researcher be sure that the research does not have negative psychological consequences for the children studied? Can the research make the children or the pedagogues feel they were exploited? How can a researcher predict what consequences her research has for further research? A researcher can have the best intentions to help and support children or the pedagogical practice, but an example of what can happen was when a Danish researcher was studying children's language acquisition in institutions and afterward was quoted for saying that many Danish crèches are so bad for the children that they should be shut down. Maybe some pedagogues afterward will say "no" if they were asked to participate in research? According to Bryman (2008) this implies a responsibility on the researcher to explain in appropriate detail, and in terms meaningful to participants, what the research is about, who is undertaking and financing it, why it is being undertaken, and how it is to be disseminated and used.

When researching children's life in preschools, ethical considerations connected to the research is not enough. The researcher has to deal with ethics in pedagogy as well, because, as van Manen wrote (1990, p.162), "pedagogical research cannot step outside the moral values that grant pedagogy its meaning." According to van Manen a pedagogically oriented human science researcher needs to be aware of that the research may have certain effects on the children with whom the research is concerned. The research can lead to feelings of discomfort or anxiety or the research can stimulate the child's learning and strengthen the child's insight in him or herself. The researcher must also be aware of that there are possible effects of the research methods on the institutions in which the research is conducted. For example, the pedagogical practices may be challenged or changed as a consequence of the increased awareness of how children experience, i.e., physical activities. The research methods used can have lingering effects on the actual "subjects" involved in the study. For example, participant observations and interactions may lead the child to new levels of self-awareness and to possible changes in activities and priorities.

Children's Everyday Life in Preschool

Children are physical, cognitive, social, and emotional active participants in their own and each other's developmental process through interactions and play and though a dynamic interaction with an environment which itself is dynamic and in progress as well as the child affect and is affected by the values and rules in the societal institution. This means that a study of children's development cannot just focus on the individual child but also has to include a study of the practices the children are part of with his or her individual motives and competences and investigate the conditions for learning and development (Hedegaard 2009; Vygotsky 1982), i.e., in children's physical activity play in preschools. Children grow up and develop in dialectical relationship with other people in different institutional contexts, and, therefore, the development of the child must be understood related to the actual conditions for the child (Vygotsky 1982, 1987, 1998; Rogoff 1990).

Young children in a modern society spend a good part of their everyday life in preschool together with peers and pedagogues. The pedagogues are significant parts of the pedagogical practice in preschools and they have to act in ethical ways too.

Pedagogues in day-care institutions do their job under the ethical and economic conditions decided by the society. The Danish day-care legislation from 2007 formulates that the purpose of the law is to promote the well-being, development, and learning of children and prevent negative social inheritance and exclusion. In addition to this, the children have the right to participate when decisions are made for them and the pedagogues must learn the children about democracy.

Play is the leading activity for preschool children, according to Vygotsky (1966, 1982). But play is not only a pleasurable activity for the child. Through play the child develops motives and competences and play stimulates the child to more activity and learning. According to Hedegaard (2008, 2009) the pedagogical practice and children's activities are the pivotal point in theories of child development. Preschools which offer inspiring and challenging conditions for children's play and experiences present a better frame for children's learning and development than preschools with restricted possibilities, i.e., physical activities and play (Quante 2011; Sandseter 2009).

Through *actions and interactions* in social situations in the pedagogical practice in preschool, children develop motives and competences as a result of the situated learning. Also, the child's self-awareness and well-being are influenced by the child's participation in social situations because the child learn about her or himself through social interactions (Hedegaard 1990, 2009) and through play children strive to learn about the life as adult (Fleer, Chaps. 1 and 2, this volume).

Children's social and cognitive development is closely connected to the activities they are engaged in. When the child engages in an activity or a dialog, it is because the activity or the dialog has a meaning to the child. She or he has a motive to engage, even if the motive is not very obvious to the adult observer. A deeper analysis is necessary as well as developing new concepts and methods to understand children's motives (Sørensen 2012).

Differences and Similarities in Ethical Considerations in Child Research and in Pedagogy

In the recent formulated ethics for pedagogues in Denmark, it is pointed out that the purposes of the pedagogical work in preschools are to promote children's well-being by ensuring all children's human rights, support children individually and socially, and create conditions for a safe and secure childhood in social communities (Aabro 2010). To meet these ethical objectives, the pedagogue must be proactive and take initiatives in interactions with children, which is different from what is demanded by the researcher. The pedagogues do have some learning and developmental goals for the children's development as the researcher do not have. It is expected by the pedagogue that she or he will lead the children somewhere in the process of learning. The aim of a cultural-historical researcher is to observe and learn from the observed subjects and their activities, and the researcher is expected to create scientific knowledge on children's development and learning.

But, there are also some similarities. The researcher and the pedagogue have to meet every child and family with respect and have to understand her or his responsibility for creating a good relation.

In the following part I will unfold the ethical considerations in my empirical study of children's physical activities and play in the pedagogical practice in preschool.

The Empirical Study

Focus in this study was on the pedagogical practice and on 5–6-year-old children's activities, especially on the interactions between the pedagogical practice in preschool and children's physical activities.

The Study Design

Research Question: What role and function does physical activity have in children's play in different preschools?

Participants: Fifty-five children aged 5–6 and their pedagogues in three different preschools, one sports preschool and two mainstream preschools in Denmark. Two physically active children, one girl and one boy, from each preschool were chosen as focus children in cooperation with the pedagogues.

Method: In the study participant observations were combined with video observations of the focus children in their activities especially trying to capture their physical activity play. As it was expected that physical activity play was more likely to occur on the playground and not inside the preschool (Grøntved et al. 2009), the researcher spent most of her time outdoor on the playground. According to Flick (2002) participant observation comes closest to a conception of qualitative research as a process, because the method assumes a longer period in the field and in contact with persons and contexts to be studied.

Analysis: The analysis of the video observations was conducted using the interaction-based method of observation based on the dialectical-interactive research approach formulated by Hedegaard (1990, 2008). The analysis focused on the children's intentions related to their physical activity play, on the interactions in the play, on conflicts in the play, and on the children's development of motives and competences through the physical activity play.

Findings: The study concluded that physical activity can have an important role in children's play and have several roles and functions. There seem to be positive effects of physical activity on children's development of social and personal competences and on their cognitive and emotional development as well. Video observations showed considerable differences in the conditions for children's physical activities in play in different preschools, and the sports preschool offered the best possibilities. Children in the different preschools had the same motives and intentions related to physical activity in their play. The children were physically active in play, because it was fun and it was nice to be with friends in a physical activity. And children achieved or qualified a special competence and challenged their own competences as well as the other children's competences. The pedagogical practice in preschools can support children's joy of movement and the pleasure of using the body in an active way and also support children's testing their own competences. Through physical activity children can support their own development and strengthen their feeling of self-assurance. The pedagogical practice can also set limitations for children's physical activity and their joy of movement and body activity.

Participant's Informed Consent: All researchers who want to study young children in preschool must, besides getting the children's informed consent first and foremost, get acceptance from the children's parents and the pedagogues to get permission to visit the day-care institution. The manager and the public authorities must also give acceptance to the study. This process can be more or less troublesome. It is very likely that because this study is part of a larger study of how children's health, well-being, and development are related to their conditions of physical activity in preschool, the study did not meet as much resistance from authorities, parents, or pedagogues as other researchers must deal with (Stanek 2011). I was allowed to visit and conduct video observations of all children in the preschool. My interest area was in the 5–6-year-old children, but I predicted that I would meet situations where younger children participated in play with the 5–6-year-old children. I also obtained acceptance to use the visual data in my dissemination.

Intentions and Motives in Research

Before conducting the video observation, I considered my intentions and motives for the specific part of the research process and for my participatory role in the interactions with the children and my actions in the empirical process (Table 11.1).

Before Undertaking the Video Observations

As a researcher I cannot be neutral and without any influence on the research situation, because I am part of the same cultural-historical social situation as the researched persons are. So I must communicate how my aims are different from the pedagogues' and the children's aim in the situation (Hedegaard 2008; Schutz 2005).

Table 11.1 Researcher's intentions, motives, interactions, and actions in the empirical process

Time	Intentions and motives	Interactions and actions
Before undertaking the video observations	To introduce myself and my camera To inform the children about my project to get their consent to participate To inform the children about what they can expect from me, and what I expect from their participation To make the children feel safe in the research situation	Telling who I am, not a pedagogue nor a playmate, but I am interested in watching and taping their activities Showing the camera, let children hold it in their hands and sense it Telling when I will tape, and when I will not tape, e.g., I have decided not to tape children in situations where they could not walk away from the camera
While undertaking video observations	To show respect to the children's play and activities To show my interest in their activities and thoughts To be seen as a reliable and responsible adult who will intervene if a child needs help	Answering children's questions about me, the camera, and anything else Appropriate admiration of the children's activities and competences like their cakes baked in the sandpit and so on Changing position from researcher to "ordinary adult" like most adults in preschool
After video observations	To show my respect and recognition and to be an "ordinary adult in preschool" To show my interest in the children as persons not only as research objects	Talking with children and pedagogues Participating in meals and other community activities Taking photos when a farewell to the oldest children's party was going on in preschool

This means that the researcher must share the aims of her activities as well as her motives and intentions. Preschool children are used to interact with different adults in preschools and can be expected to continue their play activities when the researcher has told about herself and the research (Hedegaard 2008). The pedagogues can be expected to work even more carefully in the beginning of the research period, and therefore their intentions will be clearer (Rønholt et al. 2003).

The main focus in this study is the children's physical activity, but children's physical activity cannot be seen isolated from the children's other activities especially the play, which is the children's leading activity in preschool age (Vygotsky 1978; Fleer 2009).

It is obvious but important to mention that before conducting the video observations, the researcher must decide who is in focus for the observations and what she wants to tape. In this study the aim of the research was to gain insight in what role and function physical activity has in children's play in preschool and so the researcher pointed the camera on the focus children when they were physically active in activities organized by the pedagogues or in self-organized play. In a study like this the researcher can find out when the organized physical activities are expected to take place but she cannot control when situations with physical activity will occur in children's play and has to wait for it to turn up naturally. When the researcher chooses focus children who according to the pedagogues use to be physically active in their play, she can expect good opportunities for physical activity to occur on children's initiative in natural situations in preschool. The researcher must try to be at the right place at the right time – and she has to be patient, not forcing activities so children eventually can get into awkward or dangerous situations.

My aim in this cultural-historical research was not to try to describe practice objectively independent of the participants (Robert-Holmes 2005) but to describe children's perspective on physical activity.

At my first meeting with the children, there were around 20 children aged 5–6 years, and their pedagogue placed in a circle, sitting on pillows on the floor.[4] My intention was to introduce myself as a researcher with an interest in watching and filming their activities with the purpose to learn about how it is to be a child in their preschool and learn about what children are engaged in when playing. I also wanted to inform the children about my project to get their consent to participate and to inform the children about what they can expect from me, and what I expect from their participation. I told the children that I was neither a pedagogue nor a playmate, but I would be happy to talk with them and watch their play activities. I showed the camera, let children hold it in their hands and sense it, and let the camera circulate so all children could try to hold it. I told when I have planned to tape and when I would not tape.

I wanted to make the children feel safe in relation to me and in the research situation. And to create a positive relation and let the children know that I was a kind of adult who would be friendly, nice to talk with, and an adult who would give a serious answer to any question. I wanted to contribute to the interaction with the children as Bae (2009) underlines as important for teachers, but this is also important for a participant researcher. This consideration meant that I wanted to follow children's initiative, and let the children choose what they wanted to do and what I could video-film. In addition to this, I strived to form responsive and playful interactions with the children.

While Undertaking Video Observations in Preschool

Constantly while doing my participatory research and undertaking video observations, I considered the ethics in my participation in the everyday life in preschool and made sure I had the children's consent at any time. I acted like a friendly and

---

[4] Sitting like this in a circle before lunch talking about what is on schedule in the preschool or what happened at home in the weekend is a daily activity in many preschools, so this was a well-known situation for the children.

responsible adult without taking part of the child-rearing tasks as the pedagogues are required to, according to the day-care legislation. My goal was to be seen as a reliable and responsible adult who will intervene if a child needs help.

When filming I held the camera in front of me, in waist height, so my face was visible and I could have eye contact with the children I communicated with, the same way Quiñones (Chap. 7, this volume) held her camera. I answered children's questions about my person, the camera, and anything else, and I strived to show appropriate admiration of the children's activities and competences like their cakes baked in the sandpit and so on. In that way I showed respect to the children's play and activities and my interest in their activities and thoughts as well.

Sometimes while I was filming, I found myself in situations craving that I left my role as observer and instead intervened appropriate in relation to a child. I acted according to my knowledge about children, to my insight in the pedagogical work, to my ethics as a psychologist, and of course, as a responsible and ethic researcher (Schutz 2005; Stanek 2011). One example was when a child was hanging with her head down on a fence and suddenly realized that she did not know how to get back on her feet again and cried out loud. I stopped filming and helped her down.

Another example was when I was filming Elizabeth and Victoria walking on stilts on the playground and they several times contacted me:

> Elizabeth and Victoria are walking on stilts in the grass, holding hands and both wearing a big, happy smile. While reaching the observer they shout in one voice: *We are coming closer and closer and closer...* The observer smiles back and continue filming.

The two girls contacted me in a happy and playful way with an expression of self-awareness showing that it was very funny and inspiring for their play, that they by walking on stilts were as tall as adults and thereby in eye level with the observer.

There were several situations where children contacted me, as they did contact the pedagogues. Jeff and Michael asked me to confirm their understanding of the English word "good-bye." In that situation I was nearby them and they saw me as one, whom they expected to know something about language. If a pedagogue has been there, she or he would have been asked. Another question was asked by Marwan, who wanted to know if a killer snail really could kill. I heard the question as serious and answered him seriously.

When a child directly or indirectly expressed that she or he did not want to be filmed, I accepted and went away to film the other focus child in the preschool. Especially Jeff sometimes showed that he did not want to be filmed by asking *Why do you always film here by me?* In other situations he seemed to like my attention, for example, one day where he was on the swing, swinging high and jumping off, and told me that if it had been a competition, he would have won it.

The pedagogues saw me as a responsible person with pedagogical insight and interest related to children's well-being and safety but without wanting to enforce every rule in the preschool or joining the child-rearing task. This agreed with the function I wanted to have as a researcher and with the way the children conceived me. For example, I filmed some children playing with a skipping rope as they were not allowed to do without adult supervision. The pedagogues told me afterward that they were sure that I would shift from a role as an observer to a role as a pedagogue if the situation asked for it.

After Video Observations

When I had finished conducting video observations for the day, or had a break, when children and pedagogues were engaged in routine activities as having a meal, walking to the library, or a birthday party, I continued my participation. For example, I continued talking with children and pedagogues, showing that my interest was in them as subjects not only as "research objects" so I continued to be an "ordinary adult in preschool." In one preschool I took some photos while there was a farewell party for the oldest children, who would leave preschool and start school in the summer break. By my acting as an ordinary adult in preschool, it is my opinion that I and my video observations had a minimum of disturbing effects on the everyday life in the preschools. Video equipment was well known by most of the children, and when they had seen the camera, touched it, and looked into the screen, the children felt safe about the camera, and because I participated in the everyday life in preschool as an ordinary adult and interacted in positive and friendly ways with the children and the pedagogues in several days, it is my opinion that both children and pedagogues felt safe and acted as they would have done in the situation, also without me being present.

Beneath I will present how I analyzed and interpret a social situation where I video observed and interacted with Sophia.

Did You Get It on the Tape?

As I have mentioned earlier, a researcher must constantly be aware of the ethical implications related to her interaction with children. A child must be seen as a subject who through her activities and interactions with a researcher and her camera and who as it can be seen in this transcript, develops societal knowledge as well as knowledge about herself and competences. The researcher must be aware of that she intervenes in the child's development and self-understanding and must act ethically.

This transcript also shows that through standing behind the camera, the researcher had an active role in the interaction with Sophia when she wanted to replay the situation, where she fell of a flying fox and was frightened. The example shows how the researcher's ethical considerations expand a child's self-image by showing that she was an important person for the researcher.

Transcript of Video Observation

Participants in the social situation were the focus girl Sophia (6 years, 3 months) and researcher, Hanne. The setting was the playground on a nice summer day, and Hanne was following and video-observing Sophia's activities (Fig. 11.2).

Sophia climbs to the top of a tree trunk and she asks Hanne: *Will you tape me jumping down from here? Will you?* Hanne: *Mmm… yes.* Sophia: *Will you film me?* Hanne: *Yes, I am filming you.* Sophia jumps down looking at Hanne: *Are you filming now?* Hanne smiles, nodding her head, and answers: *Yes.* Sophia: *Did you film?* Hanne: *Yes, I did.*

Sophia takes a ride on the flying fox along with two other children. The first time they sweep around and ride down while they are laughing out loud. They run up on the landing to take a trip more. Second time Sophia falls of and lands on her stomach in the sand. She cries very loud, and the other children walk toward her. One of them asks if she is all right. There are no pedagogues at sight. I turn off the camera and also walk toward her, I help her on her feet, brushes the sand of her clothes and comfort her.

When Sophia realizes that I did not film her when she felt off the flying fox, she suggests that she can show the accident again, so I can get it on the tape. I agree and Sophia walks to the spot where she fell off, and she places herself on the ground, gazing to me and the camera.

Sophia: *Do you take it?* Hanne: *Yes, I film now.* Sophia makes crying sounds, while she is kicking in the ground, imitating what she did before, when she really fell off.

Sophia takes one more trip on the flying fox and let herself fall off on the ground again.

Sophia: *Did you tape it?* Hanne: *Yes, I did.* Sophia runs for another trip on the flying fox, shouting to Hanne: *Are you ready?* Hanne: *Yes.* Sophia: *Now.* She slides down, watching the camera, and lets herself fall off again nicely in front of Hanne and the camera.

After playing the accident again she continues toward the tree trunks, balances back and forth, looks at Hanne and says: *Taadaa – and now you must tape me jumping down.* She jumps down. Stands with the arms stretched out, like an actor. *Did you tape me?* Hanne answered: *Yes I did.* Sophia ran toward Hanne with a happy smile on her face.

Interpretation of the Activity

Sophia was very active in the communication and interaction with the researcher. She knew that a replay could ensure that the researcher got her accident on the tape, and she seemed to like the idea of being taped; she was playing up to the camera, smiling, and stretching the arms (Fig. 11.3).

Like Løgstrup wrote it, I was holding Sophia's life in my hands, when we interacted by the flying fox. When I stopped the video camera and helped her up, after she fell on the ground, I showed her that she was more important than the video observation and the research. And when I agreed to tape her replaying of the accident, I showed her that her experience was important for me and my research and for other people to learn how it feels to fall of a flying fox. If I had not stopped the camera, I would have reduced myself from being a reliable adult to be an un-empathic onlooker to others' misery, which would express a very unethical attitude to children.

Fig. 11.2 Sophia on the flying fox, just before she fell off

Fig. 11.3 Sophia shows the researcher what happened

Fig. 11.4 Did you get it on the tape?

With Sophia's creative replay of her accident (Fig. 11.4), she showed that she could connect her story about her experience with falling of a flying fox together with an imagination of the researcher's interest, and it also showed her level of cognitive development. She did not just recall the situation, she replayed it for an audience and she reflected on her experience in her interaction with me and the camera, and thereby she showed in action what Vygotsky (1987) wrote that memory activity is not only about recalling an experience but about reflecting on it and making it meaningful in the sociocultural context. The development of imagination is linked to the development of speech and to the development of the child's social interaction with those around her (Vygotsky 1987). Through Sophia's interaction with me, she actively contributed to the cultural-historical research on the learning possibilities in physical activities. She proved how her imagination of the researcher and the audience watching her accident would contribute to the knowledge of what is going on in a preschool. And she was able to convince the researcher of the importance in the situation and make her video film a replay of the accident. She imagined the researcher's perspective and concluded that the researcher might think that something was missing in the research if the accident was not filmed.

The situation also showed that the researcher's way of interacting with Sophia is critical to her learning from the interaction. By acting as an engaged and empathic adult, the researcher contributed to the image of Sophia as a competent and clever girl.

What motives and intentions did Sophia have? Did she remember that my research goal was to show what is going on in a preschool and thought that the accident would be important to include, or did she enjoy interacting with a friendly adult? My interpretation is that she through the process of interaction imagined the importance of showing the accident, and thereby the interaction in the social situation of filming the accident contributed to Sophia's learning and development and to the researcher's learning and development as an ethical researcher too.

If I as an observer and a powerful adult had not stopped the camera and comforted Sophia when she fell from the flying fox, I would have acted unethically. If I had continued to video observe, I would have broken the ethical codes both for pedagogues who are responsible for children's development and well-being and the ethic codes for proper research behavior. I would have reduced her to be a research object, not a subject in her own right.

What Does the Surveillance Camera Say?

In the next situation when the researcher interacted with Mark about being video-filmed, it was a bit hard to judge if Mark was serious about asking what the surveillance camera had caught (Fig. 11.5). Was it all playful or was he really anxious? I interpret it mostly as a part of a play including some spy activity parallel to the physical activity play on the playground.

Transcript of Video Observation

Participants in this social situation were Mark and three other boys, Victor, William, and Jonas, all 5–6 years old, and Hanne with the camera. In this situation my focus was on Victor, but I became interested in Mark because of his insisting on

Fig. 11.5 What does the surveillance camera say?

communicating with me about the surveillance camera. The setting was the playground a day in spring time. I was following the boys to video observe their physical activity play on the playground.

> Mark and some other boys are looking after toys in a big box. They find some and bring it with them in a smaller box. Mark asks researcher: *What does the surveillance camera say?* Hanne answers: *It says there is plenty of activity on the playground.*
>
> Mark repeats his question: *Hey, what does the surveillance camera say now?* Hanne answer: *It says that there are children playing on the playground, and that the sun is shining.* Mark: *Is somebody playing?* Hanne: *Mmm, yes.*
>
> Mark walks in front of the camera, waving. *Hey, what does the surveillance camera say? Does it say that somebody is waving?* Hanne: *Yes it does.*
>
> The boys put the toy in a wheelbarrow. They talk while they walk around on the playground, so if I want to film them, I have to follow them around. I tried to be close enough to see what they were doing, but on a distance to make them feel free to do what they wanted. Mark look back over his shoulder to see if they are being followed by researcher.
>
> After a while they stopped at a small tower with a slide. Victor and William stood on the tower. Victor said: *I dare to jump down there, and turn around in the air.* Mark looked at Hanne, and said: *He is doing it, he is doing it, Hanne.*
>
> Victor stood on the edge of the slider, jumps down, as he planned to do. Mark said, with some admiration in his voice: *He did it, did you see, he did it, while he was turning around in the air.*
>
> The five boys were playing around the tower for a while and then they took a walk around on the playground. They talked with some girls playing on a slide. Mark told the girls that they are under surveillance, one of the girls answer him: *No, we are not.* Mark turned around and walked in front of Hanne, and asked: *What does the surveillance camera say? Is somebody walking around on the playground?* Hanne smiled and answered him: *Yes.*

Interpretation of the Activity

Mark was very consistent in asking the observer about the surveillance camera and in the situation I had to consider if it would be ethical to continue video-observing his activities. I interpret his actions and interactions as he was inspired to the spy play because of the camera and me observing him and his playmates and maybe because he wore a balaclava helmet that could associate to a helmet wore by a spy or another person who would not like to be caught by a surveillance camera and the play was on this basis (Fig. 11.6). Maybe he was not quite sure of what suspicious activities a surveillance camera would catch, so he pointed out Victor's jumping down from the tower as something important for me to video-film.

There were several other situations where I left my role as a researcher and became a responsible adult. Another example was when Johanne learned how to hang on a fence with her head down and Annlisa also tried to do it, but had to give up and cried for someone to help her. In that situation I stopped filming and helped Annlisa back on the feet again.

Fig. 11.6 Mark and the other
boys looking after toys

Dissemination

The process of documenting the data comprises mainly three steps: recording the
data (Fig. 11.7), editing the data (transcription), and constructing a "new" reality in
and by the produced text. All in all, this process is an essential aspect in the construction of reality in the research project and Dahlberg et al. (2007) emphasized
that documentation never can be an innocent activity. Documentation has always
got social and political implications and consequences. With reference to Foucault
they connect the production of knowledge to the production of power. Documentation
can be used to stigmatize children in different categories or pedagogues as lazy and
uninterested in children, as the Danish researcher mentioned earlier in this chapter
did or documentation can potentially open new perspectives and understanding, so
that pedagogical practices in preschools in the future will offer more opportunities
for children's physical activities in play by renewing playgrounds and allowing
exciting activities.

Conclusion

In this chapter I have discussed the importance of the researcher's ethical considerations when researching children's activities. With examples from my study of
children's physical activities, I have shown how it can be realized in cultural-historical
research using video technology.

My conclusion is that because I have a degree in early childhood education,
several years of experience in the field and in child research, I could participate in the
children's everyday life in preschool. I could conduct video observations and gain
insight in the children's motives and intentions related to the physical activity and
their learning and development of competences through physical activities as well.

Fig. 11.7 Walking on the playground

Because my primary aim was to be a researcher, not a pedagogue, I sometimes decided not to intervene in children's activities, although the activities could be against the rules in the preschool, i.e., when children were playing with something they were not allowed to play with. But when a child was scared of falling down, or was hurt, I intervened of ethical reasons being a responsible and reliable adult, who cared about the children's self-understanding and self-confidence.

I will end this chapter with providing some guidelines on how to deal with ethics and children in research. The researcher must

- Have a thorough knowledge on children's learning and development in institutional practices
- Have insight in the legislation and the purpose of the researched institution
- Be familiar with the children to be researched
- Be ready and able to change position from researcher to responsible adult in every situation

References

Aabro, C. (Ed.) (2010). *Pædagogers etik – en antologi* [Ethics in pedagogy – An anthology]. Copenhagen: BUPL.

Bae, B. (2009). Children's right to participate – Challenges in everyday interactions. *European Early Childhood Education Research Journal, 17*(3), 391–406.

Bayer, S. (2010). Etikkens kultur eller kulturens etik. In C. Aabro. (Ed.), *Pædagogers etik – en antologi* [Ethics in pedagogy – An anthology]. Copenhagen: BUPL.

Bryman, A. (2008). *Social research methods* (3rd ed.). Oxford: Oxford University Press.

Dahlberg, G., Moss, P., & Pence, A. (2007). *Beyond quality in early childhood education and care: Languages of evaluation* (2nd ed.). Great Britain: Routledge.

Fleer, M. (2008). Using digital video observations and computer technologies in a cultural-historical approach. In M. Hedegaard, & M. Fleer with J. Bang, & P. Hviid (Eds.), *Studying children: A cultural-historical approach*. Maidenhead/New York: Open University Press.

Fleer, M. (2009). A cultural-historical perspective on play: Play as a leading activity across cultural communities. In I. Pramling-Samuelson & M. Fleer (Eds.), *Play and learning in early childhood settings*. London: Springer.

Fleer, M., Edwards, S., Hammer, M., Kennedy, A., Ridgway, A., Robbins, J., & Surman, L. (2006). *Early childhood learning communities – Sociocultural research in practice*. Frenchs Forest: Australia Pearson Education Australia.

Flick, U. (2002). *An introduction to qualitative research*. London: Sage.

Goldman, S., & McDermott, R. (2007). Staying the course with video analysis. In R. Goldman, R. Pea, B. Barron, & S. J. Denny (Eds.), *Video research in the learning sciences*. Hillsdale: Lawrence Erlbaum Associates.

Grøntved, A., Pedersen, G. S., Andersen, L. B., Kristensen, P. L., Møller, N. C., & Froberg, K. (2009). Personal characteristics and demographic factors associated with objectively measured physical activity in children attending preschool. *Pediatric Exercise Science, 21*, 209–219.

Hammersley, M., & Atkinson, P. (2010). *Ethnography: Principles in practice*. London: Routledge.

Hedegaard, M. (1990). *Beskrivelse af småbørn* [Describing young children]. Århus: Aarhus Universitetsforlag.

Hedegaard, M. (2008). The role of the researcher. In M. Hedegaard, & M. Fleer, with J. Bang, & P. Hviid (Eds.), *Studying children: A cultural-historical approach*. Maidenhead/New York: Open University Press.

Hedegaard, M. (2009). Children's development from a cultural-historical approach: Children's activity in everyday local settings as foundation for their development. *Mind, Culture and Activity, 16*, 64–81.

Hjort, K. (2010). Om velfærdsstatens forandringer og pædagogers professionsetik. In C. Aabro (Ed.), *Pædagogers etik – en antologi* [Ethics in pedagogy – An anthology]. Copenhagen: BUPL.

Løgstrup, K. E. (1956). *Den etiske fordring* [The ethical challenge]. Denmark: Gyldendal.

Nuremberg Code. (1949). *Trials of war criminals before the Nuremberg Military Tribunals under Control Council Law No. 10* (Vol. 2, pp. 181–182). Washington, DC: U.S. Government Printing Office.

Quante, S. (2011). *Self-efficacy and climbing. "I can do it" – How to enhance self-efficacy beliefs in children aged 4–6 through physical activity and climbing in kindergarten.* 21st EECERA annual conference, Switzerland.

Robert-Holmes, G. (2005). *Doing your early years research project*. London: Sage.

Rogoff, B. (1990). *Apprenticeship in thinking: Cognitive development in social context*. New York: Oxford University Press.

Rønholt, H., Holgersen, S.-E., Fink-Jensen, K., & Nielsen, A. M. (2003). *Video i pædagogisk forskning* [Video in pedagogical research]. Denmark: København.

Sandseter, E. B. H. (2009). Risky play and risk management in Norwegian preschools – A qualitative observational study. *Safety Science, 13*(1), 1–12.

Schutz, A. (2005). *Hverdagslivets sociologi*. København: Hans Reitzels Forlag.

Sørensen, H. V. (2012). *Børns fysiske aktivitet i børnehaver* [Young children's physical activities in preschool]. Ph.D.-thesis, University of Southern Denmark.

Stanek, A. (2011). *Børns fællesskaber og fællesskabernes betydning – analyseret i indskolingen fra børnehave til 1. klasse og SFO*. Roskilde Universitet. Denmark: Roskilde

UNESCO. (1989). *The convention on the rights of the child.* www.unesco.org

Van Manen, M. (1990). *Researching lived experience. Human science for an action sensitive pedagogy*. Albany: State University of New York Press.

Vygotsky, L. S. (1966). Play and its role in the mental development of the child. *Voprosipsikhologii, 12*(6), 62–76.

Vygotsky, L. S. (1978). Mind in society. In M. Cole, V. John-Steiner, S. Schribner, & E. Souberman (Eds.), *The development of higher psychological processes*. Cambridge: Harvard University Press.

Vygotsky, L. S. (1982). *Om barnets psykiske udvikling* [Child development]. Denmark: København.

Vygotsky, L. S. (1987). *Problems of general psychology* (The collected works of L. S. Vygotsky, Vol. 1). New York: Plenum Press.

Vygotsky, L. S. (1998). *Child psychology* (The collected works of L. S. Vygotsky, Vol. 5). New York: Plenum Press.

Part IV
Central Concepts for Researching with Young Children Using Digital Visual Tools

Chapter 12
Method, Methodology and Methodological Thinking

Nikolai Veresov

> *Culture itself profoundly refines the natural state of behavior of the person and alters completely anew the whole course of his development. (Vygotsky 1997, p. 223)*

Introduction

I would like to start this concluding chapter with two references which, as I see them, create a 'contextual space' and might help to identify the place of this book within this space. At first glance these two references have no connections with each other; however, a closer look might open a new perspective, which, as I will try to show, is strongly methodological.

The first quotation is from the book *Methodological Thinking in Psychology: 60 Years Gone Astray*? As Toomela (2010) claims:

Analysis of common textbooks on research methodology in modern psychology... as well as everyday research practices of scholars shows that scientific thinking does not go beyond cookbook type behavioral recipes that are supposed to underlie scientific studies... Validity is a notion that should describe whether a test measures what it is supposed to measure. Modern psychology, instead, understands validity as a question of how test scores (i.e., behavioral 'external' outcomes of test-filling behavior) fit with some theory; and the validity is proved by a set of statistical data analysis procedures with the test scores. (p. 8)

In line with Toomela (2010), I argue that one central methodological problem is that statistical data analysis cannot in principle answer two basic questions: (1) Does the attribute that is being supposedly measured by a test really exist? (2) Do variations in the attribute causally produce variations in the outcomes of the

N. Veresov, Ph.D. (✉)
Faculty of Education, Monash University, Melbourne, Australia
e-mail: nikolai.veresov@monash.edu

M. Fleer and A. Ridgway (eds.), *Visual Methodologies and Digital Tools for Researching with Young Children*, International Perspectives on Early Childhood Education and Development 10, DOI 10.1007/978-3-319-01469-2_12,
© Springer International Publishing Switzerland 2014

measurement procedure? There is no way to prove whether one or several different mechanisms underlie behaviour encoded as a variable, and there is also no way to prove a causal relation from the pattern of covariations between variables (Toomela 2010, p. 8).

The second reference comes from Kilderry et al. (2004). These authors have undertaken a critical analysis of the field of research in early childhood and conclude that new ways of researching with children are being explored within the early childhood education sector.

> 'There is a strong tendency of researching *with children* rather than researching *on children*. This transformation is not only changing the nature of discussions about educational research in early childhood, but is also changing the positioning of such research. This reconceptualised view of early childhood research has the potential to change the way research looks where *children* can benefit from being part of the process and can tell their own story' (p. 25).

These two references reflect the contemporary tendency of rethinking the research methodology both in psychology and in early childhood studies. Such a rethinking is not only about limitations of statistical methods, measurements and validity issues, it is about searching for new ways in research and therefore a new methodology per se. This methodological book addresses these issues and suggests new ways of rethinking the research methodology in educational and psychological studies of young children. This book is not a collection of answers but rather an invitation to researchers from the field to start rethinking research methodology from within the theoretical paradigms of both cultural-historical framework and critical and poststructuralist theories.

However, what do we mean by 'research methodology', 'research methods' and 'methodological thinking'?

The term 'methodology' might be used in two contexts. Firstly, by 'methodology' we mean a set of concrete specific tools and instruments of research selected by the researcher according to his/her research question and theoretical framework. Briefly, it might look like an answer to the question: 'What are specific research settings, design, instruments and procedures I should use to answer my research question?' Nowadays, this understanding of methodology is common in academia; however, looking from a historical perspective, this meaning is not the only one (see, e.g. Bickhard 1992).

Another meaning of 'methodology' is a general view on methods and principles which constitute scientific knowledge. This understanding comes from European pre-Second World War tradition. It is specifically important in relation to Vygotsky's school since in Russian scientific tradition 'the methodology of science' is used exclusively in this sense (see, e.g. Kornilova and Smirnov 2007). Interestingly, in all Vygotsky's texts, the term 'methodology' (or 'methodological') was used exclusively in this context.[1] In other words, methodology is this sense of the word might

---

[1] For example, Vygotsky's view 'the one-sidedness and erroneousness of the traditional view …on higher mental functions' is 'in an incorrect basic understanding of the nature of the phenomena being studied…Putting it more simply, with this state of the matter, the very process of development of complex and higher forms of behaviour remained unexplained and unrealised methodologically' (Vygotsky 1997, p. 2).

look as a series of questions: How do researchers formulate their research questions? How do researchers create their research strategies and experimental designs by selecting appropriate and relevant methods according to their research questions? What are the principles of organising, conducting, monitoring and validating of experimental procedures? What are the principles of collecting and analysing of research data? This is consistent with the approach taken by the authors of the chapters in this book regardless of their theoretical framework.

The two approaches to methodology discussed here presuppose two different types of methodological thinking. The first type is thinking about your research methods, tools, instruments and procedures. Second type of thinking is a reflection on where your research question came from, what are the main principles of your selection of the research methods and procedures and whether your research question and methods fit the theoretical framework.

To make this point clear, I would use an example of Toomela (2010):

> I have found four questions to be very helpful to be asked and answered in any study and by any scientist:
>
> 1. What do I want to know, what is my research question?
> 2. Why I want to have an answer to this question?
> 3. With what specific research procedures (methodology in the strict sense of the term) can I answer my question?
> 4. Are the answers to three first questions complementary, do they make a coherent theoretically justified whole? (p. 9)

Answering all four questions is what the methodological thinking in the second sense is about, whereas only one question in this list directly relates to the methodology in the first sense. We could reformulate the last question into two subquestions: What theoretical and experimental tools do I need in order to create a research strategy to answer my research question? Are my theoretical tools (concepts and principles) of research and experimental research tools (methods, settings, procedures) in correspondence with each other?

This is one of possible examples of methodological thinking; in this case methodological thinking is focused on how the design of the research strategy corresponds to the research question and theoretical framework. What makes this book unique is that it contains several examples of methodological thinking of this type. Since they are presented implicitly, what I am going to do in this chapter is to 'unpack' them in order to show several directions of how cultural-historical methodology (in wide sense) informs research methodology (in strict sense). The same arguments could be applied when using critical theory (Agbenyega, Chap. 9, this volume) or poststructuralist theory (Sumsion et al., Chap. 10, this volume).

Cultural-Historical Theory and Research Methodology

We need cultural-historical approach as a methodological framework (in wide sense) because it focuses the researcher's lens on child's development. Yet, what does it mean 'to be focused on child's development'? What is child development as an object (process) under study, and how research *with children* rather than research *on children* would help to keep our lenses focused on development?

This book invites us to start rethinking these matters. Fleer puts forward this challenge:

> ...how can cultural-historical theory inform research into a child's development in ways which offer something new and help with gaining new understandings of children's development? Would a cultural-historical theory better inform our research practices than traditional maturational theory? (Chap. 2, this volume)

The content of this book provides answers to this challenging question. The core idea of cultural-historical theory is that child development is a social-cultural process where every higher mental functions originated in social environment is such a way that every child's 'higher mental function was social before it became an internal strictly mental function; it was formerly a social relation' (Vygotsky 1997, p. 105).

In other words, social relations in which a child as an active participant has his/her voice is the source of his/her development (Vygotsky 1998, p. 203). This theoretical framework does not only recognise the fact that child development takes place in a structured social world (Agbenyega, Chap. 9, this volume), this framework opens new perspectives in formulating research questions and developing research strategies.

These new perspectives, which are widely presented and discussed in this book, could be summarised in four key directions:

1. Changing the focus of research questions from stages of development to the process of development
2. Changing the focus of research strategies from investigation of child's behaviour to analysis of sociocultural contexts and institutions
3. Changing the focus from investigation of results ('fruits') to the processes of transformations of 'buds' into 'fruits'
4. Changing the focus from 'classical observations' to observations in existing or specially created experimental conditions

These directions are discussed in turn followed by a broad discussion of methodological principles, concluding with a theorisation of the role of researcher.

Methodological Principles

In this section, I take Toomela's questions on methodology and apply these to the content of this book in order to illustrate the central principles of the new methodology for theorising the study of young children. Together these four principles provide a new methodological foundation for childhood studies.

1. *Changing the focus of research questions from stages of development to the process of development.* Research questions and strategies based on traditional

maturational theories are mostly focused on developmental stages and milestones. Cultural-historical theory allows to study not only stages of development but to investigate development *as a process* of transitions from one stage to another through revolutionary qualitative changes and reorganisations. Vygotsky's books contain a number of examples of experimental studies of thinking (Vygotsky 1997, p. 198), memory (Vygotsky 1997, pp. 180–182), attention (Vygotsky 1997, pp. 153–177) and volition (Vygotsky 1997, pp. 207–219) from developmental perspective, i.e. as experimental investigations of complex processes of reorganisation and transition from 'natural' forms of these psychological processes to cultural forms, mediated by cultural tools.

Cultural-historical theory provides valuable research tools for investigation of transitions in dialectical perspective, i.e. through contradictions, collisions and their resolutions as moving/driving forces of development (for details see Fleer, Chap. 2, this volume; Veresov, Chap. 8, this volume).

2. *Changing the focus of research strategies from investigation of child's behaviour to analysis of sociocultural contexts and institutions.* As Hedegaard argues: 'Children's development takes place through participating in societal institutions.... Development can also be connected to the change in the child's social situation (i.e. when the child moves from one institution to the next or as a result of change in a particular practice within an institution)' (Hedegaard 2008, p. 11). Social and cultural institutions such as daycare centres, schools, families and communities do not only define certain developmental pathways for children.

Cultural-historical approach opens an opportunity to investigate sociocultural environments in a new direction, i.e. 'from the point of view of the relationship which exists between the child and its environment at a given stage of his development' (Vygotsky 1994, p. 338).

The concept of social situation of development obtains an important role in this respect. Social situation of development is 'a unique relation between the child and social reality [which] is an initial moment of all dynamic changes in development' (Vygotsky 1998, p. 198). The importance of the social situation of development is that it 'determines wholly and completely the forms and the path along which the child will acquire ever newer personality characteristics, drawing them from the social reality as from the basic source of development, the path along which the social becomes the individual' (Ibid.).

Therefore, cultural and social relationships are understood not only as backgrounds, environments or ecological systems where the child is located and where the child's development takes place, they are investigated as integral components of social situations of development. Cultural-historical theory provides powerful conceptual framework to investigate socially and culturally constructed pathways, milestones and transitions; however, what is more important is that this theory allows to create research strategies for studying unique individual trajectories of development of the child within these sociocultural contexts. It also allows for the study of these contexts, which are unique for each child, from the point of view of their developmental potentials through investigations of the qualities of social situations of development they contain. By 'the quality of social situation of development' I mean its developmental potential, i.e. a unique combination of developmental conditions and cultural tools the social situation contains. As such, sociocultural environments become objects under study not because they influence development but because they contain social situations of development as initial stage of processes of development.

In line with this, Li (Chap. 3, this volume), in presenting her research project, mentions that not many researchers focus on the ways in which adult interactions and communication contribute to children's heritage language development. The weakness of these research strategies is that those studies ignored the real social situations that determine the development of speech, specially, speech interaction (Li, Chap. 3, this volume, pp. 35–53). Li claims that cultural-historical approach creates new dimensions of a research by providing an opportunity of studying children's bilingual heritage language development *from* an analysis of the situation of development and the situation of speech interaction in home contexts.

> ...children are able to name, remember and categorise objects, not as a result of innate capabilities, whereby meanings exist in some kind of prior "language of thought", but because of the process of their interactions with others using communicative language, which verbalises these psychological processes. From this point of view, the methodological approach to studying children's bilingual development must be oriented by children's interactions and dynamic movements within their surroundings. (Li, Chap. 3, this volume)

Ridgway's research project (Chap. 4, this volume) aims to expand the researcher's capacity for investigating how institutional practices are formed, both temporally and dynamically, and thereby influencing children's development. Using a visual narrative methodology and the *past-present dialectic* as a research tool allows a researcher to factor in temporal, cultural and local historical perspectives of child development when examining the epistemological origins of various practices as phenomena over time.

Quinones (Chap. 7, this volume) argues that researchers following cultural-historical theory focus on capturing the wholeness of the different perspectives such as kindergarten and family practices through video-recording observation of these. Introducing 'visual vivencias' as a methodological tool for capturing children's moments of intense emotion and intellect/affect, Quinones analyses these moments through the prism of the context the child is participating in with others as a significant affective relationship which determines children's learning and development.

3. *Changing the focus from investigation of results ('fruits') to the processes of transformations of 'buds' into 'fruits'*. In her chapter, Monk (Chap. 5, this volume) refers to Vygotsky's basic methodological principle: 'what must interest us is not the finished result, not the sum or product of development, but the very *process of genesis or establishment ... caught in living aspect'* (Vygotsky 1997, p. 71). The question is how this general methodological principle informs research in early childhood, and how it helps to identify the research question of concrete study. Two of Vygotsky's metaphors help to answer these fundamental methodological questions. Veresov (Chap. 8, this volume) draws attention to the fact that at each age there is always a complex nexus of (1) functions that have not yet developed but are in the process of development, (2) functions that will develop but are currently in an

embryonic state and (3) developed functions. Metaphorically they could be defined as 'buds', 'flowers' and 'fruits' of development. This creates a basis to change the focus of research question from 'What psychological process am I going to investigate?' to 'Which stage of development is the process/function under study in?'

The second metaphor which complements the first one is that of the 'fossil'. As Fleer (Chap. 2, this volume) puts it, 'Vygotsky (1997) uses the metaphor of the "fossil" to make visible to the reader how the study of development in his time had focused primarily on the study of what had already formed and was complete, rather than what was in the process of development. Vygotsky (1997) argued that the research tools and their accompanying methodologies were designed to study *psychological fossils* "in a petrified and arrested form in their internal development"' (Vygotsky 1997, p. 44). He suggested that

'The beginning and end of development is united in them. They actually are outside of the process of development. Their own development is finished. In this combination of plasticity and fossilization, initial and final points of development, simplicity and completeness lies their great advantage for research, making them incomparable material for study' (Ibid.).

Reframing research questions from investigations of the 'fossils' or 'fruits' to the study of living, dynamic and contradictory *process* of sociocultural genesis of child's mind is what the cultural-historical approach requires.

As Monk states, 'Vygotsky's desire to study the process of development required methods of investigation that moved away from studying separate and developed functions to methods that were suitable when studying multifaceted, dynamic, socially formed whole processes' (Monk, Chap. 5, this volume). Her chapter, based on this general methodological principle, provides a brilliant example of a study of the process of child development from 'flowers' to 'fruits' within specially organised social contexts.

4. *Changing the focus from 'classical observations' to observations in existing or specially created experimental conditions.* Vygotsky introduced a new type of research methodology which 'artificially elicits and creates a genetic process of mental development' (Vygotsky 1997, p. 68). Due to this, researchers obtain an opportunity 'experimentally, in the laboratory, to elicit a certain development' (Ibid.). This means that a researcher not only observes child's behaviour in order to 'capture' changes and transformations but *observes* developmental conditions in children's everyday practices *or actively creates* such conditions to elicit a developmental process.

Thus, Monk (Chap. 5, this volume) introduces the intergenerational family dialogue as a tool which offers a new approach to researching everyday family practices 'holistically highlighting and at the same time uncovering the complexity and uniqueness of individual intergenerational families' (Monk, Chap. 5, this volume, pp. 73–88). An intergenerational dialogue therefore is presented in her research as a means to study a process of intergenerational development and learning in motion. As the author argues, 'it is a methodology anchored in a concrete historical setting and at the same time contributes towards an understanding of the *general conditions* that support child development' (Monk, Chap. 5, this volume, pp. 73–88). The author shows them situated in specific everyday practices of individual families that have been formed and transformed across generations and, at the same time, these specific practices are indicative of the everyday practices occurring in the wider society of which the family is a part (Ibid.).

Veresov (Chap. 8) introduces principles of cultural-historical experimental methodology focused on specially designed developmental conditions and provides an example of Vygotsky's experimental study of development of memory. Chapters of Monk and Veresov are examples of two main strategies of experimental research within the cultural-historical framework: (1) observation and analysis of existing sociocultural interactions in child's everyday life *as developmental conditions* and (2) creating and examining social situations/interactions from the point of view of the quality of developmental conditions they contain.

Cultural-historical theory itself was a result of methodological rethinking of the core question: 'What is a nature of development of human mind?' (Vygotsky 1997, p. 2). Child development manifests itself in transitions from one developmental level to another, but it is not limited by this aspect only. Underwater streams always remain hidden from direct observation of the surface. Child development is a complex process of how the social becomes the individual; it is a process originated and rooted in social situations of development and going through dramatic contradictions between demanding sociocultural contexts and child's experiences and resulted in qualitative changes in child's mind. I think that contributors of this book clearly demonstrate how cultural-historical theory can inform research into a child's development in ways which offer new perspectives and help with gaining new understandings of children's development. Cultural-historical approach informs research practices better than traditional maturational theories since it provides methodological possibilities of studying development not only as transition from one developmental level to another but as a complex, contradictory and unique process of becoming of a child's mind. This methodology makes it possible to investigate the very process of development from its initial form (social situation of development) to the final form ('fruits of development'). Cultural-historical methodology is a general framework where all specific research methods and procedures (experimental research tools) are selected in strong correspondence with the theoretical concepts and principles (theoretical research tools) and therefore make a coherent whole. This coherent whole of theoretical and experimental tools is what could be called 'cultural-historical research methodology'.

Cultural-Historical Theoretical Framework and Visual Methodologies: A Possible Meeting Point?

Agbenyega (Chap. 9, this volume) raises very important issue in respect to contemporary visual methodologies. He argues that despite visual approaches are increasingly becoming sophisticated in contemporary early childhood research, in many cases the visual is being used as appendages for textual data. In his opinion, critical reflexivity should become a key component of visual methodology because it enables researchers to be aware of the implications and effects of theory in relation to the social world they conjure up in their research. I would agree with Agbenyega's strong conclusion that without critical reflexivity visual research becomes depersonalising, objectifying, and compartmentalising and treats research participants in mechanical terms, neglecting visual research as lived experience (Agbenyega, Chap. 9, this volume, pp. 153–168).

On the other hand, experts in visual methodologies address these issues from different perspective. Thus, in recently published book 'Advances in Visual Methodology', Pink (2012) argues that an area of academic and applied research demonstrates particularly powerfully that the relationship between theory, technology and method should not be separated. Understanding methodology is concerned with comprehending how we know as well as the environments in which this knowing is produced. Research methods and the practical engagements they entail are inextricable from this process. It is therefore important to engage with both simultaneously and, in doing so, depart from the theory/methods divide.

> In the case of visual methodology this means understanding and engaging not only with the newest and latest theoretical developments in our fields, but also with the ways that these are co-implicated with technological developments and media practices. (Pink 2012, p. 3)

The task of critically reflexive rethinking the place and role of visual methodologies comes to contemporary agenda. In fact, this aspect of critical reflexive rethinking is about the relations between visual methodologies and theoretical frameworks; in other words, the question is not about how visual methodologies should be used within various theoretical frameworks but how visual methodologies can enrich theories and how theories can enrich visual methodologies. I believe this volume contributes to this general discussion by bringing a specific aspect which can be presented in short formula: 'What are ways of rethinking the role of visual methods as research tools in study of *processes* of child development?'

Thus, Fleer claims that building a methodology for the use of digital visual technologies has become an important research need for the study of young children's development (Fleer, Introduction to this volume). Standard approaches to making observations of children have been dominated by traditional views of development where progression is captured as a linear movement following maturational developmental norms. It becomes clear that these theories are limiting possible research strategies by excluding sociocultural contexts and sources of development. However, what kind of methodology of the use of visual technologies is needed?

Cultural-historical theory understands development as a process of sociocultural genesis of child's mind; it is not about 'fruits of development' or psychological fossils, and it requires to study development as a live process unfolding in space and time. The uniqueness of cultural-historical approach is that it makes it possible to expose and uncover the processes of development which, like underwater streams, underlie changes on a surface but remain hidden from direct observation and analysis. Cultural-historical framework makes them visible and, therefore, observable. Within this framework, visual methods of collecting data obtain an essential and crucial role.

This volume discusses some possible ways of theorising visual technologies as research tools by looking at them from the cultural-historical framework. On the other hand, it examines various directions of how visual methods might enrich the cultural-historical theory. In a certain sense, this volume implies a possible meeting point of visual methodologies and cultural-historical theory.

I totally agree with Fleer's claim that digital video observations provide detailed accounts of how, in everyday life, cultural development is shaped by and shapes the social situations of development. Digital video analysis allows these cultural interactions to be examined and re-examined, in ways which include the researcher and the researched, the material world and the past events that are active in the moment (Fleer, Chap. 2, this volume, pp. 15–34).

In other words, visual methods make possible not only to visualise the very process of how the social becomes the individual but allows to analyse this process in all its dialectical complexity. Ridgway (Chap. 4, this volume) uses video technology for recording of past-present dialectic as a research tool which shows the invisible relations of the 'past-present', in an early childhood site and its community. This study demonstrates a new direction of use of video technologies so that 'early childhood researchers more rigorously employ new tools for data gathering and analysis in the theoretical field of cultural-historical theory' (Ridgway, Chap. 4, this volume, pp. 55–72).

Visual technology also increases the cultural-historical researcher's awareness of research context while investigating children's development. As Li maintains, visual methodology offers a platform to support the researcher 'in capturing children's communication and interactions with their families at home, so as to discover how they develop their bilingual heritage language in relation to family pedagogy' (Li, Chap. 3, this volume, pp. 35–53). Video research using the wholeness approach enables multiple viewpoints by recording the dynamic and evolving nature of the social situations and interactive events in which children are located, where they construct their knowledge across institutions (family, community groups and preschool). Visual methodology provides a new dimension for understanding the dynamic interactive process between parents and children in order to find out how parents engage in children's bilingual heritage language development (Li, Chap. 3, this volume).

Cultural-historical framework provides possibilities of changing the role and place of visual research tools. They obtain a new status as they make it possible *to record* the processes, which become visible and observable being studied by cultural-historical methodological tools. They allow researchers to collect unique data, and even more, they allow the researcher to analyse these data, keeping a researcher focused on the process of (1) how the social becomes the individual (2) through transitions and reorganisations of child's mental functions (3) by obtaining and mastering of various cultural tools. Thus, Shin Pennay (Chap. 6, this volume) shows an excellent example of how video technologies which draw upon Hedegaard's (2008) framework provide unique possibilities for three levels of data analysis: (1) common sense, (2) a situated-practice level which included identification of interactions across all time-related categories (morning, school, after school, evening) and settings (kindergarten, class and family) and a (3) thematic level (of how conflicts and demands within interactions give rise to the formation of new demands). These three levels of data analysis allow the researcher to analyse the dynamic character of developmental processes in order to trace how contradictions drive development.

Cultural-Historical Methodology and the Position of Researcher

What has been central in all of the chapters of this book is the role that the researcher takes in cultural-historical research but also in critical theory and poststructuralist theory. The research of Quinones reflects an important aspect of visual methodologies driven by cultural-historical theoretical framework. She claims that 'visual methodologies offer not only a visual path to understanding and seeing the child but also a tactile, affectionate and perceptual path where not only the "eye" is needed but an affectionate sense and touch from the researcher' (Quinones, Chap. 7, this volume, pp. 111–128). Following this, Li states that visual methodology 'creates the conditions for the researcher to be an insider of the research setting in order to investigate young children's activities and engage in the social practices of everyday life, as well as examine people's different perspectives, including the researcher's own point of view' (Li, Chap. 3, this volume, pp. 35–53). This aspect of cultural-historical research methodology discovered and presented in this volume brings to agenda a task of further methodological rethinking of the role of a researcher.

Cultural-historical observations offer the *doubleness of the researcher* (Hedegaard 2008) where the researcher acts as a researcher and, at the same time, creates a research context by establishing the relationship to the children and the other adults. This is important since to examine how young children interact with adults and other peers within the family, community and educational institutions they participate in, cultural-historical research requires the researcher to be an active partner with the researched person within the activity. In other words, visual methodology within cultural-historical framework creates the conditions for the researcher to be an insider of the research setting in order to investigate young children's activities and engage in the social practices of everyday life, as well as examine people's different perspectives. For example, in research of Li (Chap. 3, this volume) visual methodology provides a new dimension for understanding the dynamic interactive process between parents and children in order to find out how parents engage in children's bilingual heritage language development. 'Being with' principle provides a range of opportunities for the researcher to be able to make sense of what is happening in the video by conducting research *on* the children and family (Li, Chap. 3, this volume, pp. 35–53).

Monk (Chap. 5, this volume) argues this issue from another perspective. In describing her research settings, she considers that

> 'Traditionally data analysis work involved in research has been carried out by the researcher or research team away from the research site, as a separate activity that does not involve the participants of the study. However, during intergenerational family dialogues family members and researchers have opportunities to work with and analyse data together' (Monk, Chap. 5, this volume, pp. 73–88)

What is important is that the intergenerational family dialogue as a qualitative tool combines the use of visual and verbal methods while involving family members (adults and children) as coresearchers generating and analysing data (Ibid.). In Monk's study the researcher engages in two roles: that of research partner with the family members and researcher undertaking an investigative study. While engaged in the intergenerational family dialogue, the researcher must conceptualise his or her participation within the research setting moving in and out of these two roles.

This view on the researcher's role corresponds with Quinones's approach. The aim of her research (Quinones, Chap. 7, this volume) was to investigate how the researcher is positioned when studying everyday life of children in a Mexican rural community. Quinones suggests a new concept of *affective positioning* where the research participants give a role to the researcher, as having an important place in their lives and relate to the researcher affectively.

Another example of the methodological rethinking of the role of a research is given by Shin Pennay (Chap. 6). The author claims that making a research from cultural-historical perspective requires the researcher to strategically embrace subjectivity and leverage its ability to capture what supposedly 'objective' methodologies cannot.

> The researcher is not the proverbial 'fly on the wall' but a communication partner who can ask leading questions (and perhaps even answer them depending on the situation) and has her own research intentions. Validity is defined by how well she is able to capture and interpret the different perspectives of participants in their everyday practices. (Pennay, Chap. 6, this volume.)

Pennay (Chap. 6, this volume) introduces the 'Four R Framework' which includes rapport, respect, reliability and reflexivity as core aspects of researcher's active participating position. In her view, looking from cultural-historical perspective the researcher is best positioned to assess when and how standard research practices should be incorporated or adapted to the research context. With cross-cultural studies, in particular, open communication and a clear understanding of both the theory and methodology within the research team (including translators and coresearchers) are essential to understanding context.

I believe that this book suggests several original ways of rethinking visual research methodology and the position of a researcher; it discusses insightful directions of reconceptualising the change of focus from researching *on children* to researching *with children.*

Conclusion

Concluding this chapter and the whole volume, I would like to come back to Toomela's (2010) questions about methodological thinking and answers of the contributors of this book to these questions.

1. *What do I want to know, what is my research question?* Our research questions are different, but they are focused on studying the process of child's development

which we understand as sociocultural genesis of child's mental functions. Our aim is not to describe or measure observable phenomenological superficial changes in children behaviour and activities; we are interested in finding new ways of analysis and understanding of 'underwater' streams of development which are hidden from direct observation and manifest themselves in these changes. It follows from Vygotsky's methodological claim that cultural-historical analysis '...proceeds from disclosing real connections that are hidden behind the external manifestation of any process. It... asks about origination and disappearance, about reasons and conditions, and about all those real relations that are the basis of any phenomenon' (Vygotsky 1997, p. 69). Cultural-historical methodology provides opportunities to generate processes of development by creating various types of social conditions and social situations of development for children. Creating these conditions we disclose hidden developmental processes and make them observable/recordable and therefore accessible for analysis.

2. *Why I want to have an answer to this question?* Investigating developmental qualities and potentials of these conditions, we are interested to develop new types and strategies and educational practices to be introduced and implemented in early childhood education in order to improve their developmental potential.

3. *With what specific research procedures (methodology in the strict sense of the term) can I answer my question?* Digital visual tools are very important parts of our research strategies. Their specific role is that they make possible to study the process of development of how 'the social becomes the individual' in three aspects: (a) in researching sociocultural conditions and environments of the child, i.e. the social plane of development; (b) in researching dynamical characteristics of developmental processes, i.e. transitions from the social plane to the individual plane and (c) in discovering of transformations and reorganisations of child's mental functions, i.e. qualitative changes of the individual plane of development.

4. *Are the answers to three first questions complementary, do they make a coherent theoretically justified whole?* Answers to the three first questions are complementary and make a coherent theoretically justified whole because (a) they follow from principles of cultural-historical genetic research methodology and (b) experimental tools and theoretical tools of analysis are in strict correspondence with each other.

There is one more aspect of the research methodology discussed in this book; this is the place and role of the researcher. How the researcher could position himself/herself in defining and constructing the research strategy? There are two possible positions: (1) a researcher as an 'independent observer' withdrawn from the process under study and (2) researcher as an insider, an active participant of the process under study. We believe that second position provides more possibilities in researching the process of how the social becomes the individual. Since according to the cultural-historical theory the development begins from social interactions and relationships, the researcher could take the role of active participant of such interactions and the researcher could introduce challenging situations, creating a zone of proximal development to the child. In cooperation with the child, the researcher facilitates child's activities providing tools the child can use in resolving these challenging tasks. In other words, the researcher actively created developmental conditions and social situations of development.

Here the researcher is not an independent observer; the researcher organises and even initiates the process of development on the social plane and, at the same time, observes the changes and transformations of the social plane into the individual plane of development. Another aspect of this position of researcher is that the child (and in many cases her family) is involved in research. In a certain sense the child and his social surrounding (parents, peers, teachers, i.e. people with whom the child interacts) are coresearchers. This makes it possible to investigate young children from the perspectives of the children themselves (Sumsion et al., Chap. 10, this volume). Cultural-historical framework provides methodological tools to change the position of a researcher from researching *on children* to researching *with children*; this is the answer of the contributors of this volume to challenging new trends in developmental psychology and studies of early years.

References

Bickhard, M. H. (1992). Myths of science: Misconceptions of science in contemporary psychology. *Theory & Psychology, 2*(3), 321–337.

Hedegaard, M. (2008). A cultural–historical theory of children's development. In M. Hedegaard & M. Fleer (Eds.), *Studying children: A cultural-historical approach* (pp. 10–29). London: Open University Press.

Kilderry, A., Nolan, A., & Noble, K. (2004). Multiple ways of knowing and seeing: Reflections on the renewed vigour in early childhood research. *Australian Journal of Early Childhood, 29*(2), 24–28.

Kornilova, T., Smirnov, S. (2007). *Metodologicheskie osnovy psihologii.* Saint Petersburg Publishers.

Pink, S. (Ed.). (2012). *Advances in visual methodology.* London: Sage.

Toomela, A. (2010). Modern mainstream psychology is the best? Noncumulative, historically blind, fragmented, atheoretical. In A. Toomela & J. Valsiner (Eds.), *Methodological thinking in psychology: 60 years gone astray?* (pp. 1–26). Charlotte: Information Age Publishing.

Vygotsky, L. S. (1994). The problem of the environment. In J. Valsiner & R. Van der Veer (Eds.), *The Vygotsky reader* (pp. 338–354). Oxford: Blackwell.

Vygotsky, L. S. (1997). *The collected works of L.S. Vygotsky, Vol. 4: The history of the development of higher mental functions.* New York: Plenum Publishers.

Vygotsky, L. S. (1998). *The collected works of L.S. Vygotsky, Vol. 5: Child psychology.* New York: Plenum Publishers.

About the Authors

Dr. Joseph Seyram Agbenyega (Ph.D.) is a senior lecturer in Early Childhood and Inclusive Education in the Faculty of Education, Monash University. He is a visiting fellow to State University of Jakarta, Indonesia, and University of Cape Coast, Ghana. His research focus addresses alternative theories of child development and inclusion, exploring new directions in early childhood educational research and practice and inclusive teaching and assessment of young children. He is recipient of the Sir John Monash Award, International Golden Key Award, International Monash Post-graduate Award, Monash Research Graduate School Award and Australian Leaders Fellowship Award and is joint managing editor of the *International Research in Early Childhood Education* journal at Monash University. He can be contacted at joseph.agbenyega@monash.edu.

Professor Benjamin Bradley (Ph.D., M.A., B.A.) is foundation professor of psychology at Charles Sturt University, Australia. Ben has been researching communication in early infancy since the mid-1970s. His first book *Visions of Infancy* (Polity Press, 1989) argued that infancy has provided a blank canvas for the projection of psychologists' theories, raising the following question: How do infants themselves experience their worlds? In keeping with Charles Darwin's proposals about the human psyche – another of Ben's interests – his more recent research has focused on demonstrating the capacity and content of babies' communication in infant-peer groups: in the laboratory, in families and in day care. Ben can be contacted by email at bbradley@csu.edu.au.

Sheena Elwick (B.Ed. EC) (Honours) is a doctoral candidate with Charles Sturt University, Australia. Sheena has a broad range of experience in Early Childhood Education and Care both as a practitioner and as a teacher educator. As a practitioner, she has worked in long day care, mobile childcare and also primary school settings. Her current research interests include infants' lives in early childhood settings. She is particularly interested in the potential of philosophy for engaging with the

M. Fleer and A. Ridgway (eds.), *Visual Methodologies and Digital Tools for Researching with Young Children*, International Perspectives on Early Childhood Education and Development 10, DOI 10.1007/978-3-319-01469-2, © Springer International Publishing Switzerland 2014

difficulties and uncertainties of researching with infants and for revealing new possibilities for understanding participatory research with infants. She can be contacted by email at selwick@csu.edu.au.

Professor Marilyn Fleer (Ph.D., M.Ed., M.A., B.Ed.) holds the foundation chair of Early Childhood Education at Monash University, Australia, and is president of the International Society for Cultural and Activity Research (ISCAR). Particular research interests and expertise include cross-cultural research, family studies, early childhood science education, technology education and the building of new theoretical tools to support early childhood development and education. Professor Fleer has published over 150 works. She may be contacted at marilyn.fleer@education.edu.

Dr. Liang Li (Ph.D. M.E. (EC), M.E. (TESOL International), Grad. Dip. ECE, B. Law) is a lecturer teaching undergraduate and postgraduate students and an early career researcher in Early Childhood Education at Monash University. Liang recently graduated with her PhD that drew upon Vygotsky's cultural-historical study to explore how immigrant families support their preschoolers' bilingual heritage language development. Her research interests focus on child development, family study, play and pedagogy, early childhood teacher education and visual methodology. Her most recent jointly written book is *Asia Pacific Education: Diversity, Challenges and Changes* (Monash University Publishing, in press). She may be contacted at liang.li@monash.edu.

Dr. Hilary Monk (Ph.D., M.Ed. (Adult Ed), B.Ed.) is a lecturer in Early Childhood Education at Monash University, Australia. Hilary has extensive experience in Early Childhood Education both as a practitioner and as a teacher educator having taught in New Zealand, Australia, Hawaii, Tonga and Singapore. Her research interests include family pedagogy, early childhood education, cultural-historical theory, the use of visual methodologies and adult education. She was awarded the Monash Silver Jubilee Postgraduate Scholarship while undertaking her doctoral studies from 2007 to 2010. She can be contacted by email at hilary-monk@monash.edu.

Sijin Agnes Shin Pennay (M.Ed., B.A.) obtained her master's degree at Monash University under the guidance of Professor Marilyn Fleer and her bachelor's degree in Economics at Princeton University. She became interested in early childhood education after witnessing her own children's development, having previously worked in the corporate sector in various industries and countries. Her own multicultural upbringing and family life keep her research interest focused on the role of language and culture, particularly in the everyday context. This is her first published work and is based on her master's thesis research.

Dr. Gloria Quiñones (Ph.D., M.Ed. EC, B.A.) is a lecturer in the Faculty of Education, Monash University, Australia, and teaches both undergraduate and postgraduate students. She was born in Monterrey, NL, Mexico, where she was an early childhood teacher. She has researched family and teaching practices, children's play, and science and technology in early childhood settings in Mexico and Australia. Gloria uses cultural-historical theory to understand the role of emotion in children's learning and development. Gloria is currently researching with Dr Avis Ridgway preservice teacher's understandings of play and pedagogy. Her PhD focuses on how *perezhivanie/vivencia* occurs in the everyday life of children. She can be contacted at gloria.quinones@monash.edu.

Dr. Avis Ridgway (Ph.D., M.Ed., GDEA, B.Ed.) is an early career researcher and lecturer in the Faculty of Education, Monash University, Australia. Avis' work has been recognised with an Australian College of Education, Victorian Chapter Excellence in Teaching Award for "Innovative Practice in Early Childhood Education." Avis is an honorary life member of the Reggio Emilia Australia Information Exchange, an editorial board member of the Challenge Journal and coeditor of this book. Her research draws on cultural-historical approaches using visual narrative methodology to theorise historical influences in early childhood learning and development. Research interests include play and pedagogy, early language acquisition, innovative teacher practices and arts-based methodology tools. Avis' work is published nationally and internationally. She can be contacted at avis.ridgway@monash.edu.

Dr. Hanne Værum Sorensen (Ph.D.) is a lecturer in pedagogy and child psychology at VIA University College, Aarhus, Denmark. Her research examines pedagogical practices in preschools as conditions for young children's physical activity. Her focus is on children's participation and perspectives on physical activity, with a particular interest in how physical activity influences children's learning and development. Hanne has published works on *sport, play and movement* in pedagogical practice. She may be contacted by email at hsor@viauc.dk.

Tina Stratigos (B.Ed. ECE) (Honours) is a doctoral candidate with Charles Sturt University, Australia. Tina has worked as an early childhood educator in preschool, primary school and outside school hour settings. She is completing her doctoral studies as part of the *Infants' Lives in Childcare* project with a particular focus on the infants' experience of belonging within a family day care setting. Tina is interested in the use of visual methodologies and working with the concepts of Gilles Deleuze in her research. She can be contacted by email at tstratigos@csu.edu.au.

Professor Jennifer Sumsion (Ph.D., M.Ed., B.Ec., Dip. Ed.) is foundation professor of Early Childhood Education at Charles Sturt University, Australia. She is also co-director (with Marilyn Fleer) of the Australian Government-funded Excellence in Research in Early Years Education Collaborative Research Network. Her current research interests include infants' lives in early childhood settings, the politics of early childhood curriculum and inter-professional practice. She can be contacted by email at jsumsion@csu.edu.au.

Nikolai Veresov (Ph.D.) is an associate professor of Early Childhood Education at Monash University, Australia. His research interests focus on child development, cultural-historical theory and genetic research methodology. He has published over 70 works (including four books) available in nine languages. He may be contacted at nikolai.veresov@monash.edu.

Index

Lightning Source UK Ltd.
Milton Keynes UK
UKOW01n0354051017
310445UK00008B/336/P